"Serious studies of race and identity in the [...]
a highly charged and complex history that [...] .... us today. As a new
attempt to see through those dark waters, Andrew K. Frank's *Creeks and Southerners*
is a welcome and courageous work of scholarship.... [It] is a valuable effort
to gain insight into a neglected area of southern scholarship."
—William L. Ramsey, *Journal of American History*

"Elegantly written, impeccably organized, and deeply researched in English and
Spanish sources, *Creeks and Southerners* is a welcome addition to the
booming field of pre-removal Creek history."
—Kathleen DuVal, *Western Historical Quarterly*

"*Creeks and Southerners* provides useful insight into the formation of Creek identity.
It would be useful to historians studying European–Native American relations or
Creek history.... Frank's story offers a good deal of insight into the various
conflicts and increasing tensions that ended with forced Indian removal."
—Jeremy Pressgrove, *Southern Historian*

"A valuable addition to the scholarship on the Creek Nation in pre-removal times.
While others debate when the Creek Confederacy began, Frank uses the analysis of
biculturalism and kinship along the Creek frontier to shed light on how the
confederacy gradually emerged over time. This approach provides a thorough
understanding of how culture and kinship affected internal and external relations
such as trade and alliances. *Creeks and Southerners* is a nice contribution
to the literature on the history of the southeastern Indians."
—Rebecca Seaman, *Journal of Southern History*

"An interesting source for studying the effects of early biculturalism."
—*Denver Westerners Roundup*

"Frank compiles useful details on Creek kinship structures during the late colonial
period and these, in turn, enable him to explain the intimate connections that
linked them—to a point—with their Anglo-American neighbors."
—H-Net Book Reviews H-Florida

"This insightful and well-researched volume analyzes the common ground between
the Muscogees and white Americans in a shared environment and persuades readers to
think about mixed-blood Creeks who participated in two cultures at the same time."
—Donald L. Fixico, *Montana: The Magazine of Western History*

CREEKS & SOUTHERNERS

Indians of the Southeast

Michael D. Green
University of North Carolina

Theda Perdue
University of North Carolina

ADVISORY EDITORS

Leland Ferguson
University of South Carolina

Mary Young
University of Rochester

Creeks & Southerners

Biculturalism on the Early American Frontier

ANDREW K. FRANK

University of Nebraska Press
Lincoln and London

An earlier version of chapter 6 was published as
"The Rise and Fall of William McIntosh:
Authority and Identity on the Early American Frontier,"
Georgia Historical Quarterly 86 (Spring 2002): 18–48.
Courtesy of the Georgia Historical Society.

Library of Congress Cataloging-in-Publication Data
Frank, Andrew, 1970–
Creeks and Southerners: biculturalism on the
early American frontier / Andrew K. Frank.
p.   cm.—(Indians of the Southeast)
Includes bibliographical references and index.
ISBN 0-8032-2016-2 (cloth: alk. paper)
ISBN 978-0-8032-6841-8 (paper: alk. paper)
1. Creek Indians—History.
2. Creek Indians—Cultural assimilation.
3. Creek Indians—Ethnic identity.
4. Creek children—Southern States—Social conditions.
5. Children, White—Southern States—Social conditions.
6. Indians of North America—First contact with
Europeans—Southern States.
7. Whites—Soutern States—Relations with Indians.
I. Title. II. Series.
E99.C9F73 2005
975.004'97385—dc22
2004018512

For Lisa

Contents

Acknowledgments   ix

Series Editors' Introduction   xiii

INTRODUCTION
The Problem of Identity in the
Early American Southeast   1

CHAPTER 1
The Invitation Within   11

CHAPTER 2
"This Asylum of Liberty"   26

CHAPTER 3
Kin and Strangers   46

CHAPTER 4
Parenting and Practice   61

CHAPTER 5
In Two Worlds   77

CHAPTER 6
Tustunnuggee Hutkee and
the Limits of Dual Identities   96

CHAPTER 7
The Insistence of Race   114

EPILOGUE
Race, Clan, and Creek   129

Abbreviations   133

Notes   135

Selected Bibliography   171

Index   187

Acknowledgments

More than a decade ago a young historian told me to prepare for the isolating nature of graduate school and historical research. Although I forged a love-hate relationship with my computer and frequently found myself in distant and quiet archives, I have not found this to be the case. My debts are many and my regrets are few.

This book began as a dissertation at the University of Florida, and my greatest debts belong to my fellow graduate students and my doctoral committee. First on this list must be Bertram Wyatt-Brown. He has always encouraged me to follow my interests even when they deviated from his own. His intellectual support, personal friendship, and generous use of the Richard Milbauer fund made my time at the University of Florida rewarding on every level. Without the prodding of John Moore, I never would have pursued Native American studies. My interest in Creek history began during a routine office visit, turned into a semester project, and then became a personal obsession. My manuscript also benefited from early assistance from Jeffrey Adler, Augustus Burns, Betty Corwine, Glenn Crothers, Stan Deaton, Thomas Gallant, Mark Greenberg, Daniel Kilbride, Chris Koehler, Marcus Harvey, Gary Kroll, Susan Lewis, Andy Moore, Marcus Nenn, Louise Newman, Chris Olsen, Jason Parker, and Frankie White. I also owe a special thanks to Anita Rutman and Darrett Rutman. I am lucky for having known them and learned from them, and I hope they would see some of their questions in my answers.

My intellectual debts go beyond the University of Florida. Michael Green and Theda Perdue, perhaps unbeknownst to them, have been my unofficial advisers for a few years. They have been generous with their time and have constantly challenged me to become a better ethnohistorian. They are exemplary scholars and model human beings. My thanks also extend to Kathryn Holland Braund, Steven Bullock, Stanley Burstein, James Taylor Carson, Chris Endy, Philip Goff, Cora Granata, Steven Hahn, Cheryl Koos, Peter Mancall, Greg O'Brien, Joshua Piker, Ann Plane, Charles Romney, Susanah Shaw, Pete Sigal, and Mark Wild. Clark Davis, who was tragically taken from us, deserves a special mention. I was fortunate to have known him as a scholar and even luckier to have had his friendship. I would also like to acknowledge my former colleagues at California

State University, Los Angeles. They made studying the South in the Southland a joy. More recently the staff, history faculty, and librarians at the Florida Atlantic University have helped me put the final touches together on this manuscript. Special thanks to Zella Linn, Steve Engle, and Harry Kersey for their encouragement and assistance.

Scholars cannot succeed without the help of archivists and librarians. I was aided by the knowledgeable and professional staffs at the Alabama Department of Archives and History, Auburn University, Emory University, Florida State University, the Georgia Department of Archives and History, the Georgia Historical Society, the Library of Congress, the Mississippi Department of Archives and History, the National Archives, the Newberry Library, the Southern Baptist Historical Library, the University of Georgia, and the P. K. Yonge Library at the University of Florida. Special thanks must be extended to the academic community at the Huntington Library. The beauty of the people there exceed even that of its legendary gardens. Thank you, Roy Ritchie, Susi Krasnoo, Christopher Adde, and the many readers who helped make the Huntington my academic refuge for several years.

This project would not have been possible without the support from various organizations and universities. This project has been supported by a Phillips Grant for Native American History from the American Philosophical Society, a Michael J. Kraus Grant from the American Historical Association, a Meyers Fellowship from the Huntington Library, the Newberry Library, and the National Society of the Colonial Dames of America in the State of Florida. The University of Florida provided me a McLaughlin Dissertation Fellowship to finish the dissertation, and more recently California State University, Los Angeles provided me a Creative Leave to help complete the manuscript. I would also like to acknowledge the Georgia Historical Society for granting me permission to include materials from an article I published in the *Georgia Historical Quarterly*.

I would like to express my gratitude to the staff at the University of Nebraska Press and the anonymous reviewers of my book proposal and final manuscript. They caught many mistakes, unstated assumptions, and inconsistent arguments. Without their assistance, this book would have many more errors than it inevitably does.

My greatest thanks go out to my family. Howard and Marilyn Tendrich have been wonderful in-laws. I love them and my brother-in-law, Jon, and I consider it an honor to be part of the Seitlin and Tendrich clans. My brother and sister-in-law, Gary and Gail Frank, have constantly reminded me of the important things in life, giving me some needed perspective when the walls seemed to be crumbling down. Gary's advice, even when offered unknowingly, has always been invaluable. My mother and father, Paul and Judie Frank, have encouraged me to be a historian for longer than they realize. They have taught me to follow my dreams and my heart. They have encouraged me, nurtured me, and loved me. I never could have accomplished this project without them. My love for them is boundless. I also want to thank Daniel, who will be too young to read this book for several years. Although still in his infancy, he has been able to teach me the importance of family, love, and paying careful attention to details. I love you.

My greatest thanks go out to my wife, Lisa. She has been everything to me: my closest friend, most critical colleague, and perfect partner. She believed I could accomplish this project long before I did, and I hope the final result reflects her optimism. I dedicate this book to her.

Series Editors' Introduction

Hundreds, probably thousands, of Europeans entered the Native nations of the South in the seventeenth and eighteenth centuries hoping to make their fortunes in the business of exchanging the goods of Europe for the goods of the Indians. Most scholars never asked the questions that should have been obvious, such as how did the Indians define the social (as opposed to the economic) roles of the traders, how did the Indians expect to control their business activities and police their behavior, how did the Indians integrate these men who were both strange and foreign into their worlds. Focusing on the Creeks, Andrew Frank addresses these questions in this book. He looks at the Creek kinship system and shows how the rules of kinship, ancient but adaptable to novel circumstances, applied to control both the traders and the trade. Variations were possible, as people moved into and out of the Creek country their status and condition changed, and new questions arose. But the Creeks continually found answers. An important strength of this book lies in Frank's skillful documentation of the range of options and possibilities. By building out from Creek cultural systems, Frank then explains the social and political impacts of the traders and their descendants on the history of the Creek Nation during the eighteenth and early nineteenth centuries. We welcome Andrew Frank's important new book to our Indians of the Southeast Series.

Michael D. Green & Theda Perdue

CREEKS & SOUTHERNERS

Introduction

The Problem of Identity in the Early American Southeast

In 1783 a belief in the connection between race, culture, and identity nearly resulted in hostilities between Spanish Floridians and Creek Indians. The problem began in early February, when an English-born and English-speaking man named Andrew Brissert entered the Gulf Coast town of Pensacola hoping to sell two African American slaves. Soon after he and his Creek wife arrived, the trader purchased some coffee, sugar, and hardtack and found a place to spend the night. That evening Brissert's host offered the guests some rum before the married couple fell asleep. The following morning, soon after Brissert awoke, Spanish officials arrested him. His crime was not that of slave trading—for selling African Americans was a legal and common occurrence in the Spanish colony and port town. Nor was he arrested for his drunkenness or for purchasing rum. Brissert's offense was that in being "dressed and painted as an Indian," he broke an ordinance that prohibited men from wearing disguises in the city. The local magistrates arrested him on their "Suspicion of his being a Spy."[1]

Brissert's wife and Indian family did not passively watch events transpire. The well-known Creek diplomat and trader Alexander McGillivray voiced his disapproval of the capture of his faithful assistant and tried to get the Spanish officials to explain their actions. Brissert's wife and several members of her clan similarly objected to the arrest, claiming that this was a case of mistaken identity. These initial protests hardly impressed the Spanish officials, who chose to ignore "the supplications and threats of his Tallapoosa Creek wife" and to ship Brissert off to receive punishment in New Orleans "with other English prisoners." This stranger, they claimed, was not a Creek man and definitely not an Indian; he was an English slave trader and spy who cleverly used Indian paints and clothes to conceal his true English identity. After all, when stripped of the elaborate paints and his Native costume, Brissert looked, acted, and sounded like an Englishman.

While Brissert sailed to New Orleans, where he would have been detained until a suitable punishment could be determined, the threats from Fus-hatchee villagers and Wind clan Creeks became more explicit.[2] They vowed to cut off trade relations and hinted that their warriors might take immediate retribution if the Spaniards did not promptly return Brissert to his home. The seizure of their trusted neighbor, they claimed, was tantamount to a declaration of war.

Commandant of Pensacola Arturo O'Neill took these new threats seriously and shared them with Luis de Unzaga, his superior. After some deliberation O'Neill and Unzaga concluded that they had no choice but to return Brissert to his village. If the Creeks claimed that Brissert was one of their own, the Spaniards were in no position to disagree. Race, culture, and language, they reluctantly conceded, had deceived them.[3]

Men like Brissert, his Creek children, his Creek wife, and her family form the core of this study. In the eighteenth and early nineteenth centuries hundreds of European American men entered Creek villages, married and cohabitated with Native women, and fathered an unknown number of Creek children.[4] These European American men often embraced the customs and behaviors of their hosts, at least enough to live relatively inconspicuously, and adhered to the expectations of their new families and communities. In these instances they became known as "Indian countrymen." At the same time, these newcomers to Indian life, at least in the eyes of many European American colonists, did not always blend into their communities. In villages located in what is now Florida, Georgia, and Alabama, many of the early American newcomers recognized their newly obtained Creek obligations even as they held what appeared to be European American economic and social practices. They held and sold African slaves and participated in the annual Green Corn Ceremony. They herded cattle and fenced their lands, while they partook of the ritual black drink and painted their skin. They held positions in European trading firms, even as they catered to the interests of their wives' clans. They spoke English, Spanish, or French while also interpreting it into Muskogee, Alabama, and Hitchiti. Their behavior and appearances defied simple identification. In short, Brissert was not the only resident of the early American South who, at least on occasion, looked, acted, and sounded like both a Creek Indian and a European American colonist.

Brissert's two or three Creek children, much like the offspring of other Indian countrymen and Native mothers, further blurred the distinctions between European American and Creek. In Native villages, where the overwhelming majority of these children lived, the children of Indian countrymen were considered Creeks because they obtained their matrilineal clan and village identities from their mothers, who in nearly all instances were Creek. When these children left their matrilocal homes and traveled into European American society or when European Americans entered their villages, however, their paternal identities and physical appearances often created confusion. Sometimes even more so than their Indian countrymen fathers, these Creeks had ambiguous appearances, participated in all elements of Creek life, and yet still seemed to be Englishmen, Scotsmen, or Spaniards in disguise. As much as they pierced their ears and noses, shaved their hair according to Native custom, and plucked their beards, they could not and often did not want to cut their ties to European American society. Many spoke English or Spanish, held positions in the region's deerskin trading firms, owned property in colonial society, and had European American wives. In short, Indian countrymen and their Creek children made the disparity between race, culture, and identity rather common in the early American South.

In the two centuries since the Spanish officials arrested Brissert for disguising himself as an Indian, most scholars have continued to rely on race, culture, and language to categorize their subjects. Traditional anthropological fields are devoted to tracing and categorizing people according to their physical, cultural, and linguistic traits, and historians frequently impose similar methods of defining peoples of the past. At times this methodology seems to work, as these often overlapping traits have historically defined the boundaries of many communities. Such a schema, though, cannot be used to understand the multiracial, multiethnic, and nonracial societies of the past. Nor can it effectively deal with instances in which cultures met and overlapped. In these instances the trilogy of race, culture, and language has led scholars to see boundaries and fixed cultures where fluidity reigned.

Even though scholars have long recognized the ethnic diversity within Creek and other Indian communities, the rigid logic of race continues to shape most interpretations of Indian countrymen and their Native children. These individuals exist in the background, if not the core, of every recent book on the southern backcountry and southeastern Indians. These works refer to many of the children of intermarriages, their European American fathers, and their centrality to the region's economy, social structure, culture, and political affairs. Their omnipresence, not surprisingly, has not led to a consensus about their place in Indian society. Instead scholars have split into two opposing interpretive camps.

One group of ethnohistorians points to the problems inherent to racial and cultural hybridity and recognizes that the children of intermarriages were often seen as European American intruders. These scholars emphasize the "disruptive role" that they played in Native communities, declare them to be "double-agent[s]" who helped American "divide and conquer" ambitions, and cleverly demonstrate how they were "cultural breakers" rather than cultural brokers.[5] Perhaps James Merrell's assessment of Andrew Montour, a child of an Indian–European American intermarriage, best epitomizes this approach. "Trying to be both" Indian and European American, Merrell concluded, "Montour ended up being neither. . . . There was no place in between, there were no words to describe the sort of person he was."[6]

Other scholars declare that in matrilineal communities the children of Native women were necessarily Natives. These historians contend that the children of intermarriages should be understood entirely within the Indian contexts in which they lived. Theda Perdue, for example, persuasively explains that the children of Native women in southeastern matrilineal societies must be treated as fully Native. Their clan identities and village ties can lead to no other conclusion. Terms such as *mixed-blood* and *half-breed*, which imply racial categories and partial Indianness, betray the ways in which Native peoples determined kinship and identity in the eighteenth- and early-nineteenth-century southeast. Children of mixed parentage took the identity of their mothers. James Taylor Carson similarly counters the idea that the children of intermarriages lived on the fringes of Native communities, even when they seemed to be fully immersed in European American commerce. Belonging, in a southeastern Native society, did not have a racial component or a singular cultural perspective. Even when these children embraced the most "cosmopolitan" attitudes, they did not defy Native custom or become marginal figures. Instead, they came to represent a legitimate, although not the only, Native outlook.[7]

Creeks and Southerners integrates the strengths of these previous studies and illuminates a new way to understand the children of intermarriages, especially those who served as cultural brokers on the early American frontier.[8] Rather than treating identity as an either-or situation, this book explores how individuals simultaneously obtained and maintained their central roles in both Creek and European American societies. It demonstrates how intermarried individuals and their families bridged the gap between southern and Creek societies with their kinship networks, cultural practices, political power, and economic functions. As long as the interaction between Creeks and European Americans served the needs of both communities, these families found seemingly limitless opportunities on the southern frontier. The result of such interaction is an inclusive understanding of race and identity on the early American frontier.[9]

The experiences of European American husbands and their Creek children were rooted in a historical context, but the rules of kinship that controlled their entrance into Creek society remained remarkably consistent throughout the pre-removal era. As a result *Creeks and Southerners* does do not have a strictly chronological structure. Instead the volume contains chronological bookends, with chapter 1 investigating the importance of contact and the creation of the Creek Confederacy in the early eighteenth century and chapter 7 considering the connections between race and forced removal in the early nineteenth century. In between, chapters 2 through 6 explore themes and stages in the lives of Indian countrymen and their Creek children. The book begins by examining the factors that led European Americans to enter Creek society and the ways in which Creeks incorporated them. It then assesses how Creeks used mutable traits to determine identity and thus allow non-Creek outsiders to become kin and neighbors. Next *Creeks and Southerners* details how the children of Creek–European American intermarriages obtained bicultural skills in the eighteenth century. Then the book explains how these skills and dual identities frequently allowed the children of intermarriage to serve as cultural brokers and to live in two worlds simultaneously. Finally, chapter 6 studies the life of Tustunnuggee Hutkee to detail the limits of biculturalism and dual identities.

Creeks and Southerners avoids the mistakes made by the Spanish magistrates in 1783, men who initially viewed the Creeks as a racially defined community and treated the Creeks as a fluid, multiethnic confederacy. A pan-Indian identity would slowly emerge in the nineteenth century, and race would eventually become an important factor of Native identity in the twentieth century, but this was not the case during the eighteenth and early nineteenth centuries.[10] Throughout the pre-removal era Creeks used a matrilineal system of clans to determine membership in their community, and they occasionally adopted various ethnic outsiders and embraced them as kin. They did not believe themselves to be, nor did they behave as if they were, a part of a biologically connected group called Indians. Brissert, despite the pigment of his skin, the color of his hair, and the place of his birth, lived completely immersed in Creek society. He had Creek children, a Creek wife, and a series of obligations to her clan and the Fus-hatchee village. He, like other immigrants in the Creek villages, learned to look, act, and sound like his neighbors. He painted and tattooed his skin, wore appropriate clothing, accepted the matrilineal kinship structures, and otherwise lived according to Creek custom. Brissert made these changes in his behavior and appearance, even as he participated in the domestic slave trade and worked for the region's largest deerskin trading firm, the Panton, Leslie, and Forbes Company. In this way he could look and act the part of both a Creek and a European American.[11]

Had Creeks defined themselves in racial and nonmatrilineal terms, Indian countrymen and their Creek children would not have played significant roles in Native communities. That they did testifies to the fact that eighteenth-century Creeks neither understood nor used the language of blood quantum or hybridity. In addition, it demonstrates that they did not turn a blind eye to European American appearances, behavior, or paternity. These biological or racial attributes simply did not determine Creek identities. Similarly, Creeks did not possess a singular or essentialist understanding of Creek culture. Instead they recognized that their boundaries existed in flux, with new peoples and technologies constantly entering their community. Nothing prevented Creeks from speaking English, herding cattle, owning slaves, having blond hair, or marrying non-Creeks. The boundaries between insiders and outsiders, and between kin and strangers, were not as clear-cut as the Spanish officials who detained Brissert desired and often demanded.

Erasing the racial language and logic from the history of Creek society is not an easy task. In part, interaction with European Americans prevents us from totally removing the concept of race and the importance of paternity from early American Indian history. As the behavior of the Spanish magistrates in 1783 demonstrated, many European Americans behaved as if race and identity were logically connected. Throughout the eighteenth century many European Americans, whether Spanish or English, shared a belief that immutable differences separated humankind into several races. This understanding of human difference, though, was not as clear as even the Brissert case indicates. Diplomatic concerns and the danger of the Spanish losing the Creek trade to the United States certainly contributed to the arrest and then the release of Brissert. O'Neill, who initially supported the arrest, did not consistently believe that race and identity were inevitably connected. Prior to 1783 he voiced his fears that Spanish settlers and soldiers might embrace an Indian lifestyle and family. O'Neill's experience dealing with Brissert, who was an adopted member of Creek society, must have buttressed his anxieties that Europeans could become Indians. A half year after Brissert's arrest, O'Neill urged fellow magistrates to "keep the friendship of . . . Englishmen [who] are married and have Indian children, since in what other fashion can you be assured of the trade and friendship of the Indians."[12] In short, while Creeks did not use race to divide the world into static categories, European Americans such as O'Neill presupposed biological divisions between peoples but accepted the reality that a racial barrier did not permanently prevent European Americans from becoming Indians.

European American views of Indian communities also contained a racial logic, one that necessarily shaped the views and treatment of Indian countrymen and their children. Most European Americans viewed Indian tribes as ancient creations with primordial roots rather than modern social and political entities that connected clans and villages. As a result European Americans frequently struggled to comprehend the migration and incorporation of new peoples into these Native communities. They insisted that African Americans or European Americans who entered Indian villages, unlike Native newcomers, necessarily maintained their racial and therefore premigration identities even if they lived as members of Creek society. Fugitive slaves and white colonists could reside in Creek villages, but European Americans frequently insisted that they were out of place. Their race, at least in the eye of some onlookers, prevented them from being racially Indian and therefore from truly being Creeks. European Americans similarly misunderstood the children of Indian countrymen. Even as they lived in matrilineal villages, sometimes without the presence of their biological fathers, European Americans often insisted that the background of their fathers mattered. Thus, when paternity was known, they frequently treated the Creek children of Indian countrymen differently than they did other Creek villagers.

The experiences of African Americans among the Creeks contrast sharply with those of European Americans. Southern racism and concerns about slavery made it nearly impossible for most African Americans to take advantage of their biculturalism and serve as cultural intermediaries on the early American frontier. Many African Americans intermarried and became residents of Creek villages, but they could hardly move freely in the American South. Once they found homes in Creek villages, they almost always fought to maintain their anonymity and thus their freedom. Repeated attempts by European Americans to force them back into bondage further convinced most African American refugees to immerse themselves in their new lives. Even the Creek children of African Americans faced restrictions that other Creeks did not. The ethnic backgrounds of African American Creeks closed more doors than they opened. As a result this book primarily deals with the interactions between Creeks and European Americans. Other historians have explored and will continue to explore the fascinating and complex history of African Americans and southeastern Indians.[13]

Unfortunately, men like those Spanish officials who insisted on seeing Brissert as an Englishman and Creeks as a racial group wrote most of the primary sources used to study eighteenth-century Creeks. Very few works were written from a nonracial or matrilineal perspective. As a result historians must confront a myriad of misleading terms that pervade the available sources. For example, the terms that eighteenth-century English colonists used to distinguish the children of intermarriages have implications today that counter their original meanings and even confused contemporaries who employed them. Our modern sensibilities often recoil at the racist implications of the terms *half-breed*, *half-Indian*, *half-blood*, and *mixed-blood*. They connote biological attributes, genetic percentages, levels of acculturation, and political loyalties. Furthering the imprecision of these terms, English-speaking eighteenth-century Americans usually used *half-breed* and *mixed-blood* as general terms for individuals of any "mixed" background, whether Indian, African, or European. Context, rather than the terms themselves, determined their precise meaning. Most importantly, and the major reason that these terms are not employed within this text, they prioritize racial and paternal identities, two concepts foreign to the worldview of eighteenth-century Creeks.[14]

The non-English terms used to denote racial intermixture in the eighteenth century contain shortcomings of their own. The problems with the term *mestizo* parallel those associated with *half-breed*. To a non-native speaker this term may appear innocuous, but the biological and cultural implications of *mestizo* cannot be ignored. In addition to having class connotations that placed *mestizo* above *Indio* (Indian) and below *blanco* (white man), the term also inferred African mixture and signified Spanish origins and identities. Although Spanish men fathered many Creek children, they did so less frequently than residents from England, Scotland, and the United States. Even in instances where Creeks had Spanish fathers, the term *mestizo* remains imprecise. *Mestizos* traditionally obtained their identities as residents within colonial Spanish society, not as members of an Indian society, where nearly all of these children lived.[15]

Some scholars of southeastern Indians use the French term *métis* to refer to the children of intermarriages, but it too has inappropriate connotations for Creek society. The Métis were and are an autonomous and recognized ethnic group in Canada. It may not be an offensive term, but when used in the southeast it falsely implies the presence of a distinct, self-conscious culture and community. The children of intermarriages in the southeast, at least in the pre-removal era, did not become conscious of their paternal commonalities or form a cohesive community. Just as importantly, the actual history of the children of intermarriages betrays the explicit meaning of the term *métis*. Rather than a people "in between," as the term literally means, most of the children of intermarriages lived in only one of their parent's worlds (Native or colonial). Even those who brokered two worlds normally lived in only one of them.[16]

Even the Muskogee language, at least in the eighteenth century, did not provide a term to demarcate the children of intermarriages. The Creek's matrilineal society, which persisted throughout the pre-removal era, had no need for words that indicated the status of a father. The matrilineal Creeks treated the children of European Americans in the same way that they treated all children. Children with Creek mothers were Creeks, members of a particular village, and members of a clan. Creeks also had various ethnicities, such as Muskogee, Alibamo, and Hitchiti, but matrilineal descent controlled this aspect of identity as well. For most of the pre-removal period, paternity and race had little effect on identity. The children of Creek women were *este mvskoke*, the children of non-Creek women were not.

In short, neither eighteenth-century European Americans nor Creek Indians created an accurate or extensive vocabulary to label the children of European American men and Creek women. Although there have been some recent attempts to create a scientific vocabulary to account for multiracial people, these efforts have usually resulted in little more than new jargon and ahistorical understandings of the past. As a result this volume does not intend to create a new vocabulary or impose a new one onto the past. In most instances the term *Creek* will be used to identify those individuals, regardless of their racial or ethnic heritage, who lived as accepted members of Creek society. Those European American men who were adopted into a clan and the children who were born into their mother's clan are treated just as Creek society treated them at the time, as full members of their Native community.[17]

Despite the problematic nature of the primary sources available for the study of pre-removal Creek society, the European American concern for paternity and racial bias actually made the writing of this book possible. As this volume explains, racial assumptions within European American society provided the means for many children of intermarriages to participate in the diplomatic and economic community that connected Creek and European American communities. They became deerskin traders, interpreters, and travel guides, and they participated in treaty negotiations as village chiefs and advisers. These contexts provided the bulk of the sources available for the study of pre-removal Creeks, and therefore a written record of their presence remains. Furthermore, European Americans who encountered the Creek children of intermarriages or Indian countrymen frequently found it necessary to comment on the apparent disconnect between race and identity. As with many human instances, the exceptions to commonly held rules garnered more attention than the assumed rules themselves and those who seemed to adhere to them. As a result eighteenth- and early-nineteenth-century documents constantly refer to the presence of Indian countrymen and their Creek children.

This volume, in part because of the biases inherent to the available sources, contains an intentional and perhaps inescapable bias. This book focuses on the minority of the Creek children of intermarriages, the handful of mostly men who became prominent traders, interpreters, diplomats, village chiefs, and warriors. It focuses on the options and opportunities that they received because of their mixed parentage and the competing definitions of identity in the eighteenth century. It demonstrates how European Americans entered Creek society, explains how paternal identities affected the children of Indian countrymen, and then explores how these paternal ties enabled some Creeks to mute their Creek pasts and become European Americans. Clearly these were the exceptions to the rule. Not all children of intermarriages helped mediate differences between Creeks and European Americans, and most did not become famed leaders in Creek society. The majority lived beyond the prying eyes of the European American observers, hunting rather than trading and speaking Muskogee rather than interpreting it into Spanish or English. Most viewed their maternal uncles as their male role models and turned to their clans in times of crisis. Born into villages and clans, these Creek children grew up and otherwise lived indistinguishably from the rest of their people. In these instances neither paternity nor race mattered.

CHAPTER 1

The Invitation Within

Throughout their pre-removal history in Georgia, Florida, and Alabama, Creek Indians welcomed countless African, Native, and European outsiders into their villages. Creeks often took the newcomers as spouses and occasionally adopted others into their families. This attitude toward ethnic outsiders was rooted in a political structure and a dynamic culture that fostered inclusivity. Formed as a conglomeration of declining chiefdoms in the eighteenth century, the Creek Confederacy contained various ethnicities and cultures from its inception. The term *Creek* therefore refers to dozens of ethnic groups, the largest being the Muskogees, who formed social and political alliances in the eighteenth century. Strict rules that applied to all members of Creek society governed the process of incorporation. Creeks consistently incorporated outsiders into their eighteenth- and early-nineteenth-century villages and struggled to maintain a sense of who and what belonged in their villages. Creek villages rejected individuals who—regardless of their race, birthplace, or ethnic identity—did not live by various cultural norms.

The rules that governed acceptance into villages remained remarkably constant until the nineteenth century, when new ideas about race resulted in regulations for intermarriages between Creeks and European Americans. Incorporation required that ethnic newcomers cede some of their customs and authority to that of the larger Creek community. Yet it did not demand a total negation of past traditions, personal interests, and original identities. Instead most members of Creek villages had multiple identities, reflecting their ethnic, village, clan, and eventually national ties. The divergent concerns of individuals, families, villages, and the confederacy coexisted in an uneasy balance. Some forces united villages into a complex network of relations and obligations, but ethnicity, geography, kinship, politics, and village loyalty divided Creek society.

Underneath these differences, however, most Creeks spoke a common hegemonic language, Muskogee; were organized socially through a matrilineal kinship system based on clans; practiced several common religious ceremonies and rites; lived in a polity with merit-based authority figures; participated in an economic system that organized agriculture, hunting, and trade on strict gender lines; and shared a political identity. An ethic of reciprocity also connected individuals into familial networks of exchange. Throughout the century that preceded removal, these characteristics extended to all members of Creek society, regardless of their birthplace and ethnic backgrounds.

A Creek identity, even if it was not called Creek for much of the eighteenth century, emerged as a product of the disruptions caused by European contact. Recent scholars commonly refer to the existence of a "New World" for both Europeans and Native Americans after contact, one that looked remarkably different than the one that preceded the arrival of Europeans. This implication of contact was wide-ranging, affecting everything from dietary norms to the rules of warfare, and from the nature of diplomacy to cosmological understandings of the world. The arrival of European Americans also had geopolitical ramifications, and in the lower southern interior, this meant the gradual formation and constant reformation of a loose social and political framework that became called the Creek Confederacy.[1]

When Hernando de Soto plundered through the southeast in the 1540s looking for gold, a Creek Confederacy did not exist. De Soto and his soldiers encountered dozens of large Indian chiefdoms: among others, the Coosa, Altamaha, Apalachee, Talisi, and Alibamo chiefdoms. These Mississippian societies, which formed between AD 700 and AD 900, were complex and generally contained paramount chiefs, hierarchical structures, institutions of centralized power, specialized labor forces, complex systems of tribute, and sophisticated agricultural practices. In palisaded cities these southeastern Indians spoke numerous languages, relied heavily on agricultural production, had diverse cosmologies, and competed for power and territory as distinct political entities. Once de Soto's hostility to these indigenous societies became evident, Indian guides led him into the swamps from which the warriors from several chiefdoms chased his forces out of the southeast. De Soto and his men were no match for the well-organized Native Americans. Natives outnumbered the Spanish conquistadors, and their technology was well suited to warfare in the southeastern terrain. The Spaniards fled Florida, but not before de Soto and his men introduced deadly pathogens, for which these chiefdoms had no answer.[2]

The newly introduced diseases resulted in "virgin soil epidemics" throughout the southeast. Smallpox, measles, and other European diseases continued to arrive as unintended consequences of the constant interaction between Natives in Cuba and Florida.[3] Like elsewhere in the Americas estimates of the population decline vary, but even conservative estimates of southeastern Native depopulation conclude that the chiefdoms experienced dramatic devastation (at least an 80 percent decline) as a result of European diseases. Throughout the Americas, epidemics initiated political, social, and cultural upheavals that, in the southeast, led to the dismantlement of the pre-Columbian chiefdoms. Spiritual leaders, unable to heal the sick, struggled to maintain their power. Smaller populations could not support the elaborate systems of tribute that supported the hierarchical structures, and with the decline of the chiefdoms, the southeastern societies simplified. They could no longer fully support the hierarchical structures of the chiefdoms, the full range of specialized crafts, and the elaborate spiritual rituals. Disease irrevocably altered the lives of southeastern Indians.[4]

When Spanish explorers Tristán de Luna (1560) and Juan Pardo (1568) returned to Florida a generation after de Soto's last visit, only remnants of the large chiefdoms remained. The Coosa, Timucuan, Talisi, Ichisi, and other large chiefdoms of the southeast had experienced drastic depopulation and decentralization. The hierarchical settlement systems that de Soto observed had recently collapsed, the Natives no longer constructed the ceremonial mounds that dotted the southern landscape, and many of the rituals of the region's Indians became less extravagant. Grave goods, for example, became less frequent and networks of tribute less extensive. Smallpox, measles, and influenza epidemics continued into the seventeenth century, further plaguing the declining chiefdoms. Once powerful enough to chase de Soto and his men out of the region, the Indians of the southeast were no match for the next wave of Spaniards.[5]

It seems unlikely that the Indians passively watched their kin perish and their communities collapse. At first, they probably resorted to traditional remedies. They may have called upon their spiritual leaders for guidance and turned to herbal remedies such as the black drink to purge the impurities from the community. They likely held ritual busks, such as the Green Corn Ceremony, fasted and performed ceremonial dances and sacrifices. Some blamed the newcomers for their troubles and tried to escape the calamity by moving to interior settlements. Those who stayed adapted their diets and lifestyles to fit the changing situation. For many southeastern Indians this meant enslaving other Natives in return for bounties offered by the Spanish newcomers. After decades of turmoil, times when traditional responses to the chaos could not create stability, many of the Indians from the interior southeast pursued a new solution. Completely regrouping, these culturally diverse peoples became a new and flexible entity that outsiders eventually called the Creek Confederacy.[6]

The confederacy formed slowly and unevenly over the seventeenth and early eighteenth centuries. At first, marriages and families connected the survivors of various villages in the region. Over time, kinship ties slowly led to ceremonial exchanges and diplomatic alliances. Village leaders began to attend busks and other ceremonies at neighboring towns, and by the mid-eighteenth century several villages began to meet in multivillage political and diplomatic councils.[7] The result eventually became known as the Creek Confederacy.

Ethnic Muskogee Indians formed the core of this new polity, the heart of which Creek tradition locates in four towns: Coweta, Abihka, Kasihta, and Coosa. Other villages quickly joined. To bolster their size and strength, the Muskogees muted their cultural differences and past conflicts and invited the remnants of other nations and villages into their confederation. Many newcomers came from the southeast, others originated from more inland and northern Native nations. Muskogees incorporated these newcomers, despite their strange dress, odd physical appearances, and equally peculiar religious beliefs. By the eighteenth century thousands of non-Muskogee Indians from dozens of ethnic groups had made a home among the ever-expanding confederacy.[8]

During the eighteenth and early nineteenth centuries the Creek Confederacy continued to expand. Although slave raids and disease continued to take a toll on Native communities, Creek society enlarged by turning six particular types of ethnic outsiders into *este mvskoke*, or fellow Creeks. The confederacy took in Indian nations that it had routed in war, refugees from other tribes, prisoners of war, remnant Native groups that had been defeated by the European military powers, individuals whose communities had succumbed to European diseases, and various non-Creek men who married Creek women. For the most part the incorporation of these types of ethnic outsiders began early in the confederacy's history and continued into the 1800s. As a result the Creek Confederacy remained in a constant state of re-creation.

Like other Indian confederacies, the Creeks expanded by conquering and absorbing neighboring villages. Many of those who could not resist Creek war parties, frequently cited by both Natives and Europeans as one of the more powerful military forces in the pre-removal era, survived by allying their villages with the Creeks. Big Warrior, an early-nineteenth-century chief, told Baptist missionary Lee Compere that in the eighteenth century the Creeks were so powerful "that the Uchee tribe they made [into] tributaries. That they were then a great people & their warriors pressed on into the lower part of what is now Georgia & South Carolina."[9] Other conquered peoples similarly became residents of Creek villages. Ethnic groups such as the Uchees, for example, entered the confederacy with their own clans and quickly intermarried with their Creek hosts. Many Yamasee Indians joined the confederacy after ruinous warfare with South Carolina in 1715. These wartime refugees included Tomochichi, a chief who as an elder represented the Yamacraw Creek community in negotiations with Georgia from 1733 until his death in 1739. Still, neither the Yamacraws nor

Yamasees lost their ethnic identities when they joined the Creeks. Generations later, many Creeks continued to distinguish descendants of the Yamasees or Yamacraws from Muskogees and other ethnicities. In some instances Creeks recalled the conquest behind their incorporation and often referred to them as outcasts.[10]

The Creeks also grew in size when individuals opted to flee neighboring Indian communities and enter Creek villages. Native American immigrants came from several neighboring southeastern nations, including the Cherokee, Choctaw, Chickasaw, Catawba, and Shawnee nations. These individuals, often described as outcasts from their original villages, frequently used marriages to enter Creek village life. Although marriage itself did not make a newcomer a Creek, it did provide certain privileges and obligations through the clan of a wife. For others, especially women and the young, adoption into a clan turned non-Creek fugitives into village residents. In 1750, for example, South Carolina governor James Glen observed that a "few Renegade Chickasaws 30 or 40 in number who being banished [from] their own Country live" among the Creeks.[11] Memory of the presence of individual immigrants from vibrant nations endured into the twentieth century. In 1938, for example, Creek Sam J. Haynes, who claimed that one of his grandfathers was a white deerskin trader, also recalled that generations earlier several refugees from "the Catawba Indians were adopted by the Creeks."[12] Most probably the refugees' ancestors left their villages in search of asylum among the Creeks. Many of these newcomers, especially those from the Choctaws and Chickasaws, spoke a Muskogee language similar to that spoken among the Creeks and came with worldviews similar to those held within Muskogee villages. For Cherokees and other non-Muskogee speakers, however, the entrance into Creek villages meant learning new languages, and for all new newcomers entrance into the Creek Confederacy meant abiding by new cultural rules. Loyalty to clan, village, and confederacy seemed the essential core of these rules. Not surprisingly, several Creek myths normalize the incorporation and adoption of outsiders, people and animals, into their communities.[13]

Other non-Muskogee individuals became residents of Creek villages as captives of war. Not all prisoners, however, became Creeks. Captives typically faced four options: death, ransom, adoption, or enslavement. This process continued into the nineteenth century. Georgian Eunice Barber, captured in 1818, watched as Creeks determined the futures of several dozen captives including herself. Barber recalled that the immediate decision, to kill them or to let them live, was made by any Indian who "had lost a friend in the expedition. [He] had the power to determine [the captive's] fate, either to adopt him in the place of the deceased, or to doom him to savage torture." The decision resulted from estimation of the individual's ability to become immersed into the community even as it symbolically killed the captive before giving him or her a new life in the Creek community. Barber failed to recognize the other two options available, slavery and ransom, but she did identify the two extremes of captivity: complete adoption and ritualized torture and death.[14]

Creeks, like many other Natives, frequently adopted war captives to replace relatives who died young, whether in war or from disease. The need to obtain replacement kin often led Creek warriors to wage war against weak neighboring villages and to capture small parties of enemy warriors. In 1747 St. Augustine governor Manuel de Montiano explained this practice, one known to anthropologists as the "mourning war." "In order to increase their numbers" the Creeks implement a policy of "killing the men and carrying off the women and children. They marry the former and raise the latter according to their customs." The importance of replacing deceased kin was not lost on captives. If deemed adoptable, Eunice Barber noticed that each prisoner "was unbound, taken by the hands, led to the cabin of the person into whose family he was to be adopted, and received with all imaginable marks of kindness." He would then be "treated as a friend and a brother," and the new families "appeared soon to love him with the same tenderness as if he stood in the place of their deceased friend." Adoptees obtained a clan and therefore a place within a Creek community, but they did not enjoy complete freedom. Each adopted captive "had no other marks of captivity, but his not being suffered to return to his own nation, for should he have attempted this, he would have been punished with death." Creeks expected adopted newcomers to accept their new Creek identities and otherwise live as full members of their families and villages.[15]

In addition to replacing deceased kin and forming surrogate kinship ties, Creeks also chose to incorporate captives or newcomers who possessed skills of which they could make use. Many captives or fugitives within Creek villages were linguists, seers, blacksmiths, shamans, gunsmiths, and cobblers. Individuals without such skills had less to offer their Creek hosts and so had less chance of being adopted. Throughout the era Creeks tried to lure blacksmiths to their villages. By incorporating newcomers with desired skills, the Creeks adhered to their Mississippian roots, which encouraged the incorporation of new ideas.[16]

Not all captives became Creeks. In comparison to the "tenderness to those whom they adopt," the cruelty of punishments for nonadopted captives shocked many colonial observers. One European American resident among the Creeks succinctly summed up the stark dichotomy between torture and adoption. "Hospitable and kind as these people are to friends, they are, if possible, still more inveterate to enemies."[17] Barber recalled "particulars of many of the instances of barbarity exercised upon the prisoners of different ages, and sexes." Careful not to offend her audience with descriptions of "too shocking a nature to be presented to the public," Barber ensured that her audience would assume that the "savages" were capable of the most depraved acts. Rather than describing the tortures, she asserted that "it is sufficient here to observe that the scalping knife and tomahawk, were the mildest instruments of death—that in many cases torture by fire, and other execrable means were used."[18] Other descriptions of punishments did not leave the nature of the "savage cruelty" or "tomahawk torture" to the vivid imagination of frontier Americans.[19] Philip Georg Friedrich von Reck, in 1736, for example, vividly described the cruelty that southeastern Indians displayed to "their war captives. . . . They either take off their skin from the top of their heads, or burn them while they are still alive," he claimed. "Sometimes the captive, before he is entirely consumed by the fire, is thrown into the river, where the boys shoot arrows at him until he is dead." Throughout this tortuous process, the captors admired the courage of their captives, found a way to demonstrate their dominance, and in some instances saved captives who proved their worth.[20]

Creeks often rejected the alternatives of vengeance and adoption. Throughout the eighteenth century European Americans and Native Americans offered the Creeks ransoms or prisoner exchanges for the return of captives. In other instances Creeks incorporated the newcomers in social positions analogous to slavery. More often the Creeks chose to return captives to their American or Indian families or to sell escaped slaves back to their masters.[21] During the American Revolution, for example, the Shawnees paid a ransom for "a Peoria Woman who was a prisoner among the Creeks [in order to return] her to her nation."[22] The lucrative business of selling African slaves for ransom led many Creeks to steal slaves solely to claim the rewards. Missionary Francis Le Jau, for example, recognized that many Creeks waged wars solely to obtain captives to sell into slavery. By the nineteenth century some Creeks turned to individual acts of theft to obtain and then return African slaves back to their masters. European American captives occasionally faced similar circumstances. Alexander McGillivray, for example, successfully "ransomed [Jane Brown and two of her children] from slavery and entertained them at his house for more than a year" before assisting her return to her family in North Carolina. Her son, George, however, remained "in one of the upper Creek villages, doomed to a still longer captivity." McGillivray could arrange the freedom for Jane, as she was taken from his sister's village. George, who lived in a different village and under the control of another clan, was not so fortunate.[23]

Just as thousands of ethnic outsiders joined the Creeks through migration, captivity, and intermarriage, the Creeks lost considerable numbers through out-migration. After they were fully integrated into Creek society, the Seminoles emerged as a distinct ethnic and political identity prior to the American Revolution before splitting off entirely in later years. Several villages and individuals rescinded their Creek identity, stopped attending the annual councils, and charted a distinct cultural and political course. The Seminole migration to Florida occurred in several waves. Throughout the late eighteenth and early nineteenth centuries the Creeks lost hundreds of members to the Seminoles.[24] Other individual Creeks moved to neighboring Cherokee, Choctaw, and Chickasaw villages, and still other Creeks left their villages when they married non-Creeks. This process helped limit the population growth that was achieved by in-migration, as the children of some Creek men and women lived outside Creek villages.[25]

The out-migration of Creeks aside, the Creek's policy of incorporating ethnic outsiders allowed it to experience sustained population growth in the pre-removal era. Fewer than ten thousand and perhaps as few as seven thousand Indians lived in Creek villages in 1715. Despite the fact that death rates remained higher than birth rates, by 1750 the Creek population was rising. It soared to nearly seventeen thousand in 1780, and in 1825 on the eve of removal, the Creek population hovered near twenty thousand. The success of the Creek policy of incorporation did not go unnoticed by European American observers. James Adair commented that "their artful policy of inviting decayed tribes to incorporate with them" worked. "They have increased double in number within the space of thirty years." This had dramatic consequences for frontier Americans. "These reduced, broken tribes," Adair continued, "have helped to multiply the Muskohge to a dangerous degree." The successful strategy of incorporating ethnic outsiders allowed thousands of southeastern Indians to survive and prosper despite the arrival of Europe's destructive diseases and aggressive European policies.[26]

The Creek Confederacy incorporated non-Muskogee ethnic groups but did not force complete assimilation upon them. Throughout their pre-removal history Creek Indians spoke several languages. An Indian trader (probably George Galphin or Lachlan McGillivray) learned that within the Creek Nation "live the remains of seven Indian nations." Each of these remnant groups "usually conversed with each other in their own different dialects, though they understood the Muskohge language; but being naturalized, they were bound to observe the laws and customs of the main original body."[27] Occasionally the Creeks needed interpreters to facilitate discussions between neighboring villages. Although the shared and hegemonic language of the confederacy was Muskogee, many Creeks continued to speak the diverse and mutually incomprehensible languages of their ancestors. George Stiggins, for example, asserted that ethnic Alabama Indians preserved their traditional language within Creek villages. "While in the assemblies they use the Creek tongue, but in their local concerns they use their own tongue or language."[28] In part, Alabama Indians may have insisted on using their own language as a sign of ethnic solidarity and proof that they may have been incorporated but they had not been eliminated. From their origins Creek communities allowed both multilingual and non-Muskogee speakers. Speaking Muskogee, however, proved essential to the handling of diplomatic affairs between Creek villages.

The survivors of the disintegrating southeastern Indian chiefdoms created new ethnic identities, a flexible political structure, and a means of confronting the realities of the New World in the southeast. The survivors did not completely abandon the ethnic identities of the pre-Columbian chiefdoms. Generations after the collapse of the southeastern chiefdoms, southeastern Indians referred to themselves in terms of more ancient pedigrees. As ethnohistorian J. Leitch Wright Jr. concluded in *Creeks and Seminoles*: "The trouble with all this is that the Indians considered themselves what they had always been—Yuchis, Cowetas, Coosas, Alabamas, Shawnees, Tuskegees, among many others."[29] Context determined the identities, whether racial, ethnic, or national, of Creek Indians.

Many Creeks cherished the knowledge of their ethnic origins. Several groups, in particular, maintained their ethnic identities for generations after their incorporation. The Natchez, Uchees, Alabamas, and Hitchitis all earned reputations for vigorously maintaining their pre-Confederacy identities.[30] In 1824 a British traveler observed that "the few individuals of the once powerful nation of Natchez who escaped the murderous greed of their pursuers were lost among the Chicasaws and Creeks, who took them in and befriended them, and among whom remnants of their language are still found."[31] Non-Creek ethnic identities often persisted in the twentieth century. In 1938 Turner Tiger recalled the peculiarities of his ancestors' incorporation. "The Natches tribe was one that was adopted into the Muskogee-Creek tribe and each Natches family did not live alone but they lived in the same house with another Muskogee-Creek family." A full century after the Creeks experienced forced removal, Turner Tiger recalled that his Natchez ancestors became a part of the larger nation, not as a Natchez village but by joining new villages, most probably through adoption and intermarriage.[32]

Throughout the pre-removal era European American outsiders recognized the cultural and ethnic diversity within Creek society. Georgia officials, in 1747, summarized the Creek polity best. They were "a loose and fluctuating Body of People frequently increasing, decreasing and changing their Places of Abode."[33] In 1775 Bernard Romans observed that they were "a mixture of the remains of the *Cawittas, Talepoosas, Coosas, Apalchias, Conshacs* or *Coosades, Oakmulgis, Oconis, Okchoys, Alibamons, Natchez, Weetumkus, Pakanas, Taënsas, Chacsihoomas, Abékas* and some other tribes whose names I do not recollect."[34] Two decades later an Englishman who lived among the Creeks and learned about their oral traditions discovered that "the Creeks, who call themselves Muscokies, are composed of various tribes, who, after tedious wars, thought it good policy to unite to support themselves against the Chactaws, &c." Despite the ties that created cohesion, the Englishman recognized that "they consist of the Apalakias, Alibamons, Abecas, Cawittas, Coosas, Conshacs, Coosactes, Chasihoomas, Natchez, Oconies, Okohoys, Pahanas, Oakmulgis, Taensas, Talepoosas, Weeterminas, and some others.[35] George Stiggins wrote in the nineteenth century that the "Muscogie body is composed of the following tribes who retain their primitive tongues and customs viz; the Alabamas, Hitcheties, Uchies, Puccunnas, Aubihkas, Ipso-co-gas, Natchez." Despite their historical differences, Stiggins claimed that "these tribes are inseparably united by compact and consolidated by individual and national interest."[36]

Several forces served to counteract the polarizing tendencies of ethnic diversity and competing identities. A kinship system based on matrilineal clans helped structure the Creek Confederacy and its component villages. Generally Creeks considered anyone with a Creek (or clanned) mother to be *este mvskoke*, or a fellow Creek. Every member of the Creek Confederacy belonged to one of several dozen clans. Being a member of a clan conferred on individuals a specific social place within Creek society. Usually named for an animal or a natural phenomenon, clans served as extended families, and Creeks believed them to be traceable to a single progenitor. Children, as members of their mother's clan, owed only minor obligations to their father's clan. For these reasons the Creeks forbade marriages to fellow clan members, or to relations of their mother, because they considered them incestuous.[37]

Although some clans had reputations for having greater political or spiritual influences and obligations than others, the most important factor in Creek society was simply belonging to a clan. Those who lived among the Creeks but did not belong to a clan were deemed nonentities, outsiders, or guests. Marriage ties mitigated the marginal position of non-Creek men, as the relations of their wives could provide protection and various forms of informal assistance. Nevertheless, residents without Creek clans had no rights, received no assistance or protection, and could not claim a Creek identity. Clans served a number of functions, including connecting members of distant villages into a single kin group and thus helping link distant villages into a unified entity. Larger clans existed in almost every village, thus uniting members of different villages with kinship ties. Smaller clans, although often present in only a handful of villages, also assisted the cohesion between villages. By forcing individuals to look farther for their spouses, the incest taboo also served to unite clans and villages and alleviate the potential for splintering along clan and village lines. As George Stiggins wrote, "[the clan system] is the strong link of their political existence, a complete curb and cement to their ferocious and vindictive nature when irritated."[38]

As stated earlier, Creek communities determined identities through a child's mother and her clan. This importance extended to the children of all inter-marriages, whether the fathers were European American, African, or Native. Tecumseh, predominantly known by nineteenth-century contemporaries as a Shawnee, had a different identity among the Creeks. The child of a Shawnee father and Muskogee mother, Tecumseh may have lived among the patrilineal Shawnees, spoken Shawnee, and dressed like a Shawnee. However, the matrilin-eal Creeks accepted him as a fellow Creek. When he visited the Creek Nation in 1811, Tecumseh could not speak Muskogee, had no official Creek residence, and had none of the physical markings associated with the Creek Nation. Still, the kin and clan connections of his Creek mother's matrilineage afforded him the right to speak at the Creek Council, albeit through an interpreter.[39]

Kinship bonds created extensive social obligations throughout Creek society. Matrilineal clan ties determined who would be included in hunting parties, reli-gious rituals, village meetings, national councils, and peace negotiations. In ad-dition to clustering their residences around their extended families, clan leaders served as advisers, provided spiritual guidance, and helped arrange marriages. Creeks also protected their fellow clansmen and usually avenged their deaths. On several occasions U.S. Indian agent Benjamin Hawkins complained that the obligations of kinship prevented "justice" from taking place and ensured that a cycle of vengeance would ensue instead. The Creeks' pursuit of "satisfaction," he complained, prevented a centralized and regulated system of enforcement. Clan loyalty and obligations, Hawkins bemoaned, profoundly affected every aspect of Creek life.[40]

Intermarriage offered non-Creek men opportunities to attach themselves to a Creek clan. Although husbands could not become members of their wives' clan, they could enjoy many of the protections and connections that a clan provided. In other words, they could find an acceptable place in Indian society and cease to be intrusive outsiders. Because the Creeks were also a matrilocal society, or a society where men joined the household of their wives at marriage, marriages to Creek women also provided ethnic outsiders a place to live. Men could enter their wives' villages, enjoy the hospitality of their wives' matrilineage, and become connected to their wives' social and kinship networks. On occasion, adoption provided outsiders with full memberships in a clan.

Individuals with Creek residences who did not have clan ties often had to appeal to Creek leaders for protection. Powerful heads of alliances sometimes took personal interest in who could and could not cross the frontier. Nineteenth-century historian Albert James Pickett credited Alexander McGillivray with controlling the southern frontier with an iron fist. "No one ventured into the nation without making way to him for protection," Pickett wrote.[41] Other clan and village leaders also helped regulate the borders of Creek society. The most explicit use of this power related to the fates of hundreds of fugitive slaves who were returned to their American masters rather than being embraced by Creek villages.[42] Without the leaders' permission, non-Muskogee residents could find themselves in serious trouble. Clan leaders often controlled marriages, and village leaders punished vagrants. The Creek Indians carefully regulated entry into Creek life. In at least one instance the Creeks prohibited an intermarried resident, Charles McLatchy, from leaving his Creek village.[43]

Creek ceremonies, much like the system of clan, also helped counteract the factionalism within individual villages and the larger Creek community. The Green Corn Ceremony, also known as the busk or *poskita*, was the most important annual ceremony. Although not all villages held this ceremony before joining the Confederacy, once they became members they either adapted a former ceremony to fit the purpose of the busk or adopted the Creek version. Each village conducted its own Green Corn Ceremony, and residents of all clans attended. Those who refused faced physical punishments and social ostracization. Through extensive invitations to neighboring villages and the expectation of reciprocity, the festival helped cement political alliances between neighboring villages and smooth over tensions with distant enemies. The Green Corn Ceremony also had sacred significance. It reinvigorated the spiritual base of the community and re-sanctified relationships and the village. During the ceremony, which lasted about a week, divorces became final, crimes were forgiven, and villagers otherwise feasted.[44]

Other rituals served to unify the ethnic diversity between and within Creek villages. The customs surrounding the black drink served to minimize mistrust among Creeks and between Creeks and outsiders. Creeks drank this heavily caffeinated tea before councils, entering the village square, returning from the hunt, and other occasions. They offered the tea to guests and expected that it would literally and symbolically cleanse the individual who drank it. Participants confirmed the cleansing aspect of the ritual by vomiting the tea and the contents of their stomachs. When Moravian missionaries came to the Creeks in the early nineteenth century, they recalled participating as "the 'Black Drink' or cleansing tea was served. One of the Indians went from man to man more than twenty times singing while all were drinking. The Indians immediately ejected it, but it did not effect me that way."[45] Drinking the tea was not enough to become welcome in the community. The missionaries apparently alienated the Creeks by keeping their drink down. They remained polluted outsiders, and perhaps as a result the missionaries soon found themselves unwelcome in the community. For outsiders to be welcome in Creek communities, the ritual needed to be complete. Many Americans, especially traders and government officials, learned the importance of the black tea in creating trust among the Indians. They came to believe that the "black drink . . . [has a] superstitious efficacy; alleging that it brightens their ideas, and enabled them to form more correct and just decisions upon any subject that may come before them."[46]

Finally, ethnic and cultural diversity forced upon the Creeks a flexible political structure. The leaders of specific *Talwas* or villages consulted each other in times of war and pledged allegiance in case of attack. Collective Creek actions in the eighteenth century resulted from temporary coalitions of cooperating autonomous units. Each of the approximately fifty Creek villages acted autonomously, and villages did not necessarily heed the desires of fellow villages, but each village shared similar political structures. Creeks divided authority along civil, military, and religious lines. Each village selected a *Mico* or head chief and numerous assistants and advisers. Each village also had the same structural arrangement of religious and military leaders. Creek villages may have had the ability to act autonomously, but they each shared remarkably similar structures.[47]

Creek leaders had little coercive power to dictate actions or decisions. Civil leaders obtained their positions because their fellow villagers believed that they could best lead the community toward consensus. They delayed decisions and often hoped that time, persuasion, or migration would lead to village consensus. When towns split over issues, they would often split into mother and daughter towns, with the latter forming when the minority party physically moved. Military leaders won their ranks through valorous actions in battle. New names and tattoos followed on the heels of battlefield deeds. According to Joel Martin, religious specialists were "distinguished by an unusual birth (twins), extraordinary experience (visions), unique clothing, the gift of divination, and mastery of an esoteric or archaic-sounding speech."[48] Like the power of other appointed

Creek leaders, religious leaders' power only lasted while their advice worked. When they issued false prophecies or could not offer spiritual guidance, others took their place.

The fragmentation and shifting alliances within the Creek Confederacy frustrated many European Americans. Land cessions and treaties promoted by leaders of one village might be condemned by those in another. In times of war some Creek villages might remain neutral, while others lined up on opposing sides. During the American Revolution most Creek villages initially supported a policy of neutrality but then slowly moved into the British camp. However, the machinations of trader George Galphin successfully turned some villages and individuals into allies of the American revolutionaries. Unfortunately, European Americans frequently assumed that the Creeks acted as a single entity, not as coalitions of villages or clans. Consequently, they viewed internal dissent among the Creeks as signs of "Indian instability" and proof that they could not be trusted to keep their word.[49]

The alliances within the Creeks often took on a geographic dimension, with the most significant split between "upper" and "lower" towns. The lower villages, being closer to British or American settlers, became more involved in European trade and were often willing to adopt aspects of American "civilization." These lower towns were located on the Flint and Chattahoochee rivers and included, among others, Coweta and Kasihta. The upper division primarily consisted of the villages on the Coosa, Alabama, and Tallapoosa rivers and included Coosa, Fus-hatchee, and Tuckabahchee. Although this geopolitical division does not explain all factionalism within the Confederacy, Europeans believed that these alliances remained relatively constant.[50]

In conclusion, ethnic diversity formed the backbone of the Creek Confederacy. In the early American South, Creek villages eagerly embraced outsiders in an attempt to overcome the struggles associated with the demographic and spiritual disruptions of European contact. Ethnic outsiders shared technological skills, rituals, and information; they helped create a formidable set of military and diplomatic relationships; and, most fundamentally, these alliances served as the basis for a new geopolitical entity. The flexibility of this unit allowed Creeks to maintain some of their ethnic heritage while compelling them to follow the obligations of their clans and live in accordance with cultural norms.

The inclusive policy toward ethnic outsiders helps explain the presence of European Americans in eighteenth- and nineteenth-century Creek villages. Creeks could incorporate and regulate these newcomers much the same way that they controlled other non-Creek immigrants. Transgressors could be punished, evicted, and killed while those who lived within the rules of Creek society could be embraced, married, and occasionally adopted. Newcomers did not need to abandon their past in order to become residents of Creek villages. Just as Alabama and Hitchiti Creeks retained their languages long after their incorporation, many Indian countrymen continued to speak English and inter-act with colonial kin without threatening their Creek identities. Just as Creeks could embrace some of the rituals and ceremonies of their non-Creek kin, some Creeks could embrace the folkways of the Indian countrymen.

CHAPTER 2

"This Asylum of Liberty"

During an official tour of the Creek Nation in 1790 and 1791, U.S. Army lieu-tenant Caleb Swan estimated that at least three hundred European American men lived in Creek villages. Some of these men, known as Indian country-men, cohabited with and married Native women, raised Creek children, and seemed to be incorporated into village life. Swan noticed that they lived in every village and apparently adhered to the community's mores. This, as Swan and others noticed, was not the case for all European American villagers. Some did not intermarry, ignored local customs, and otherwise lived as tolerated presences rather than accepted members of Creek communities. Creek leaders, neighbors, and especially customers of the European American traders watched these residents carefully, demanded that they follow certain rules, and often expelled or punished transgressors. If an outsider were to remain in a village for long, violations of Creek norms had to be kept at a minimum, and marriages with Creek women and ties to Indian clans seemed almost essential.[1]

Swan easily categorized the motivations that brought the bulk of these Eu-ropean Americans into Creek villages. Most Indian countrymen, he explained, arrived with connections to the highly competitive deerskin trade. As a result "every town and village has one established white trader in it, and there are sev-eral neighborhoods, besides, that have traders. Each trader commonly employs one or two white packhorsemen." Swan recognized, though, that not all Indian countrymen had connections with the trade. "There is in almost every town one family of whites, and in some two, who do not trade," he explained. "These last are people who have fled from some part of the frontier, to this asylum of liberty."[2] Swan's division encapsulated the motivations of the European Ameri-cans who became residents of pre-removal Creek villages. They came in search of economic opportunities, who desperately needed refuge, or both.

Swan's estimate that three hundred "whites" lived in Creek villages hardly rep-resents an accurate demographic assessment of the Indian countryman expe-rience in the century before removal. It may not even be an accurate snapshot for 1790. Swan's visit stretched from the summer until the start of the winter, a time when Creek men predominantly hunted on lands outside the village. Had

Swan stayed through the winter he would have undoubtedly seen more men in the villages, but he insisted that this was not an option. After all, he explained, he "could not have remained in the country through the winter season without suffering the inconveniences of cold, and probably of *hunger*, and these without an associate or companion." Even when Swan briefly participated in the hunt, he only observed part of the male population. As Swan himself noted, Creeks hunted with their kin or clan and in rather small groups. His guide and host, Alexander McGillivray, did not participate in the hunts, further limiting his interaction with Creek men. As a result his count may have underestimated the number of incorporated European American men. Swan also necessarily miscounted those "whites" whom he "saw." The military official did not differentiate the long-term residents, many of whom had adopted Indian dress and markings, from those newcomers who returned to colonial society in the weeks and months that followed. Thus Swan may have not "seen" those European Americans who embraced their Creek lives while simultaneously counting as residents those who were there for the short term.[3]

Swan's population estimate also suffers from slippery definitions of "white" and "Indian" and from the confusion caused by the racial status of the Creek children of intermarriages. In the late eighteenth and early nineteenth centuries countless European Americans cohabited and had children with the offspring of earlier European American–Creek sexual relationships. These families usually lived within Creek villages, followed Creek customs, and rarely adhered to European American or Christian norms. Some European Americans considered these relationships to be intermarriages or interracial relationships; others did not. Swan apparently tried to include only European American newcomers in his count, apparently excluding several children of intermarriages, including a "Scotch half-breed" from his count of intermarried residents, even though he insisted that "like all half-breeds, [he] is very proud of being white-blooded."[4]

Finally, Swan counted only the men he observed and thus failed to mention the presence of women. Although there were comparatively few intermarried women, other records reveal that at least two dozen European American women had Creek husbands. This oversight may have resulted from Swan's diplomatic mission, which was to establish guidelines for Creek-American relations and extend the sovereignty of the United States over Indian territory. The omission also resulted from the highly segregated nature of Creek society. Men and women lived "separate lives" in southeastern Indian villages.[5] Few eighteenth-century travel accounts mentioned Creek women at all, especially inside the home. Even Indian countrymen spent much of their lives far from the households of women. Frenchman Louis Milfort, with whom Swan spent much of his time hunting, hardly recorded anything about women's life in his memoir about the Creeks. Other intermarried men experienced a similar separation from women. Even though he had two Creek wives and had lived in Creek society for twelve years, Thomas Marshall admitted that he "had not entered 3 of the Indian houses." When he had "business . . . with the men he went to their doors, mentioned it to them, said and did what was necessary."[6] After five years of residence among the Creeks, David Hay had a similar experience. After entering his first Indian hut, he told his companion "that probably he should never enter another."[7]

Despite its shortcomings, Swan's account provides the only statistical overview of the eighteenth-century Indian countryman experience for the Creeks. Fortunately, some European American officials compiled lists of licensed traders, while various missionaries, diplomats, and traders recorded the names of prominent "white" and "mixed" families. U.S. Indian agent Benjamin Hawkins, for example, recorded in his letters and diary the names of at least eighty-eight Indian countrymen and their Native families in Creek society between 1786 and 1816. Thomas Woodward and George Stiggins combined to name more than fifty-five Indian countrymen and their Native families in their early-nineteenth-century accounts. After stopping one list of intermarried families at twenty, Woodward apologetically explained that there were a "great many other whites and half breeds whom I have known and could name, [but it] would be too tedious." These accounts never intended to be comprehensive or exhaustive, and they rarely included those not involved in the deerskin trade or in diplomatic affairs. As a result the identities of many Indian countrymen, especially those who sought refuge in Creek villages, will never be known.[8]

The bureaucratic aspect of the removal crisis of the 1820s and the 1830s confirmed the long history and continued presence of Indian countrymen in Creek villages. In 1832 the United States charged Enoch Parsons with compiling a census of the Creek Nation before their forced removal west. Parsons almost immediately recognized that this project meant more than simply counting and listing. It also required him to determine who was and who was not a Creek. Indian countrymen and their Creek children, he quickly discovered, created confusion. Parsons expressed several problems, a few of which directly related to determining the total population of intermarried couples. The first question related to those European Americans who had more than one Creek wife. Parsons did not help matters when he chose to ignore the Creek's matrilineal social structure and instead organized the census with the foreign concept of a male head of household. In a matrilineal society one man with two wives counted as one man in two families. Parsons assumed that the man should be counted as the head of a "common family" even though men who engaged in polygamy were far from household heads; they were marginal figures in multiple households. Parsons also questioned whether Indian countrymen should be "considered as an *Indian* & endued with the same rights" as those born in Creek society. In other words, did their racial or birth status matter? Parsons assumed that most Indian countrymen were Indians, whether they were adopted into a clan or not, but he questioned whether he should take into account the timing of the marriage. The long-term marriages that took place before the removal treaties, he assumed, were clearly legitimate relationships, and as a result the relevant Indian countrymen were sufficiently Creek. Parsons rejected European Americans who married Creek women more recently because they had not necessarily acted in "good faith." Instead, "numerous relations of the latter kind have been formed & are daily forming with such intent & which will be observed and considered sacred according to their opinion no longer than is necessary to complete their fraudulent purpose—to wit of obtaining a property in the Land."[9]

Parsons did not intend to count all the intermarried European American residents. He only needed to count those Creeks who moved west, and fortunately for him he did not have to account for the racial identities of the myriad of families like that of English trader Nicholas White. Around 1766 White married a Creek woman and had at least two sons and two daughters with her. In the years that followed, apparently, three of their children married other Creeks and the fourth married an unknown white American. Parsons did not confront the complex identities of the White family. These marriages between the children of intermarriages and European Americans occurred rather commonly, and they often took place far from the creators of written records. As a result the number of these children are far too great and the sources far too skimpy to offer any suggestion as to the precise extent of their presence. Nevertheless, anecdotal evidence points to at least several hundred marriages between the Creek children of intermarriages and European American men and women.[10]

Statistical precision may elude our grasp, but the omnipresence of relationships between European American men and Creek women does not. As Swan noticed, nearly every village had resident traders as well as other European American refugees. The population of these Indian countrymen and their children was most likely increasing at the time of Swan's visit. Earlier in the century, as alluded to by the relatively small presence of bilingual Creeks in the 1760s and 1770s, fewer intermarriages took place. Sexual relations undoubtedly occurred between Indian women and European American men, but few of the men remained in villages long enough to help socialize their Creek children. By the 1780s and 1790s, as alluded to by the increased presence of bicultural and bilingual Creeks at the turn of the century, the experience was more prevalent.

Although the number of intermarriages cannot be definitively determined, at least eight hundred European Americans found spouses and permanent or semi-permanent homes in Creek villages between 1700 and 1830.[11] These fugitives, primarily men, entered Creek villages despite their unfamiliarity with Creek culture. They fled to their new homeland because it was, they were convinced, their best alternative to the poverty, imprisonment, political oppression, forced labor, indebtedness, ethnic discrimination, and limited opportunities of their colonial lives. Through intermarriage and occasionally adoption, many of these fugitives became members of Creek villages. There they helped raise Creek children, adhered to the expectations of their wives' clans, and profoundly shaped Southern and Native societies.[12]

Not all European Americans came to Creek villages voluntarily. A handful of captives became permanent residents. Taken prisoner and adopted at age ten or eleven, Hannah Hale eventually married the headman of a Creek town (Thlothlagalga), gave birth to five Creek children, and accumulated a sizable inventory of slaves, cattle, hogs, and horses. When her Georgia parents tried to have her returned to them in 1799, she refused to separate herself from her Creek ties.[13] Similarly, the Uchees took John Hague captive when he was a young boy. He married a Uchee woman, moved into a Creek village, fathered several children, and by the nineteenth century became what one observer believed to be as "much of an Indian as you will see."[14] Even the possibility of financial ransoms did not guarantee the return of white captives. In 1792 the Creeks rebuked an attempt to ransom two white women and a child. After John O'Riley, a trader who married a Tuskegee woman, offered "to purchase them at the price of a negro, each, for their ransom . . . the Indians refused." Their explanation was simple. "They did not bring the prisoners there to let them go back to the Virginia people, but had brought them to punish and make victuals and work for them, the Indians."[15] In this instance, the Creeks' desire to "to replace our deceased friends, that our wrongs may be revenged and our name and our honour maintained," could not be altered with an offer to purchase the prisoners.[16]

Although O'Riley failed to redeem the captives, most European American captives obtained their freedom when parents, missionaries, diplomats, soldiers, traders, and even Creek leaders successfully arranged ransoms and prisoner exchanges. Unlike most Native captives, European Americans who were captured by the Creeks usually returned home to their families. Hawkins and Indian leader Alexander McGillivray both credited themselves with helping redeem dozens of European American prisoners. Furthermore, treaties between Creeks and the European American powers consistently included provisions for prisoner exchanges and ransoms. As a result the custom of taking captives did not lead to a large "white Indian" population.[17]

Consequently, most Indian countrymen voluntarily entered Creek villages to escape the economic and social problems inherent in the eighteenth-century South. The need for asylum in the colonial South prompted Christopher Gottlieb Priber to propose a settlement on the Cherokee side of the Creek border in Georgia. In 1743 Priber tried establishing the village of Cusseta as an asylum for French, English, German, and African refugees. "He expected a great resort of debtors, transported felons, servants, and negro slaves from the two Carolinas, Georgia and Virginia, offering, as his scheme did, toleration to all crimes and licentiousness, except murder and idleness." Refugees, he hoped, would bring their property to the village and create "an asylum for all fugitives." In addition, Priber planned to abolish conventional standards of sexuality within the confines of Cusseta. He proposed dissolving all marriages and "allowing a Community of Woman and all kinds of Licentiousness." In Priber's estimation the sexual mores of southeastern Indians constituted the best place for such sexual freedom. Priber's plan never realized its potential, perhaps because of his naive understanding of Indian society. In August 1743 Georgia authorities tracked down and arrested the "little ugly Man, [who] speaks almost all Languages fluently, particularly English, Dutch, French, Latin and Indian; [and who] talks very profanely against the Protestant."[18] Georgia officials stopped Priber, but they could not arrest the out-migration of thousands of white Americans. Priber's refuge disappeared, but the preconditions sponsoring it remained.[19]

Most Indian countrymen, or at least many prominent ones, had Scottish backgrounds. Some scholars claim that the Scots-Creek connection and the prevalence of Scots-Indian relations as a whole can be partially explained through the similarities between the two groups' clan systems, their love for "the manly arts," and their shared history as "indigenous peoples." Differences between the two cultures and societies make this claim unlikely. More likely, descriptions of the two groups appeared similar because eighteenth-century English writers chastised both Scotsmen and Indians for their "savagery." The reasons for the presence of Scotsmen in the deerskin trade lie elsewhere. For Scotsmen, the trade with southeastern Indians offered an escape from mounting ethnic discrimination, economic problems, and diminishing political opportunities in the eighteenth-century southeast. Scotsmen had dominated politics in early South Carolina, for example, but their influence waned as a native-born Anglo elite gradually took control of the colony. Matters worsened during the American Revolution, when many Scotsmen increased their disfavor in the South by supporting the English Crown. This alienation, especially for already struggling farmers, made entry into the deerskin trade an attractive economic opportunity. As a result Scotsmen influenced the trade to such a degree that most southern trading firms had Scottish partners, and traditional Scottish patterns became incorporated into Creek clothing.[20]

Whether of Scottish or other European nationalities, assistants and pack-horsemen usually offered their services to merchants, knowing that promotions and economic advancement frequently occurred inside Indian villages. Samuel Mims, for example, entered Creek country as the packhorseman to one of the era's leading traders, George Galphin. Decades later Mims had married a Creek woman, ran a ferry across the Alabama River, owned dozens of African slaves, grew several dozen acres of cotton, and, when civil war erupted among the Creeks in 1813, sheltered hundreds of refugee Creeks. He had become, in the words of one observer, a "wealthy Indian countryman." When Lachlan McGillivray was twenty-two, he agreed to assist his uncle, James Bullock, on a diplomatic journey through the Creek Nation. Bullock, a respected Scots trader, showed his kinsman the lucrative potential for the deerskin trade. Within two decades McGillivray became a more influential trader than his uncle ever was. Few packhorsemen or assistants could match the experiences of McGillivray or Mims, but struggling southerners saw the Creek trade as one of several options in the impoverished backcountry.[21]

Other southerners entered villages as traders. Because factors normally provided the start-up capital, credit, and goods, prospective traders only needed a passport or license from a European American official to start working among the Indians. Although some entered without a license, prospective traders could usually find someone who would give them permission to trade. Spain, Great Britain and the United States all adopted systems of passports to regulate the number and character of those involved in the trade, but the regulations proved ineffective. John Stuart's 1763 complaint that he could not regulate the trade when "each Governor of the several Provinces can grant a License to any person to Trade indiscriminately to all the Indian Nations" resonated throughout the eighteenth century. Stuart, the British superintendent for Indian affairs in the southern district from 1762 to 1779, complained with good reason. The eighteenth-century fight for control of the lucrative deerskin business and for Indian allies led Spain and Great Britain to issue competing passports. In addition, colonial South Carolina and Georgia both sanctioned Indian traders, offering licenses to nearly all applicants and for all the region's Indian nations.

Competition between the two colonies for control of the Indian trade continued until after the Revolution when the United States established the federal
factory system. Even after the Revolution, traders continued to use passports
from Spanish, British, and American sources.[22]

Creeks did not welcome all licensed settlers into their villages and frequently
tolerated rather than embraced traders who brought various goods to their
communities. Village leaders, to varying degrees of success, used marriage to
regulate the behavior of the traders. Over time, because of mounting reliance
on European material goods and debts to European merchants, marriages often
failed to control the traders.[23] Throughout the pre-removal era Creeks watched
the interlopers carefully. They demanded that traders follow certain rules, regardless of any marital connections. Many of the hostilities against traders during the Yamasee War in 1715, for example, were "owing to the continued Oppres-
sions and ill Usage they received from a publick Agent; of which [the Indians]
often Complained in vain."[24] Over the next century Creeks expelled traders for
fraud, demanded that some trading licenses be revoked, and occasionally killed
those whose actions deviated too far from acceptable behavior. Newcomers in
all the southeastern nations lived with quite similar expectations. One Cherokee, at the beginning of the nineteenth century, made this clear about one "white
man. He is an old man and has an old woman, one of our people, and I have no
objection to his staying in our Country as long as he behaves himself well."[25]

Marriages to Indian women proved the best way to obtain Native sanction to
remain among the Indians. Native wives also solicited business from fellow clan
members and neighbors, forged political connections, apprised their husbands
of impending warfare, and gathered information essential to selling deerskins.
European American traders also benefited from the labor of their wives, who
interpreted for them, collected debts, tanned and dressed deerskins, and helped
teach the language and customs of the Creeks. As a result most resident traders
had Creek wives and families.[26] On several occasions Creeks evicted traders who
lacked an Indian wife and killed a few unconnected traders for their abusive
behavior. In 1752 several Creek leaders responded to a rash of misbehaving
traders by demanding that the British punish their citizens responsible for "de-
bauching their Wifes . . . and said if his Excellency would not punish them for
it, the injured Persons would certainly put their own Laws in Execution." To
prevent further outrages, the Creeks expressed their "desire that all the strowling
white People that are not employed in the Indian Trade may be ordered out of
their Nation." Such instances made the importance of clan connections and
intermarriage explicit.[27]

The nature of the Creek's social structure limited the number of European

American women who cohabitated with Creek men in the pre-removal era. Although these relationships were not frowned upon in Creek society, the female outsiders would have had trouble finding a place within female-controlled villages. Unless they were adopted by a clan, intermarried women would not have relatives in the town, access to property, independent status, or social obligations. They would be nonentities. A Cherokee pointed to this reality at the beginning of the nineteenth century: "The white Women may stay with their Red Husbands, as men love women & women love Men—But they may stay as they please & go back when they please." Other factors, including the masculine nature of the deerskin trade and the feminized images of Indian men within European American society, further limited the number of intermarried European American women. As a result most Indian countrywomen were adopted captives rather than voluntary migrants.[28]

Kin regulated and monitored each other's actions even as they protected their fellow kin. Consequently all residents of Creek villages had to follow the community's rules. In 1798 several Creek chiefs agreed to banish six traders and packhorsemen who "meddle in public affairs, are constantly circulating reports injurious to our peace, that they have information that mischief is brewing, the American troops are coming on our land and such like stories." The Creeks gave Richard Bailey, John Shirley, William Lyons, Samuel Lyons, Francis Lessly, and Robert Killgore twenty-four days to leave the nation. Bailey left behind a Creek wife of thirty-three years and several Creek children; the others similarly left their families. Charles Weatherford, who was married to one of McGillivray's sisters and a woman of the Wind clan, was also nearly banished. Fortunately for him, the Creeks granted him a reprieve "in consideration of his family on the Indian side, and a promise made by Opoie Hutke of Ocheubofau, that he will in future attend to his conduct and endeavor to make him reform his conduct and behave well in future." Weatherford's family prevented his banishment, but even their protections had limits. "If he do's misbehave again," the Creeks promised, "he is then to be removed without any favour or affection."[29]

Weatherford's experience confirmed the protection provided by Indian wives, but he was not the first to make this observation. In 1709 British traveler John Lawson explained that "*Indian* Traders . . . [have] *Indian* Wives, whereby they soon learn the *Indian* Tongue, keep a Friendship with the Savages." This had several functions: "besides the Satisfaction of a She-Bed-Fellow, they find there *Indian* Girls very serviceable to them, on Account of dressing their Victuals, and instructing 'em in the Affairs and Customs of the Country." Without the aid of Creek women, Lawson wrote, "'tis impossible for him ever to accomplish his Designs amongst that people."[30] More than fifty years later, naturalist William

Bartram recorded a similar impression of Native women. "White traders are fully sensible how greatly it is to their advantage to gain their [Indian women's] affections and friendship," he claimed. Native wives "labour and watch constantly to promote their private interests, and detect and prevent any plots or evil designs which may threaten their persons, or operate against their trade or business."[31]

Creeks pursued their own interests in making marriages with European Americans. Clan and village leaders recognized the importance of having connections with potential deerskin traders and trusted interpreters in their midst. Creek chiefs used these marriages to impose controls on the traders and thus on the trade. With kinship ties to traders, Creeks hoped for and often received a steady flow of trade goods, fair prices for their skins, protection from debts, and access to the colonial society. The Wind clan, whose members seemingly married European Americans more frequently than other clans, obtained a reputation for having near royal status among the Creeks. It is unclear, though, whether intermarried white men spread this idea to boost their own reputations, whether access to rare trade goods increased the power of the clan, or whether this prestige predated the arrival of European Americans. In any case, ties to European American society reinforced and perhaps even created this reputation.[32]

Creeks often pursued intermarriages and invited European American residents into their villages for diplomatic reasons. In these instances Creeks repeatedly insisted that their decisions turned outsiders into Creeks. For example, in 1786 a Creek leader declared that "our old Interpreter [James] Durouzeaux . . . has grown old in our land, he ought to regard himself a Creek redman & support the Country in which he has spent the most of his days."[33] Durouzeaux, who was born to English parents, had become a member of the Creek Nation. His loyalty and residence, as well as his Creek wife and presumed adoption, made Durouzeaux a Creek man. In order to avoid confusion, Creek leaders frequently wrote to European American officials to announce their acceptance of Durouzeaux and other intermarried men, especially those who performed essential functions such as interpreting and smithing. Similar acts of acceptance extended to at least several dozen "white m[e]n naturalized as a Muscogee."[34]

Creek demands and European American desires resulted in traders cohabiting with Native women regardless of the intended length of stay among the Indians. Short-term relationships with local Creeks fostered the idea that an abundance of "trading girls," or young Indian women, eagerly awaited the arrival of Europeans. John Smythe, while traveling in the southeast in the 1780s, observed that it is "customary when a white man enters an Indian town . . . with intention of residing there for some time, if only a few months, for him to have a wigwam, or hut, erected, in which he lives with some squaw, whom he either courts to his embraces, or received from her parents as his wife and servant, during the time he may stay among them."[35] Smythe's focus on the utility of the marriages from the husband's perspective obscured the power it provided Native women and their communities. By turning traders from strangers into kin, clan leaders could regulate the actions of the traders and thus regulate the newcomers. Marriages, in other words, often served functions analogous to European American licenses.

Incorporated European American men and the children of intermarriages lived under the same clan-based regulations that governed all residents of Creek villages, and they received the same punishments for their transgressions. Historians have often been misled into believing that Creeks differentiated between the children of intermarriages and other Creeks. For example, many scholars have understood the Red Stick destruction of cattle, homes, clothing, and other forms of property in 1813 as a symbolic rejection of European American culture and a means to reorder Creek society.[36] In isolation this interpretation makes sense, but within the larger context of Creek history it may not. Years earlier, Creeks used similar forms of punishment, regardless of the transgressor's race or even cultural leanings. In 1799, for example, Mankiller and other warriors interrupted a meeting between Creek, Spanish, and U.S. officials, probably because of their opposition to rumored land cessions. Their actions outraged many Creek chiefs who demanded that the instigators be "beaten with sticks, and cropped & their houses and property destroyed and the others beaten and left naked on the Ground." Mankiller "defended Himself," but he, too, was eventually "pull'd down." They "burnt his House and destroy'd Ducks, fowls and every thing belonging to him[,] beat him until he was on the Ground as a dead man[,] cut of[f] one ear with part of the cheek and put a Sharp Stick up his Fundament."[37]

Perhaps unaware that Native customs structured the lives of Indian countrymen, some European Americans, especially those who quickly passed through Creek country, derided traders for their temporary relationships. They called the relationships "*Winchester*-Weddings," "left-handed marriages," or "casual marriages," because these relationships countered European American mores. The connotations of these relationships led many observers to use the term *wench* to describe Indian wives. Others equated "the trading girls" with prostitution because their "profession" was to "get Money by their Natural Parts." Many traders treated these relationships as temporary affairs. If they returned to European American society, they normally returned alone.[38]

At the same time Creeks did not necessarily consider the short-term relationships with "trading girls" to be marriages. The confusion resulted because Creeks did not restrict women's sexual affairs to the confines of marriage. They punished adultery severely—usually cropping the ears and hair of female perpetrators and beating male transgressors. Yet premarital sex itself carried no taboo—just rigorous rules that prohibited sex (in or out of marriage) just before battle or during certain festivals, pregnancy, or a hunt. Such "freedom" confused many European American observers who conflated sanctioned sexual intercourse and marriage. Moravian missionary Abraham Steiner, for example, failed to differentiate between the two when he claimed "one may marry for a day, a night, or a week without objections being raised." Despite Steiner's confusion, Creeks did not consider casual relations to be a form of marriage.[39]

Despite the structured nature of Creek sexual relations, Steiner and other European Americans saw "looseness" and "prostitution" in the Creek's culturally sanctioned sexual practices. Creeks offered selected visitors the "services" of single women, as gifts and as signs of hospitality. Creek attitudes toward sexuality permitted single Creek women to have casual liaisons without losing the community's respect. Even married women could be sexually active with guests, provided their husbands accepted the situation. Creeks regarded relations with married women a special privilege, and only the most notable guests enjoyed such honors. Functionally, the short-term relations with white traders provided women and their kin connections to trade goods and gave traders the protection needed to live among the Indians.[40]

Contrasts between the European American and Creek systems of sexuality created intercultural tensions, especially when Creeks did not initiate the contact. When Creek women approached colonists with opportunities for sexual relations, no disgrace accompanied rejection, and few European American men publicly objected to the overtures. When European Americans took the initiative, however, insults were likely. This was the case when Sir Richard Everard visited the Coweta village in 1741. Upon his arrival the British baron informed the local *mico*, Chigellie, "that he was a person of Distinction, and a Beloved Man of the King of England." Chigellie responded as was customary: he summoned other village leaders with the expectation of receiving "a Talk from the Great King." Everard informed the congregating Indians that he had not come to speak. Confused, Chigellie asked why he came to the nation. The Baron responded by saying that "he came there to lye with their Women." Swiftly, the meeting ended. Chigellie stood up, "took ye Barronets Gold laced Hat off his head, putting it on his own, and gave him an Old hat in Exchange." After this forced gift exchange, the Indian leader dismissed the baron, telling him "when any of his Daughters wanted an husband he would send for him." A disgraced Everard never returned. Traders who witnessed the exchange left "much offended at ye Baronets behavior, and told [Chigellie] that [they] Suspected, he had escaped from the Strong House in England."[41] Despite the rumored "looseness" of Native women, travelers did not easily find "bedfellows." Instead Creek women selectively offered their company.

Short-term marriages did occur between Creeks and European American colonists, often when potentially long-term marriages failed. Sometimes traders left their wives just as they originally planned, and other relationships ended despite initial expectations to the contrary. Joseph Fitzwalter, for example, arrived in colonial Savannah a bachelor at the age of thirty-one. He held hopes for marriage, but even Governor Oglethorpe recognized that the colony's gender imbalance might result in his and others' frustrations. There are "above 700 men more than there are women," Oglethorpe would later complain. "Most of these would marry if they could get wives."[42] A peculiar personality and his landless condition further limited Fitzwalter's hopes for marriage within colonial Georgia. However, while employed as the gardener to the Board of Trustees in 1735, his life turned around. The Creeks offered him a marriage to Tuscanies (Molly), a relation of several prominent Creek leaders. For Fitzwalter the cultural frontier did little to dampen his enthusiasm. He thought that his new wife would make a fine English bride. He hoped "that Time will wear her of the Savage way of Living." Shortly after the wedding the Creeks approached Fitzwalter with another opportunity. "The Indians," the gardener wrote to his employer, "are very much for my going to the Nation to Trade with Them and that I Refer to your [Oglethorpe's] better Judgement being unwilling to do anything without your Instructions." The governor approved, and Fitzwalter joined the deerskin trade. The marriage quickly failed, Fitzwalter's Indian spouse abandoned him, and his career in the Indian trade abruptly ended. Without the protection that Tuscanies and her clan afforded him, Fitzwalter could not remain in the Indian nation. He returned to Savannah, Georgia, where he soon remarried and worked as a tavern keeper and wharfinger until his death in 1742. Fitzwalter's short-term experience in the deerskin trade prevented him from obtaining a large estate, and at his death he left meager holdings.[43]

Unlike Fitzwalter, several European Americans forged permanent homes and families among the Indians. Although "married in the Indian way," Kendall Lewis lived with his wife for more than thirty years. Abram Mordecai moved to the Creek Nation in 1785, married a Creek woman of African descent, and remained among the Indians until his death over a half-century later.[44] Despite the common intention of returning to European American society, many deerskin traders chose not to leave their Creek villages. An English traveler explained this reality in 1763. "Some came here as traders, took an Indian woman, *possibly* intending to cast her off when they should get rich enough to retire," he explained. "But either they have not yet become sufficiently rich, or else they have come to like the Indian country and the Indian customs."[45] According to other observers, European Americans remained among the Indians because they became attached to the Creek lifestyle. Traveler John Lawson, for example, observed "that *English* Men, and other *Europeans* that have been accustom'd to the Conversation of these Savage Women, and their Way of Living, have been so allur'd with that careless sort of Life, as to be constant to their *Indian* Wife, and her Relations, so long as they liv'd, without ever desiring to return again amongst the *English*."[46] More often than not, the Indian "Way of Living" included "black eyed boys and girls" under the care of their mothers and "farms and herds, which also are yearly increasing."[47] The Creek's matrilineal structure meant that husbands who abandoned their wives also had to leave their children, lands, and cattle behind.

Most Indian countrymen, whether they came as part of the deerskin trade or not, brought material possessions with them into Indian villages. During the American Revolution nearly three thousand British Loyalists fled to the lands of the southeastern Indians, bringing their African slaves, cattle, and other moveable goods. During the war these Loyalists opted to move out of the southern colonies because of what East Florida governor Patrick Tonyn called the "cruel and unrelenting severity with which [the revolutionaries in Georgia and South Carolina] treated the loyalists." Revolutionaries confiscated property, threatened lives, and plundered farms and businesses.[48] Pressures to enlist in Revolutionary militias also pushed some southerners into Creek villages. British agent John Stuart understood that "A Great Number of Families wishing to Avoid the Calamities of a rancorous Civil War," migrated "from the different Provinces, to Seek bread and peace in those remote deserts."[49]

British refugees saw two benefits in going to Creek villages rather than finding safety elsewhere. First, a pre-existing community of European American traders with Loyalist sympathies provided them with places to stay. Harboring assumptions of returning, most Loyalists sought the comfort of these nearby temporary residences. Moreover, the permanent population of Indian countrymen ameliorated the culture shock associated with entering Indian villages. Several dozen Loyalists went to Hickory Ground to find refuge with trader Lachlan McGillivray and his Creek son Alexander. Frank Moore, for example, wrote that "in Mr. McGillivray's rice barn the ladies told me there were fifty men, women, and children." There the refugees found a plantation that resembled homesteads on the American side of the frontier, with residents who spoke English and dinner tables that offered typical colonial fare. Second, and perhaps more importantly, the Creeks represented a potential reserve of anti-American soldiers. Most Creek villages wavered between neutrality and open support of the British during the war. Loyalist refugees hoped to end the wavering and forge an anti-Revolutionary strike force.[50]

These hopes came to fruition, and Creek villages became bases for retaliatory strikes against the American Revolutionaries. Such assaults began early in the war, continued after the peace in 1787, and led to several instances where "white men dressed and painted like Indians" fought alongside Creek warriors.[51] In June 1776, seven hundred southeastern Indians "turned out against the settlements, not by order of the royal officers, but incited by about forty whites, who had fled to them from the Congaree."[52] Three years later Thomas Jefferson expressed his fear that "these Savages, [who] are employed by the British nation as allies in the War against the Americans," would unfavorably sway the balance on the southern front.[53] Jefferson's fears were somewhat warranted. By that point in the war U.S. attempts to preserve Creek neutrality had mostly failed, and American officials began to complain about the alliances between "some of your mad people and the Tories and bad people who remain among [the Creeks]."[54]

Loyalist Indian countrymen remained a presence in southern Indian society long after the war, even after the realization that the Tory cause was lost. With the cessation of violence, Loyalist refugees frequently chose not to return to their former residences. Some enlisted in British regiments, while others went to Canada, England, Bermuda, Ireland, and East Florida. Some stayed among the Creeks. James Walsh could not return to South Carolina, where he had earned a reputation as "a despisable murdering swamp Tory."[55] Others remained within Creek villages because they sought futures as deerskin traders or because they had found Indian spouses. The prevalence of British Loyalists among the southeastern Indians led John Chisholm to claim in 1797 that he could track down fifteen hundred Tories in the five southeastern Indian nations. Swan estimated that most of the three hundred white refugees in Creek villages had "been attached to the British in the late war, and of course have from loss of friends and property, or persecution, retained bitter resentments against the people of the United States."[56] Some of the most notable fugitive British Loyalists who remained in the Creek Confederacy after the war included Timothy Barnard, William Augustus Bowles, Abram Mordecai, Samuel Mims, George Wellbank, James Russell, and James Walsh.

Many Loyalists had deserted from military units and entertained no hopes of continuing the fight. After Abram Mordecai deserted his post, he never looked back. His loyalty to the Crown ended with his decision to take flight. [57] In fact, soldiers of all the region's militaries deserted to Creek villages in the eighteenth century. [58] An anonymous English traveler among the Creeks recorded that the Indian countrymen "have found their way here from different causes. Some of them are discharged soldiers, whose ties to kindred and home have been much worn, if not entirely broken off," he wrote. "They would about as lief marry an Indian woman and settle in the country, as to go back to the States." French, Spanish, British, and American officers noticed that soldiers found refuge among the Indians. [59] The loneliness of frontier posts often encouraged single soldiers to seek out the companionship to be had in Native villages. Because of this, each of the European military contingents in the southeast actively forbade interracial contacts—especially sexual relations—between soldiers and Indians. [60]

William Simory's story illustrates the path that dozens of soldiers took to obtain residence among the Creeks. Simory fled to the Creeks to escape military service to the English Crown. By 1772 he had found a position working for Robert Mackay, a prominent deerskin trader. His loyalty to his Creek family was clear: Simory reportedly stated that "he had been formerly a Soldier to the great king and run away from him and would now live and die amongst [the Creeks]." Simory may have believed himself to be a Creek Indian, but the Crown tried to arrest him for treason anyway. [61] Similarly, James McQueen deserted his military post and moved to the Creeks to avoid facing punishment for striking an officer. Spaniards stationed in Florida also found their way to Creek villages. As Thomas Simpson Woodward recalled, Jim Henry had a Chehaw mother, but his father was a "Cuban Spaniard, and one of the deserters from St. Augustine." [62]

Because of the oppressive nature of indentured servitude, the problem of runaways and revolts plagued colonial society. In 1735 the red string affair "threw [Georgia] into great confusion." Nearly fifty indentured servants, distinguished by red strings tied around their right wrists and assisted by local Creek Indians, stole guns and threatened to overturn the colonial order. Although the uprising was quickly put down by the freeholders in Georgia, the red string affair provided the means for several dozen servants, mostly Irish immigrants, to escape their legal obligations. Several found refuge among the Creeks. [63] Servants, however, did not always require communal efforts to escape their bondage. William Stephens complained in the 1740s that many of Georgia's servants fled to South Carolina and to Indian lands from which there was little hope of returning them. [64]

The observations of Stephens and the experience of the red string affair parallel a modern oral tradition. Two villages, Broken Arrow and Big Springs, according to modern Creek Indians, began in the eighteenth century as communities of escaped indentured servants. Their inhabitants, mostly if not all male, married neighboring Creek women, and the villages gradually became incorporated within the Creek Confederacy. When the southeastern Indians were forcibly removed west of the Mississippi River in the nineteenth century, the descendants of these marriages went west. Although the literal truth of this oral tradition cannot be verified, both towns obtained reputations for having large intermarried white populations, and at least several dozen escaped servants became Creek residents. If not literally "true," the oral tradition points to the incorporation of European American fugitives.[65]

Criminals from each of the neighboring European colonies formed another group of Indian countrymen in Creek villages. In 1771 Governor James Wright called Indian villages a "Kind of Asylum for Offenders who will fly from justice . . . and in the Process of time (and Perhaps no great Distance) they will become formidable Enough, to Oppose His Majesty's Authority . . . and throw everything into Confusion."[66] Forty years later, Moravian missionaries complained that Indian countrymen hindered the efforts to spread the gospel because "most of them are escaped criminals from Georgia and elsewhere who are hiding with the Indians."[67] As long as European Americans shared a border with the Creeks, they worried that criminals would find asylum among them and then commit further crimes under the Indians' protection.[68]

Although some observers may have derided Indian countrymen with reputations of criminality simply because they chose to live among the Indians, the reality of fugitive criminals among the Creeks remained real. As a result colonial officials actively tried to return criminals from the sanctuary provided by Creek villages. In 1744 Georgians tried Ambrose Morrison for the murder of Thomas Wright. For the past year Georgians had been unable to bring Morrison to trial because he had spent most of this time hiding among and working for deerskin traders. Attempts to apprehend him failed until he accompanied several other traders to Savannah in order to renew licenses. Refuge among the Creeks did more than provide Morrison a temporary refuge; it also provided him with character witnesses. The resulting trial saw Morrison exonerated, largely because of the testimony of fellow traders.[69] Ironically, a year later Morrison found a position working as a constable among the Indians, charged by Governor Oglethorpe to keep the peace.

Decades after Morrison's immersion into Native society, criminals continued to find refuge among the Creeks. In 1818 Thomas Hunter informed the governor of Alabama about "a white man named Smith who has married a squaw of the Creek nation" and engages in criminal activities with his Indian neighbors. There "surrounded by almost inaccessible hills . . . they are suspected [in] generall of giving aid and assistance not only to hostile and bad Indians but to rascals of every description." The assistance that Smith provided his fellow Indians apparently ensured his acceptance among the Creeks. As Hunter explained to Alabama's governor, capturing him would be difficult because of the thirty to forty Indian warriors who constantly surrounded and protected him. His support for "hostile" Indians proved his loyalty and guaranteed his safety within Native society.[70]

European Americans employed the same tactics to apprehend fugitives from justice that they used to capture runaway slaves. Often they proved successful. When John Logan took flight in 1822, the jailer of St. Clair County, Alabama, wrote Governor Israel Pickens asking for assistance. A reward, he claimed, would help return the fugitive who "has his family in Coosa Valley & perhaps will shelter among the Creek Indians." The Creeks returned Logan and claimed the reward.[71] Thomas L. McKenney, U.S. superintendent of Indian trade, similarly praised the 1818 arrest of "Betsy Perryman, a half breed and one of your slaves, named Nanny, grounded on information . . . that . . . [they] were at this time harboring a certain Mulatto Joe lately escaped from prison." When criminals fled to the Creeks, their freedom was not certain.[72]

Efforts to arrest fugitives frequently failed. Kendall Lewis, for example, escaped a murder accusation in Hancock, Georgia, by entering and finding a new life in Creek society. In 1808 a game of cards turned violent, and "Edward Denton of this country was murder'd by Kendall Lewis, who has absconded with an intention to escape the punishment which the law has annexed to his crime." Lewis's neighbors believed that bringing him to justice would be impossible. "It is presum'ed, from circumstances," they claimed "that he is either gone to the Creek nation, or the Mississippi territory." Lewis's flight into a Creek village paid off. He escaped punishment for murder, discarded his ignominious past, and gained influence among the Creeks. Within the span of a few years, Lewis became an interpreter and adviser to his village's chief, Big Warrior, who reportedly "would not attend any conference with the whites unless Kendall was present."[73] Because Lewis was bilingual and a blacksmith, the Creeks had little to gain but much to lose by returning him. A hundred-dollar reward could hardly compensate for his translating and metalworking skills. Lewis's Creek wife and her family further protected him from facing American justice. When Georgians came looking for him, agent Benjamin Hawkins instructed local Christian missionaries to keep him hidden. Hawkins, who relied on Lewis for his interpreting skills, understood that his Creek family would not allow his arrest. When Indian removal took the Creeks west of the Mississippi River two decades later, Lewis followed his wife, Creek children, and village to Indian Territory.[74]

The paths of refugee soldiers, debtors, criminals, and Loyalists converged into a single phenomenon when William Augustus Bowles came to the Creeks in 1778. Bowles arrived after a short stint in the British army. When the turmoil of the American Revolution struck Maryland, Bowles enlisted as a fourteen-year-old ensign to "uphold the dignity of the King." His military service, however, ended in December 1778 when he deserted his post in Pensacola, Florida. Bowles fled to the Lower Creeks, married an Indian woman, and started a family. When the Spanish attacked Pensacola in 1780, local Indians (including Bowles and other Loyalist refugees) came to its aid. When the Revolution ended and thousands of fellow Loyalists fled to Canada, Bowles returned to his home among the Creeks. Over the next two decades Bowles declared himself emissary to the British Crown, "styl[ed] himself Director General of the Muscogee," and obtained the support (and anger) of hundreds of Creeks, Seminoles, and Cherokees.[75]

In addition to his popularity in several Indian villages, Bowles attracted the allegiance of dozens of discontented white Americans and Indian countrymen. This did not go unnoticed. Benjamin Hawkins, who believed that Bowles was a threat to frontier order and American authority among the Creeks, regretted that "some of our unworthy citizens have been accomplices with Bowles."[76] Although their connection to Bowles earned them Hawkins's disfavor, their status as runaway criminals, deserters, or "unscrupulous traders" compounded his hostility. Bowles's actions confirmed the fears of neighboring Americans that the disgruntled masses among the Creeks could form a formidable force. Bowles plundered American settlements, led the Creek resistance to further land cessions, opposed traders whom he believed corrupt, led expeditions to steal horses and slaves in both Florida and Georgia, and offered runaway slaves shelter.[77]

Bowles was not the exception to the southeastern "white Indian" experience. Albert J. Pickett recalled that "hundreds of unprincipled men of vagrant dispositions like [Bowles] were to be found at this period, in all parts of the Creek Confederacy, deserters from the two armies & deserters from justice from the surrounding colonies."[78] The permeability of the southern frontier and the Creeks' acceptance of outsiders allowed men such as Bowles to escape the problems they faced in early American society. By voluntarily entering Creek villages, they could escape poverty, imprisonment, forced labor, indebtedness, political oppression, and ethnic discrimination. Once among the Creeks, the histories of these varied migrants converged. Most participated in the deerskin trade, intermarried, raised Creek children, became residents of Indian villages, and otherwise lived according to the demands of their wife's clan.

Not all Indian countrymen could completely discard their ethnic identities as European Americans, and few of them wanted to abandon their cultural assumptions. Many of them continued to adhere to the mores and use the skills that predated their entry into their Native communities. Although these refugees lived as residents of Creek villages and pledged their loyalty accordingly, their cultural traits and appearances allowed them to remain European Americans in the eyes of European American society. This convinced some in European American society to treat Indian countrymen as if they never rescinded their European American pasts. Living among the Creeks did not lead Americans to believe that their ethnic identities and loyalties had changed.

CHAPTER 3

Kin and Strangers

In the aftermath of the particularly bloody battle of Tallapoosa in 1813, U.S. general Andrew Jackson discovered an Indian infant "sucking his dead mothers breast." Jackson, apparently believing that the motherless child would not be cared for by the surviving Creeks in the village, took the fate of the orphaned child into his own hands. After feeding the infant with some sugar water, the future president wrote to his wife, Rachel, to explain that "charity and christianity says he ought to be taken care of and I send him to my little Andrew [Jackson Donelson, his adopted son] and I hope [we] wil[l] adopt him as one of our family."[1] Indeed, in the following years the family did. Jackson insisted that Lyncoya receive a grammar school education, eventually arranged a harness-making apprenticeship, called him "son," and even tried to have him enrolled at the U.S. Military Academy at West Point. The future president and advocate of Indian removal believed that Lyncoya—despite his Indian birth, lineage, and appearance—could embrace American culture and, of course, naturally desired to do so. As a privileged slaveholder and successful soldier, Jackson concluded that he had the best chance of shaping his Indian child into an American.[2]

Because of this optimism, the future president and his neighbors reportedly expressed surprise when in later years Lyncoya continued to exhibit "Indian" behavior. Jackson's frustration at Lyncoya's apparent resistance to accepting American culture, however, never diminished the president's belief that Lyncoya would eventually "mature" and Americanize. James Parton, a nineteenth-century biographer of Jackson, wrote that Lyncoya's "Indian nature" could never be erased. Despite his insistence on a connection between human biology and behavior, Parton does record the shock Lyncoya's juvenile acts—as opposed to the naturally Indian acts—received. "A lady of Nashville tells me, that when, as a little girl, she used to visit the Hermitage with her parents, this Indian boy was a terror; as it was his delight to spring out upon the other children from some ambush about his house, and frighten them with loud yells and horrible grimaces."[3]

Many eighteenth- and early-nineteenth-century white southerners shared Jackson's belief in the potential of Native Americans to learn and live by European American ideals and customs. Few believed that this process would be quick, many used this doubt to justify Indian removal, and others expressed doubt that it would ever occur. Yet a belief in the theoretical potential for Indian acculturation was widely shared. The assumption that race and culture were not linked motivated a host of religious and cultural missionaries and agents to enter Creek villages and try to foster various forms of acculturation. This belief represented a continuation of a Jeffersonian understanding of Indians, and as Bernard Sheehan and others have demonstrated, it often justified violent assaults on Indian culture and society. European Americans could feel sympathy for individual Indians and believe in their own humanitarianism, while simultaneously denigrating and destroying Native traditions and customs.[4]

Creeks also disassociated race from culture, as they defined members of their villages in ways that minimized the importance of biology and physical appearances. Instead Creeks typically determined identities and nationality with more mutable categories. Adoption rituals and an emphasis on matrilineal clans routinely turned outsiders into insiders, and strangers into kin. They used tattoos, haircuts and hairstyles, body paints, and animal greases to manipulate their physical appearances and their identities. As a result Indian countrymen and their Native children had little problem, at least physically, blending into eighteenth-century Creek society.

Few residents of the eighteenth-century South attached the modern and innate standards of "blood" or "race" to being an Indian or European American. Instead, most eighteenth-century Creeks and Americans relied on traits that could be learned, practiced, altered, contested, and concealed to determine who was who. They assumed that members of one society could become full members of the other. The savage could become civilized, the heathen could convert to Christianity, the "redman" could become white, and the Indian could become American. Conversely, some European Americans feared they might "turn Indian," Christians could "revert" to savagery, and white southerners could become Creek Indians. Members of both societies believed that Native Americans and European Americans had been separated for generations, if not since their creation. History and cultural developments, not biological inevitability, separated the two societies and made them appear incompatible.[5]

Biology did not inevitably separate Natives from newcomers; a range of mutable traits did. Eighteenth-century Creeks and European Americans relied on appearances, cultural behaviors (including but not limited to languages), kin connections, and political loyalties to determine the ethnic identities of strangers. Creeks and European Americans disagreed over how to interpret these traits, and their interpretations necessarily changed over time. Nevertheless, both cultures used the same categories to determine identities, and they recognized that the inconstant natures of these categories made Indian and European American mutable categories. Creeks expected other Creeks to appear with specific cultural markings, live within a range of culturally proscribed actions, and accept the conventions of clan ties. Those who did not were outsiders: American, Seminole, Spaniard, Georgian, African, Cherokee, Choctaw, or French. European Americans had a similar range of cultural norms that helped them distinguish themselves from outsiders. Although biology was not ignored in southern society and was often obsessed over when it came to those of African descent, many European Americans drew distinctions between the nature of the "Indian" and "Negro" races.[6]

During the eighteenth century the range of acceptable behavior within Creek society expanded to include many of the activities common within southern society. As a result, for eighteenth-century Creeks, acting like a Native often meant acting like a white southerner. Southerners and Creeks often performed similar acts for contrasting reasons and with modified rules, but still the cultural divide between southeastern Indians and European Americans was not as wide as modern scholars and eighteenth-century observers infer. At the very least the range of acceptable behaviors in the two communities overlapped. Both cultures increasingly accepted members who enslaved African bondsmen, herded cattle, grew cotton and corn, believed in the racial inferiority of Africans, and pursued market participation. Throughout the century both cultures also maintained a non-slaveholding majority, unequal distribution of American-style wealth, and an ethos that attached martial valor to masculinity. Some aspects of the two cultural worlds overlapped, and the divide that separated Creek behavior from European American blurred.[7]

Many of the changes within Indian society resulted from the demands of the deerskin trade. As the intercultural deerskin trade permeated the southeast, nothing less than a consumer revolution altered the region's Native societies.[8] The cultural trends were so clear that many Americans began to view the southeastern Indians as "civilized tribes." Although this term embodied ethnocentric assumptions about "civilization" while also having negative connotations for the other presumably "savage nations," it also implied that the Creeks and the other southeastern nations were becoming more acceptable to American sensibilities. They were still Natives, but in the opinion of many in European American society, the Creek's acceptance of African slavery, their system of agriculture, and their participation in the deerskin market made them seem to be well on the path of Americanization.[9]

The changes within southeastern Indian society led many European Americans, especially during the debates over Indian removal, to differentiate the Creeks and their neighbors from Natives to the north and west. There are two "classes" of Indians, one missionary wrote. One is "uncivilized," and "the other . . . embraces the Cherokees, Creeks, and some other southern tribes, who have become partially civilized, have instituted governments, and are practicing agriculture and the mechanic arts."[10] It also led others to describe Creeks as undergoing a "transition from a savage to a civilized state."[11] The obvious ethnocentric connotations of the term "civilized" have led to the term's modern demise. Yet scholars should not throw out the observation with its biased implications. Eighteenth- and nineteenth-century Americans perceived a difference between southeastern Indians and Natives elsewhere and believed that this difference was related to their adoption of European American cultural traits.[12]

As the Creeks became more dependent on the deerskin trade, they and American settlers in the southern backcountry increasingly relied on European-made clothing. Not surprisingly the fashions often reflected the appearances of the Scottish traders who sold them.[13] British naturalist William Bartram explicitly compared the Native style of dress to that of the Scottish Highlanders. Seemingly unaware of the changes in Native styles that occurred earlier in the eighteenth century, the naturalist wrote that "their clothing of their body is very simple and frugal. Sometimes a ruffled shirt of fine linen, next to the skin, and a flap which covers their lower parts; this garment somewhat resembled the ancient Roman breeches, or the kilt of the Highlanders." Thus, by the time of the American Revolution, Creeks and their European American neighbors could not necessarily tell each other apart through clothing alone. To no surprise many Scotsmen discovered that their Highlander styles helped them blend into both Native and American society.[14]

"Civilized Indians" could approach becoming Americans because in the eighteenth century Indians did not need to change their biological makeup to become Americans. "All" Natives had to do was replace their "savage practices" with the trappings of civilization.[15] Most European Americans believed that being an Indian was a temporary state in the development of humankind. Indians could "rise in civilization" and become Americans, while Americans could undergo "race reversion" and become Indians. The fear of Indianization, in fact, often proved more powerful in American society. "'It is very easy to make an Indian out of a white man, but you cannot make a white man out of an Indian.'—which latter remark is profoundly true."[16] Eighteenth-century Americans used terms such as "turning Indian," "Indianization," and "Americanization" to describe the transculturation of individuals. Thus, many European Americans believed that "Indian" was a temporary identity, optimistically hoped that Natives would become fellow Americans, and hesitatingly accepted that the "civilized" could become "savage." On some occasions European Americans recognized that the self-identification as an "Indian" was a choice.[17]

Without an accepted biological classification to separate Indians from European Americans, many European Americans turned to simple, ethnocentric dichotomies, and in the process their categories often reflected more about themselves than the Natives. Passionate Indians hunted and gathered, while rational Americans farmed. Indians were drunkards; Americans were sober minded. Indians were naked; Americans covered themselves with clothing. Indians lived in nature; Americans lived above it. For every positive image of themselves, eighteenth-century Americans gave Indians a condescending counterimage. Each dichotomy, however, relied on mutable distinctions, as Americans recognized that Indians could become sober, take command, don clothing, and adopt American ethics. When the Indians completed this process of giving up their "Indian" traits, they ceased to be Indians and became instead Americans.[18]

In the eighteenth century Americans used the father-child, civilized-savage, and white-red dichotomies to distinguish Natives from Americans. The patriarchal imagery of the father-child metaphor, although taken to the extreme form by Andrew Jackson, was shared by other less notable Americans and relied on a mutable definition of "American" and "Indian." It worked with the simple supposition that when children (Indians) matured, they became parents (European Americans). The maturation process, which involved mass acculturation, would occur as naturally as children inevitably became adults. Nineteenth-century southern author William Gilmore Simms explicitly understood this assumption. "In relation to the European colonists [Natives were] to be treated as children, and gradually lifted to the social eminences of civilization, by a hand, equally firm and considerate." Simms firmly believed that in due time their "nomadic life" would give way to a "rise in civilization."[19]

Many European Americans also believed that their difference from Indians could be explained by a "civilized-savage" dichotomy. This hierarchical duality was never as rigid or self-apparent as some commentators believed. Indians could reject their savagery, and Americans could slide from civility, making both Indianization and Americanization possible. In other words, Natives were simply "savage whites," and Americans were "civil Indians." Eighteenth- and nineteenth-century religious missionaries and diplomats frequently worked on this premise.[20] Baptist missionary Isaac McCoy voiced this belief. In 1830 McCoy stated, "facts declare that the Indians are only what others would have been, had they been placed in similar circumstances—neither better not worse, neither more nor less wise, or virtuous or vicious, than others, and naturally no more attached to hunting or war than others. In a word, they are precisely what we should reasonably expect to find them." McCoy believed that as the material circumstances of the American Indian became more like that of the European American, so would his culture. In due time savage Indians would become civilized European Americans.[21]

The most enduring distinction between Creeks and European Americans relied on a seemingly unalterable condition—skin color. Yet in the eighteenth and early nineteenth century many European Americans frequently contended that even the skin color of Natives would "whiten" over time.[22] Thomas Jefferson, for example, followed with great interest the story of an Indian "who for near two Years past, has been gradually whitening. It began on his Breast, and has transfused itself throughout the whole Body to the Extremities. Above half his Hands and Fingers and half his Feet and Toes are yet of the Indian Colour and his Fac pied. The Skin on the other Parts is become a clear English White with *English Ruddiness*. The Complexion and Colour of his Skin is even clearer and fairer than most white Persons with whom he has been compared. He has had no Sickness but has continued all the while in good Health." Jefferson's observations reflected the common attribution of the redness of the Indians to environmental circumstances or historical sources—not biology. Because Jefferson believed that skin color, like all of the dichotomies between Natives and Americans, was mutable, he could assert that "the ultimate point of rest and happiness for them [Indians] is to let our settlements and theirs meet and blend together, to intermix, and become one people."[23] Jacques Fontaine, a French Huguenot in Georgia, shared Jefferson's belief that time would unite the Europeans and Natives in culture and appearance. He believed that the Indian appeared different because of cultural practices. "The Indian children when born are as white as Spaniards or Portuguese," he wrote in 1757. "Were it not for the practice of going naked in the summer and besmearing themselves with bears' grease, &c, they would continue white."[24] Naturalist Mark Catesby wrote with a similar perspective in 1771. "The colour of [the Indian's] skin is tawny, yet would not be so dark did they not daub themselves over with Bear's oyl continually from their infancy."[25] John Archdale provided his description of the Indian with the same emphasis on self-manipulation. "The Natives [of the southeast] are somewhat Tawny, occasioned, in a great measure, by Oyling their Skins, and by the naked Raies of the Sun." The belief in mutable differences between Indian and American allowed Archdale to believe that "if managed discreetly . . . many of them, in a few years, [may] become Civilized, and then very capable of the Gospel of Christ." The apparently "tawny" or "reddish" color of the Indian's skin, these commentators believed, did not result from biology; it occurred because Native Americans intentionally manipulated their appearances.[26]

Philip Thicknesse, an eighteenth-century Englishman, used various cultural markings to distinguish Americans from Indians, or as he stated, "Christians" from "savages." In 1788 he wrote that "their rude dress; painted faces, sliced ears, *nose bobs!* and tattooed Skins rendered their external appearance, to us Britons, singularly savage." Still, Thicknesse was not completely repulsed by Natives because of their seemingly "savage" appearances. For several months he considered a marriage with a Creek woman, believing that she would quickly learn the attributes of civilization. Unlike his perception of Africans, Thicknesse wrote that he "could perceive no traces of that bloody and revengeful disposition among the Indians, of which we have in these later days heard so much." Instead, he discovered "by making frequent excursions to the court of *new Yamacra*, and picking up a little of their language . . . that my person, and property, was as safe at the court of *Yamacra*, as at any court in Christendom." Thicknesse discovered that the "singularly savage" "external appearance" of the Creeks was merely the cultural facade of an otherwise civil people. After his initial repulsion to the Natives, Thicknesse realized that they had some of the "better virtues" to offer him. Nothing permanent or insurmountable, he concluded, separated southeastern Indians from European Americans.[27]

The belief in the mutability of identities and behavior led several missionaries (religious and cultural) into Creek villages during the eighteenth and early nineteenth centuries. Although this diverse group of European Americans differed in their stated goals, tactics, and beliefs, they shared a pervasive belief in the ability of Indians to embrace American culture. Baptist missionary Lee Compere, who proselytized among the Creeks at Withington Station from 1823 to 1829, epitomized this group. Compere understood his religious teachings to be the key to the total transformation of Creek society. If the "motley group" of "Jews, heathens and professed christians, the children of the forest, and those of civilized life" would simply embrace his teachings, he reasoned, the entire lower South would be transformed. "How soon then would the shades of distinction disappear! for all would easily be recognized as the children of one common parent, and as destined to one common home." Compere, like other Christian missionaries to the Creeks, sought to teach more than baptism and salvation—he sought to transform gender relations, literacy, parenting, burial practices, and nearly every other aspect of Creek culture.[28] Through hard work or prayer, Compere though he could transform Indians into Americans.

Just as Compere denied the existence of permanent "Indian" traits, Creeks manipulated their appearances to indicate status and ethnic identities. They plucked their beards, cut and styled their hair, and used various oils and paints to create a "Creek appearance." Thomas Ashe observed in 1682 that "their Hair [is always] black and streight, tied various ways, sometimes oyl'd and painted, struck through with Feathers for Ornament or Gallantry; their Eyes black and sparkling, little or no Hair on their Chins."[29] His mentioning of the occasional use of oil and paint inferred that the Creeks neutralized the varied physical traits among themselves by matting down their hair and coloring their skin. A common appearance needed to be created to differentiate themselves from non-Creek outsiders. In 1734 German Protestant Salzburgers in Georgia observed that the neighboring Indians took careful measures to ensure that their appearances reflected their communal identities. Although the newcomers to Georgia did not understand the symbolism used, they recognized that the Creeks "paint their faces with various colors, especially black shaded with red. . . . They always go bareheaded, all of them have short black hair which they somewhat trim at the crown. To dress up they put small white feathers in their hair and behind their ears, which they consider a symbol of bravery. . . . Most men and women have stripes painted on their necks. . . . They have no beards, and if any would grow they pull it out." Appearances mattered, but eighteenth-century Creeks and European Americans recognized that differences between the peoples did not occur naturally. By meticulously controlling one's appearance, naturally occurring physical differences could be either overlooked or modified, and identities could be altered.[30]

Creeks also used hair, on both the head and the body, to determine the ethnic identities of Creeks, other Natives, Africans, and Europeans.[31] Alexander McGillivray, for example, learned through oral tradition that the southeastern Indians who confronted Hernando de Soto differentiated Spaniards from themselves because they had "hair all over their bodies."[32] Several eighteenth-century commentators observed that hair, or the lack of it, was culturally determined. Philip Georg Friedrich Von Reck, the Dutch traveler, discovered in 1736 that "the [Creek] men have little or no beard, because they pluck the hair out continually."[33] Thomas Jefferson used this information to critique George Louis Leclerc Buffon's thesis that an American climate created an inferior Indian. In response to Buffon's proof of the "inferior" unmasculine Native—that they "have no beard"—Jefferson claimed that "had [Buffon] known the pains and trouble it costs the men to pluck out by the roots the hair that grows on their faces, he would have seen that nature had not been deficient in that respect."[34] Southeastern Native Americans and European Americans, Jefferson believed, differed in appearance because they chose to be different.

Southeastern Indians consciously used distinct hairstyles to separate themselves from each other, Frenchmen, Spaniards, Englishmen, and other neighbors—whether Native, African, or European in origin. Some European Americans were able to learn the Native system for demarcating nationality with
hairstyles. A "Gentleman" from Augusta, Georgia, for example, could tell "a
Nottawega, by his Hair, Hatchet, and two small wooden Images, that were tied
to his neck."[35] Neighboring Choctaws earned reputations for growing their hair
long, while a tribe in Pensacola obtained the name "Hair People" because of a
similar custom.[36] These observations revealed that the range of Native hairstyles
was as distinct as the material icons that modern archeologists traditionally use
to demarcate communities. Similarly, a South Carolinian in 1763 observed that
"[the Creek Indians'] hair is always black, without curls; the men cut and dress
theirs with beads and other ornaments in various shapes, by which the tribes
easily distinguish one another."[37] Southeastern Indians altered their appearances, and to the observant colonist they did so in ways that distinguished one
Native nation from another.[38] Quite similarly the southeastern Choctaws used
cradleboards to flatten the heads of their infants and mark their status.[39]

Creeks also manipulated their appearances to delineate differences *within*
their society. In the eighteenth century a lack of cranial hair was a symbol of
shame. Creeks cropped the hair of adulterers and enemy warriors doomed to
execution. They also endowed the act of scalping with symbolic importance.[40]
Southeastern Indians also used hairstyles to indicate marital status and to state
they were in mourning.[41] In 1744 William Stephens, the secretary to the Board
of Trustees of Georgia, observed that certain markings had ceremonial uses as
well as serving as a means of personal identification. "They [the Creeks] were
all painted with Feathers in their Hair, in the manner they use when they go
to War &c."[42] Stephens's observation, much like Lawson's, reveals that Creeks
shaped their appearances to suit their social needs.

When hair color and style did not conform to Creek standards, but attitudes,
kinship, and residency did, the Creeks often embraced the difference as part of
a Creek identity. Just as the English often created nicknames for Indians with
odd physical traits, Creeks routinely did the same. A blond Indian, for example,
was known as Yellow Hair by his Creek kin. Another Creek was known as High
Headed Jim. Through this process of naming, Creeks incorporated biological
differences within a Creek identity.[43] One warrior from Pensacola alternated
between the names Kellessechuppo and Beard. In the sixteenth century another
southeastern Indian went by the name "The Bearded."[44] In other instances
Creeks minimized the importance of biological differences through various
rituals. During adoption ceremonies, for example, Creeks also used paints and

hairdressings as symbols of a new identity. At the very start of Eunice Barbor's adoption, her Creek captors "daubed my face and body with black and red paint, and dressed my head with feathers, in imitation of their own!" Various Indian countrymen also used paints to distinguish themselves as Creek warriors and spiritual leaders. Such acts of naming and dressing allowed Creeks to embrace and incorporate outsiders of various appearances.[45]

The adoption rituals of eighteenth-century Creeks also reveal that they did not believe that biology inevitably separated Creeks from European Americans. Creeks believed that adoption turned strangers into Creeks, did not differentiate European outsiders from either African or Native outsiders, and considered adoptees to be as equally connected to the ancient past as were Native-born Creeks. Thus, adoption displayed the Creeks' nonbiological understanding of ethnic identity. Through a ritualized acculturation process, hundreds of outsiders of all ethnic backgrounds became members of Creek villages in the eighteenth century.[46] Non-Creek Natives, Africans, and Europeans all entered Creek villages through a similar process of adoption. Biological distinctions did not matter. At times the adoptees obtained the identities of deceased Native kin and fulfilled their kin functions, yet others received identities as members of, but newcomers to, the Creeks. Even though the Creeks believed that clans were lineages to the ancient world, adoption allowed newcomers to be attached to a clan.[47]

Because Creeks associated appearances with identities, the use of permanent tattoos also helped Creeks and other southeastern Indians determine the identities of newcomers to their communities, whether young children or adopted adults. In 1751 Jean-Bernard Bossu recalled that when Indians living on the Arkansas River "adopted me. . . . A deer was tattooed on my thigh as a sign that I have been made a warrior and a chief. I submitted to this painful operation with good grace." Bossu clearly misunderstood or at least misstated his place in the southeastern Native community. The tattoo of a deer probably indicated his new clan affiliation, not his personal rank within the nation. Bossu's other comments about his experiences make it clear that he entered the deer clan as an adopted peer, not as a leader. Nevertheless, Bossu meticulously recorded the manner of using tattoos to mark adoptees. He reported he was sitting "on a wildcat skin while an Indian burned some straw. [The Indian who drew the tattoo] put the ashes in water and used this simple mixture to draw the deer. He then traced the drawing with big needles, pricking me until I bled. The blood mixture with the ashes from the straw formed a tattoo which can never be removed." The painful and permanent process of tattooing allowed other Creek Indians to recognize immediately Bossu's ethnic identity and social standing.

With his clan identity literally written on his body, southeastern Indians could see the obligations they owed to this newcomer.[48]

The southeastern Indians who encountered Hernando de Soto in 1543 apparently used tattoos in a similar manner. When de Soto met Juan Ortiz, a Spanish captive among the southeastern Indians, he described Ortiz as "a Christian, naked and sun-burnt, his arms tattooed after their manner, and he in no respect differing from them."[49] Ortiz had not become an Indian to the Spaniards, who hoped to "redeem" him. Yet his appearance confused the Spaniards, who initially saw him as just another Native warrior. In 1851 historian Albert James Pickett understood from his communication with several Creek Indians what it meant for "Jean Ortiz [to be] tattooed *in the manner of the Indians.*" Ortiz, his captors, and his adopted male kin used tattoos to state tangibly their identities. From before European contact until the late eighteenth century, southeastern Natives physically ensured that acculturated captives and young children could be identified by their physical appearances.[50]

Creeks also used paints and jewelry to place adoptees into a clan. European American Eunice Barber recalled that after she was taken captive, she was brought to a village where the Creeks decided to adopt her. "At the entrance of their village," Barber wrote, "they daubed my face and body with black and red paint, and dressed my head with feathers, in imitation of their own!—as soon as they had completed thus decorating my person, according to their Indian mode, they all set up a terrible yell." The ritualized transformation of a female European American into a female Creek demanded that Barber's physical appearance change, but it did not demand the more permanent tattoos that were primarily reserved for men. Instead the Creeks used ritual devices that temporarily altered her appearance but permanently changed her ethnic and clan identity.[51]

Just as kinship defined Creek identities, it was equally important on the American side of the frontier.[52] Kinship, like appearance and cultural traits, could unite Indians and Americans. Creating an intertwined American-Native kin network necessitated intermarriage. This led dozens of eighteenth-century European Americans to voice their belief that intermarriage could unite the two societies. Virginian William Byrd, for example, wrote in 1700 that the British failure to encourage intermarriage with Indians ensured separate kinship networks and intercultural hostilities. Had the British "brought their Stomachs to embrace this prudent Alliance," the Indians could have been Americanized. Intermarriage, he wrote, "[is the] only method of converting the Natives to Christianity. For, after all that can be said, a sprightly Lover is the most prevailing Missionary that can be sent amongst these, or any other Infidels."[53]

Because of the socializing influence of white fathers, many eighteenth-century Americans believed that "the mestizo sons of [intermarriages] are most inclined toward the whites." Thus, the "mixed" children of intermarriages were the key to the future amalgamation of the two races.[54]

Jefferson directly attached intermarriage with his hope in uniting Creeks and Americans into one culture. In an 1803 letter to Hawkins, he prophesized that intermarriage held the key to bringing Indians, the Creeks in particular, into American society. Tell the Indians, he said, that "your blood will mix with ours; and will spread, with ours, over this great island." The president continued by stating that "the ultimate point of rest and happiness for" Indians and Americans "is to let our settlements and theirs meet and blend together, to intermix, and become one people."[55] Jefferson, like many other proponents of Creek–European American intermarriages, assumed that these relationships cemented social connections because they created an intricate, multicultural web of kinship. Once created, the distinctions between Creek and American would gradually disappear.[56]

Unlike in the French colonies, where the government paid individuals to intermarry and learn the Indian culture, European American officials never subsidized intermarriages with the Creeks. In a few instances, usually after observing the French example in Canada and Louisiana, European Americans advanced the cause of intermarriages. In 1732, for example, the *South Carolina Gazette* carried a proposal that proclaimed intermarriage as the means to soothe over the tensions caused by the deerskin trade. By encouraging Native traders to come to established English towns, the writer explained, these Indian men "will have Opportunity by their daily conversing with the Fair Sex, and to be hoped, Encouragement sufficient, without Compulsion, to have, or take Christian Wives."[57] This early proposal for Indian men to marry white women apparently failed to attract much support, but in the century that followed some officials sanctioned relationships between Indian women and European American men. Return Meigs, who worked as a U.S. agent to the Cherokees, asserted in 1808 that "I encourage marriages between whitemen and Cherokee women. I always have and I allways will." Meigs made his rationale clear to Hawkins. "Where the blood is mixed with the whites, in every grade of it," he explained, "there is an apparent disposition leaning toward civilization, and this disposition is in proportion to its distance from the original stock."[58] Hawkins, who apparently considered and then rejected an offer of a Creek wife, was not completely convinced. Marriages did not lead to control over Indian society. Instead, he explained, "a man who keeps an Indian woman is the slave of her family and a slave to her whims and caprices." This reality made it impossible to control his subagents. As a result

Hawkins prohibited "any people in this department from having Indian wives." This regulation did not prohibit intermarriages, per se, but instead controlled the behavior of "those who are employed by the public."[59] Traders could still marry Indian wives, but those solely employed to represent the United States could not.

A similar proposal was suggested by Spanish governor Arturo O'Neil in Florida. "There is need that a good missionary should come promptly to make all the necessary arrangements to bring about marriages between the persons of these nations and some of our Europeans already distinguished for excessive fondness for the Indian women, and these equally enamored of the whites." O'Neil voiced a belief common in the Spanish colonies—intermarriages provided a means of controlling lands without literally inhabiting them. With intermarriages, he said, "in a short time the most fertile lands from the head of the Escambia River to the Tensaw River and all those on that side within sixteen leagues of this town would be immediately cultivated by friendly Indians and mestizos."[60]

Despite these beliefs in the transformative power of intermarriage, few proposals for sanctioned intermarriage were ever officially raised for Creek society, and none passed. Despite this lack of promotion, few eighteenth-century European Americans questioned the premise that intermarriage would theoretically unite European Americans with Native peoples. Some believed that the nature of the intermarriage connections was political; others saw it as economic. Nearly all believed that the French policy of promoting intermarriages gave them a diplomatic advantage.[61] Nevertheless, in the southeast, opponents found two major problems inherent in promoting intermarriage. Each problem related to the Creeks' insistence that Creek women stayed within their matrilineage's villages. First, because intermarriages demanded that European American men live among the Creeks, several critics saw a practical difficulty in getting white male volunteers. Those who could teach the "right" cultural attributes would naturally oppose leaving American culture and living among cultural "savages." Second, because intermarriages occurred in the midst of an Indian village, Natives could easily resist civilization. Instead of the husband Americanizing the village, the village tended to Indianize the husband. Frenchman J. Hector St. John Crevecoeur, for example, wrote that "there must be in their social bond something singularly captivating, and far superior to anything to be boasted of among us, for thousands of Europeans are Indians, and we have no examples of even one of those Aborigines having from choice become Europeans."[62] Kinship could unite Creeks and Americans, but Americans did not see all connections as desirable, let alone feasible. In theory, intermarriages could help bridge the gap between Indians and Americans, but few European Americans were willing to encourage the sacrifices necessary for an official policy regarding the Creeks.[63]

In the eighteenth century both Creeks and Americans differentiated themselves from each other, and like members of all societies, both distinguished insiders from outsiders or welcome neighbors from intruders. Creeks did not consider all residents of their villages, whether Native born or newcomers, to be Creeks. When Americans entered the Creek Nation in the eighteenth century, even if they were adopted or intermarried, they had to change their behavior and appearance to gain acceptance. Many traders, Tories, and other fugitives lived *among* the Creeks but not *as* Creeks. Both societies primarily relied on mutable cultural traits and did not simply use immutable biological concepts to differentiate ethnic Creeks from ethnic Americans. They both believed that identities could be chosen, rejected, and contested, and that these identities were, at least theoretically, temporary.[64] In the eighteenth century both Creeks and Americans believed that they knew the difference between a white man among the Indians and a white Indian, between an Indian countryman and a white trader, between a savage Indian and a civilized white man. Although both insisted that self-apparent differences separated Indians and Americans, they also believed that these differences could be bridged. Through intermarriage and the work of religious and cultural missionaries, Indians could reject their savagery and Americanize. At the same time both communities recognized that white southerners could reject their cultural pasts and become Creek Indians. The permeable barrier between Creek and American identities could occur because Creeks and Americans both determined these identities with mutable traits rather than biological "certainties." They recognized that appearances could be altered, behaviors could be learned, and kin connections could be created. European Americans recognized that Creeks used tattoos, clothing, hairstyles, body oils, and skin paint to alter their appearance. A distinct "Indian appearance" did not occur because of biological inevitability; instead the Creeks consciously created one.

This set the stage for the dual, and often ambiguous, identities of Indian countrymen and their Creek children. Without rigid unchanging standards to determine who was a Creek and who was an American, Indian countrymen and their Creek children could frequently assert both Creek and American identities. They often had kin connections to both worlds, knew how to appear both Creek and American, and understood the cultural rules of both societies. Creeks and Americans disagreed over the identities of these mixed individuals, as they saw the questions differently. A traditionalist Creek leader and member of the

Wind clan in one situation could be a white planter politician in another situation. Individuals could be accepted as Creek Indians in Creek society and white southerners in American society. Although this was rarely an easy situation, as the two worlds often demanded conflicting loyalties, a few individuals could seamlessly move between the two societies. The opportunities and complexities created by dual identities, in both European American and Native societies, are explored in the following section.

CHAPTER 4

Parenting and Practice

In February 1797 a Creek woman offered to arrange a marriage between her daughter and Indian agent Benjamin Hawkins. As Hawkins deliberated the proposal, concerns about cultural differences colored his decision. Since entering Indian territory a few months earlier, Hawkins had learned that marrying and having children with a Creek woman would require him to compromise his ideas about household management and parenting. "The woman and most of these Creek women," he wrote, are "in the habit of assuming and exercising absolute rule, such as it was over their children, and not attending to the advice of their white husbands." Hawkins considered this gender arrangement to be unacceptable and tried to explain this to the Creek woman. "The white men govern their families and provide clothing and food for them. The red men take little care of theirs, and the mothers have the sole direction of the children." After his comparison of American and Creek parenting roles, Hawkins demanded that if "I shall take one of my red women for a bedfellow . . . and she has a child, I shall expect it will be mine, that I may clothe it and bring it up as I please [and] I shall look upon them as my own children." The Creek woman would not budge; such an arrangement would violate the cultural foundations of her community. Hawkins had failed in his early attempt to refashion Creek families or obtain a Creek wife.[1] In subsequent years Hawkins did not change his impression of Creek households. "The husband," he later wrote to Thomas Jefferson, "is a tenant at will only so far as the occupancy of the *premises* of the women." As a result Hawkins had to live the rest of his days among the Creeks without an Indian wife and without the protections of a clan.[2]

Hawkins, although a newcomer to Creek society when he rejected the marriage offer, accurately portrayed the parenting norms within the Creeks' matrilineal society. Maternal uncles, not biological fathers, served as male role models for Creek children. Biological fathers belonged to a different clan and sometimes to a different village than their children, thus many observers concluded that European American men had no role in socializing their Creek children. Such was the case for South Carolina governor James Glen, who in 1753 regretted that the families of intermarriages "abound in Children, but none of them bestow the least Education." By indicting both the individuals who chose to marry

Indians and the Native customs that regulated family life, Glen helped forge an image of Indian life that Hawkins and other eighteenth-century European Americans shared.[3]

Even though mothers and their matrilineal kin had the dominant role in socializing Creek children, Glen and Hawkins overstated the ways in which the interests of European American fathers either were ignored or went unasserted within southeastern Indian society. Creek wives and their kin could not and often did not want to prevent European American fathers from interacting with their biological children. At times Creek mothers and European American fathers held common goals. Many Creeks chose to intermarry, or encouraged their kinswomen to intermarry, because of a desire to enter and control the deerskin trade and to obtain access to valued European resources. Creek women and clan leaders often sought access for themselves and their children to guns, ammunition, food, liquor, clothing, language skills, Western education, and an understanding of European American culture. They used intermarriage to connect themselves to the material and sacred resources of the deerskin trade and of the nonvillage world. Thus, the interests of Creek families and European American fathers did not always conflict. Creek mothers and the members of their clans hardly encouraged their children to become European Americans and move out of the village, but they perceived that there were benefits to incorporating new ideas, customs, and materials into their Creek lives. As a result many Creek women regulated but encouraged the assistance of biological fathers in the socialization process.

Not all children of intermarriages obtained the skills necessary to live and move in and out of two societies. Most could not speak English or Spanish, rejected most European American values, and were otherwise indistinguishable from their Creek neighbors. Others obtained only a few skills or trade goods without fundamentally changing their lives or outlooks. They viewed colonial society as an alien culture and lived their lives in Creek villages according to the mores of Creek culture. In these instances the backgrounds of their biological fathers—much as the fathers of most Creeks—hardly mattered at all. Similarly, some Creeks such as Tustunnuggee Thlucco (Big Warrior) learned English and other skills of European American origins without the aid of a European American father. Biology or residence in a village did not prevent Creeks from obtaining literacy, growing cotton, owning slaves, fencing lands, or herding cattle.[4]

European American fathers had limited time with and control over their children. The socialization of Creek boys and girls primarily took place inside villages or under the supervision of clan members. This oversight frustrated many European American fathers who found their abilities to raise their children constrained. As a result few Creek children became as comfortable in their father's world as in their mother's. Many, as one English traveler observed, "spoke English well, but had not been taught to read so as to make [them] proficient." European Americans could hardly thwart the socializing influences of Creek mothers and their kin, but through active participation fathers provided many Creeks with formal and informal education in American culture and mores. Together Creek mothers, their clansmen, and European American fathers schooled Creek children in European American and Native manners, customs, languages (usually Muskogee and English), cosmologies, and social norms. In this multicultural environment some Creek children discovered, consciously and unconsciously, that they could simultaneously act as an Indian and a European American.[5]

The active parenting by biological fathers defies anthropological theories about childrearing in Creek villages. "The father," anthropologist J. N. B. Hewitt concluded in 1939, "had no more to do with the discipline and education of his children than an alien."[6] Since then scholars have repeatedly demonstrated how matrilineal descent determined most aspects of family authority in traditional Creek society. The biological mother and her kin primarily socialized a Creek child. Maternal uncles taught young boys to hunt, punished them for transgressions against Creek rules, introduced them to the obligations of clan, helped orchestrate marriages, controlled scratching and tattooing rituals, and performed most of the parenting roles European Americans associated with biological fathers. In this cultural system biological fathers—whether Native American, European American, or African American—lived as outsiders to their children's family and thus had little official control over their children.[7]

Despite these gender norms, some European American fathers frequently exerted some influence in the upbringing of their Creek children. Creek men, who had extensive obligations to their sisters' children, had no cultural imperatives to raise or even interact with their biological children. Even more so, such actions could curtail their ability to meet their obligations to socialize their sister's children. Indian countrymen, however, often had different desires and expectations. Some abandoned and rejected their Creek children, much as many southern planters ignored their children in the slave quarters, but many could not escape their own society's expectations for fathers.[8] As a result many Indian countrymen insisted on participating in the process of parenting and used various methods. They arranged to have their children educated by nearby tutors and foreign schools; they used their children as assistants in the deerskin trade and other financial enterprises; they gave their children property through wills and informal gifts; and they took their children on trips into the heart of colonial society.

Many Creeks learned how to behave and appear like European Americans because their European American fathers proactively sent them to schools outside their village. In the early eighteenth century, for example, Coosaponakeesa spent nearly her entire childhood in South Carolina with her father's family. The historical record is silent over how her father, Indian trader Edward Griffin, took her out of the nation. As a young child at the start of the eighteenth century, Coosaponakeesa spent a decade almost entirely in South Carolina and outside the controls of her matrilineage. In this context she went by her English name of Mary. With the guidance of her father, she was baptized and schooled in the town of Ponpon, lived according to the cultural mores of the southern frontier, traveled extensively in colonial society, and learned the legal and financial mechanizations of colonial English society.[9] Coosaponakeesa was not the only Creek child who received a Western-style education in the early eighteenth century. Soon after Coosaponakeesa returned to her Creek home, Governor Oglethorpe observed several "half-bred Indians" coming to Savannah to obtain educations. Their parents, along with some "white" families, "leave their children here at school with Mr. [John] Wesley." Apparently many of the Creek students had already been socialized to colonial norms and blended into Georgian society so well that their Creek identities went unnoticed by Wesley.[10]

As the eighteenth century progressed, European American fathers continued to arrange private education for their children outside the village. Lachlan McGillivray, an eighteenth-century Indian trader, took his Creek son Alexander to Charleston, South Carolina, to immerse him in a European American environment and place him under the tutelage of his Scots cousin Farquer McGillivray. By living as a European American on a daily basis, Alexander became "well versed in [the] Language and customs" of colonial society, "acquainted with all the most useful European sciences," and known for his outstanding oratory.[11] When this tutelage ended, Lachlan arranged for his son to work at a mercantile firm in Savannah.[12] After several years within colonial society, the American Revolution brought the younger McGillivray back to Creek country and to the protection of his matrilineal clan. His actions among the Creeks over the following decades reveal that he understood (although not always accepted) European American conceptions of justice, the ideology of republicanism, the rules of civility, and American standards of authority.[13]

When the Revolution ended, Alexander McGillivray reinforced his image as a European American by "spend[ing] his winters on the sea-coast among the Spaniards, leaving his wife, servants, and horses at a plantation he has near

Tensau, within the borders of West Florida . . . returning to pass his summers in the nation."[14] In 1790 McGillivray put to work this experience of alternating between societies when he attended the quarterly meeting of the St. Andrews Society of the state of New York. The society chose to honor McGillivray, who was in New York to sign a peace treaty on behalf of the Creek Nation. North Carolina senator Samuel Johnson, a member of the organization, watched as "the Society, anxious of shewing their respect to the character of Col. M'Gillivray, availed themselves of his presence in the city, and unanimously elected him as an honorary member of the Society." According to a newspaper account of the event, the Creek leader "mingled with great affability in the festivity of the evening."[15]

At the end of the eighteenth century, Indian countrymen who wanted to educate their Creek children found new options outside their wives' villages. After 1783 Spanish fathers could send their children to special schools established in Florida. The Spaniards made the religious and cultural rationale for this educational policy clear. They established schools "in order that the children may learn in them to read, write, and speak Spanish, the use of their native tongue being prohibited; designating for the purpose teachers in whom are united the Christianity, competence, and good conduct, which are necessary for so useful and delicate a ministry."[16] Dozens of other Indian countrymen placed their children under the guidance of John Pierce, a man who established the first American school in Alabama in 1799. The school, which existed on the edge of Creek territory, apparently catered to the interests of European American fathers. Educational options also remained in Georgia. Pierce's Alabama school was much closer to most Creek villages, but "several of the principal half breeds," U.S. Indian agent David B. Mitchell explained, continued to "have their Sons and daughters at School in Georgia and elsewhere."[17]

A few Creeks obtained formal education in even more distant areas, only to return to use their training within a Creek context. David Moniac, for example, enrolled at the U.S. Military Academy at West Point in 1817. Moniac's experience reveals how Creek values often shaped the direction of Creek education. After David proved his martial prowess in the Red Stick War of 1813–14, Sam and Sehoy sent their son off to obtain an education in the martial arts. A few years later David returned and served as a valuable Creek warrior.[18] Another Creek boy, David Tate, was first educated "near Abernethy, in Scotland" and then later in Philadelphia. When Tate returned to his Creek village, he used his Western education among the Creeks and within Native expectations. Tate obtained a sizable holding of land near the Alabama River, and he served as an interpreter and informant to both the Creek and American governments. His comfort in American society proved helpful in 1810 when Joseph Cook sued him. Cook sought to redeem stolen property that was sold to Alexander McGillivray years earlier and then later bequeathed to Tate. Tate claimed his rights as an Indian and used his understanding of the American legal system to refute Cook's claim. Rather than denying possession of the disputed property, Tate asserted that his Native ethnic identity took him out of the jurisdiction of the United States and that the statute of limitations for the crime had passed. Tate won his case, in large part because his European American education taught him how to assert his Creek ethnic identity when it benefited him.[19]

Creek families challenged many attempts to send children out of their villages for schooling. In the late 1780s, for example, William McIntosh Sr. confronted the outrage of his Native wife and her brothers when he suggested that his two Creek sons leave the village for their schooling. McIntosh ignored their outright refusal and single-handedly arranged a compromise. He promised that he and his children would travel to his native home of Scotland and, as proof, agreed that his Creek wife would remain among her kin. This pledge appeased no one. Still, William Sr. stubbornly went ahead with his plans. While waiting for the Scotland-bound boat to leave the Savannah port, the maternal uncles successfully defended what they saw as a breach of Creek etiquette. They snuck onto the boat and "redeemed" the children back to their Creek village. Family legend states that while the children rested from the long journey to reach the boat, William Sr. "joined the other passengers in the lounge area. Later in the evening when the Captain returned to his stateroom, the two boys were missing. . . . Nothing could be done now for the ship was at sea and the Captain was taking the trip alone."[20]

In contrast to William McIntosh Sr., most Indian countrymen did not defy the wishes of their Native wives or their wives' clans. Instead, they pursued options closer to home and under the supervision of their wives and the wives' families. Just as a wave of Creeks with European American fathers came of age at the beginning of the nineteenth century, new educational options emerged within Creek villages. In many instances southeastern chiefs invited the schools into their communities in an attempt to regulate the instruction as well as obtain desired skills.[21] Under the rubric of the United States' overarching civilization plan, the Methodists and Baptists ran federally funded schools at the Asbury and Withington missions on the margins of Creek villages. Each school rarely enrolled more than twenty-five students at a time, but the students were primarily the Creek children of European American fathers.[22] Several dozen other students under the supervision of the wives and with the consent of the communities attended the Choctaw Academy, a school established in 1825 and largely supported by the U.S. government.[23]

To the chagrin of teachers and many European American fathers, Creek women carefully watched and frequently intervened in the educations of their children. Reverend Lee Compere, for example, complained in 1826 that "another of our girls has been taken home under the pretense of visiting a sick sister." Compere was not convinced of the sincerity of the excuse. "Poor girl!" he wrote. "She has a mother so entirely opposed to civilized habits, that we fear it is only a trick to persuade her own child from school, who till now has been governed by her own inclinations."[24] When missionaries preached religion rather than desired skills such as literacy, they aroused the ire of a community. In many instances the gender of the child shaped the patterns of resistance. Creek men often resisted attempts to teach young boys "agriculture and mechanics" and frequently removed their male kin from the schools in time for the annual hunts. Women usually resisted when the schools taught young girls foreign notions of cleanliness and encouraged them to replace fieldwork with learning how to spin and loom.[25] These acts of resistance, though, demonstrated more than the continuing importance of clans. They also reveal that mothers and clans frequently consented, albeit within defined limits, to the European American education of their children.[26]

When schooling was restricted or unavailable, some European American fathers tried to socialize their children within the village. Here biological fathers frequently obtained the permission, even encouragement, of their Creek wives. As stated earlier, Creek women often married European American men in order to control and attract the influx of material resources. As their children matured, some mothers urged their children to assist their biological fathers in the deerskin trade and diplomatic affairs. As a result Creek children became apprentices to their fathers, who informally taught European American customs, basic bookkeeping, language skills, and the cultural and economic necessities of slavery, cotton planting, and herding. Many Creek children interacted with fathers who established plantations, built Western-style homes, used slave labor, and fenced their property.[27]

Perhaps the most common way in which European Americans influenced their Creek children was in their teaching of English and Spanish. The omnipresence of English speaking, and sometimes of reading and writing, allowed many children of intermarriages to become interpreters for their villages. In most instances Creek families had deep-rooted reasons for encouraging rather than resisting these literacy lessons. One Yazoo Indian, for example, explained that this followed a universal custom in Native society. "In all the Indian nations there is always someone who knows how to speak the language of the neighboring nation."[28] Villages that did not have members who could speak the language of their neighbors were in the unenviable position of having to rely on strangers to be their interpreters. When necessary, southeastern Indians used the Muskogee-based lingua franca of Mobilian. Yet whenever possible it appears that Creek villages tried to use Muskogee or the language of their neighbors.[29]

European American fathers, especially when their children assisted them in frontier exchanges, helped create naming patterns that prepared some Creeks for participation in both Creek and American societies. Most Creeks received a name at birth and, as was customary in southeastern Native society, continued to obtain other names as their lives progressed. In addition to birth names, Creeks also received titles of authority, nicknames, and family names. Some European American fathers expanded this tradition by giving their Creek children English or Spanish names. These names usually consisted of the father's surname and a Spanish- or English-sounding first name. Alexander McGillivray also went by Alejandro Maguilberi and Hoboi-Hili-Miko; Josiah Francis went by Hillis Haujo; William Weatherford went by both Lamochatee and Red Eagle; and Davy Cornels went by Efau Tustunnuggee and Dog Warrior.[30]

Several children of intermarriages received "Creek names" that "passed" for English names, and when such names were accompanied by a surname, they helped buttress the perception of a European American identity. Several Creeks with the name Sioh (occasionally spelled Seah or Siah) used the first name of Josiah and a surname within European American society.[31] Similarly, several Creeks went by Milly among European American society and Malee, a traditional Muskogee name, among the Creeks.[32] On at least one occasion an Indian trader altered his surname to assume a mixed identity. Daniel McDonald took the surname of McGillivray to try to convince society of his kinship ties to Alexander McGillivray and establish his claims to the powerful leader's property. Although he fooled few Creeks or Americans, McDonald recognized that names reflected one's place in society.[33]

Using an English or Spanish surname served several functions for Indian participants in frontier exchanges. Using a name in the language of one's customers and associates helped forge bonds of trust, and it subtly provided a way for some Creeks to make their father's identity known to strangers. At the same time, using an English or Spanish name allowed Creeks to avoid many linguistic and cultural difficulties. The Muskogee language uses several sounds that exist outside of the linguistic vocabulary of most European Americans. Choosing "William" over "Thlucco," for example, allowed individuals to avoid the "thl" consonant combination that frequently appears in Muskogee names and was foreign to European phonetics. Using English and Spanish names also downplayed ties to Indian culture, and thus one's ties to "savagery," and further minimized the social distance fostered by linguistic differences. Finally, using English names helped European American customers pronounce and even remember the names of their Creek associates.[34]

European American fathers, at least those who remained in Creek villages long enough to see their offspring mature, also helped arrange marriages for their children. In many instances the children married their father's business associates. Laughlin Durant, the Creek son of a trader, married a "Miss Hall" from East Florida, and one of George Cornells's daughters married Billy McGirth, the son of a former Loyalist and trader. Similarly, trader George Colvert, married his "mestizo son" to the sister of a fellow trader. These marriages may have resulted from the interests of Creek mothers and maternal uncles—men and women who, after all, may have been following the same cultural imperatives that led to the original intermarriages. Nevertheless, the marriages would likely not have taken place without the active participation and knowledge of European American fathers. Through the active efforts of several European American men, paternal kinship networks united many intermarried Creek families.[35]

In many instances white fathers educated their children through their positions in the deerskin trade and diplomatic affairs. Timothy Barnard, for example, used his position in the deerskin trade and the Creek agency to help teach his children the values and mechanics of the market and colonial society. As his children matured, Barnard relied on several of his Creek children to relay letters and information into American society. During the early nineteenth century Timpochee, Homanhidge, and Tuccohoppe repeatedly moved between Creek and American society on official business. By arranging repeated visits to American society and constant interaction with American officials within Creek society, Barnard ensured that his children would become comfortable in two worlds. Apparently it worked. Timpochee (also known as Timothy) became an interpreter for the United States and a major in the U.S. Army. One image of Timpochee epitomized the dual nature of his life. In this portrait Timpochee appears with a full beard, something quite rare in Creek society, and in an Indian turban. Apparently the painter saw him as belonging to two worlds as well.[36]

European American fathers also trained their children by employing them at various ferries, toll roads, and inns throughout Creek territory. These enterprises, much like the homesteads that they often built, typically took place outside of the female-controlled villages and on lands at least once considered hunting grounds under male control. As a result Creek mothers could not completely oversee these enterprises. Thus, Sam Moniac helped his father run a tavern on the federal road; Adam Hollinger helped operate a ferry across the

Tombigbee River; and Jesse Wall used several family members to help run his tavern. Employing Creek children in these ventures served several functions that were quite analogous to the functions played by Creek wives in the deerskin trade. Children served as laborers and interpreters, and they provided the sanction of Creek clans. Finally, and perhaps unintentionally, employing children in frontier enterprises helped teach some European American customs.[37]

Other Creek children obtained access to financial capital through their European American fathers. Indian countrymen, even as they escaped their troubles in colonial society, often brought African slaves, horses, cattle, and other valuable goods into Creek society. Others built homes and planted orchards near Creek villages. By passing this property over to their wives and children, the fathers further helped inculcate new values and customs. These acts also allowed some children to start their own economic ventures. Several Creek children built inns, ferries, taverns, and trading stores. In these instances fathers provided the means for their children to choose cultural and economic paths that would have otherwise been closed to them.[38]

Some Creek customs made it difficult for fathers to bequeath their property to their children. Like other southeastern Indians, Creeks buried certain goods with the dead in order to protect the deceased in the spiritual world. Alabama Creeks, for example, buried their men with a knife in their hands in order to guard them from an eagle that "beset the spirit trail." Similarly, Creek warriors traditionally went to their graves with their "warlike appendages." In the case of deceased village leaders, Creeks often destroyed all of the property. Several ethnographic accounts detail a southeastern death ritual where deceased priests or chiefs are burned inside a house with all of their possessions. Most Creeks, though, did not burn their homes or destroy all their possessions. According to one tradition, some household goods were cleaned and distributed rather than destroyed. Other items remained in families for several generations before being buried. In these instances Creek custom required that property follow matrilineal lines and that landed property only be held by women.[39]

Despite these well-known burial and inheritance norms, several Indian countrymen tried to bequeath their possessions to their children. George Galphin, for example, passed cattle, slaves, buildings, and lands for "use during natural life" to several of his Indian children. As Galphin desired, his children obtained much of the moveable property and continued to live on the lands he left. With no matrilineal heirs within Creek society to make claims on the property and no impulse to bury the property with the deceased, some European Americans such as Galphin could pass on their property as they wished. In part, this was possible became the burial of possessions alongside the dead was not simply about the destruction of property. Galphin's Indian family, by allowing the transferal of property to Galphin's heirs, chose not to provide him the protection of grave goods.[40]

When heirs existed in Creek society, written wills and stated intentions rarely guaranteed that property would be passed to Creek children. Instead, as the experiences of Alexander McGillivray reveal, Creek customs normally prevailed. McGillivray originally obtained from his Scottish father, Lachlan, an unknown number of slaves and cattle and a plantation at Little Tallassee. Lachlan, who was married to a Creek woman, aroused little protest from the Creek community with these informal acts.[41] Years later, at his own death, Alexander did not have the same success distributing the same property to his progeny. In 1793 William Panton arranged to have McGillivray's sisters "yield up all the negroes and a part of the cattle for his children."[42] Panton, who acted on what he believed was McGillivray's request, ultimately did not succeed. More than a decade later, Hawkins recalled that of the "negros, horses and cattle, little . . . went to his children." Instead, the property went to "his relations on the maternal line, . . . Mrs. Duran[t] and Mrs. Weatherford, the first a sister and the other a maternal sister only." They "took possession of the greatest part of the property and have destroyed the stock of horses and cattle." In this instance the property remained in the hands of McGillivray's sisters—demonstrating that his clan owned the property all along. Nevertheless, the adherence to Creek custom did not necessarily prevent McGillivray's children from an inheritance. As members of their mother's clan, the children may have had access to the items retained.[43]

In some instances, the passing of property from fathers to their biological children protected Creek interests even as it violated traditional norms. For most of the pre-removal era, the Creeks protested the practices of intermarried traders who fled the nation when they "have gotten their hands full." Too often "they have got tired of the Country and left their wife & Children to Suffer, which we think very unjust." In 1818 the Creeks enacted a law to limit the frequency of this occurrence. In short, the law declared "if a white man takes an Indian woman, and have children by her, and he goes out of the Nation, he shall leave all his property with his Children for their support." The writers of the law made it clear that this supported rather than defied Creek interest. Rather than consolidating the property in the hands of men, as some scholars have suggested, this law kept property within the controls of the matrilineage. The phrase "his Children" clearly deviated from the Creek conception of kinship, but doing so ensured that the property would remain within the community and in the hands, albeit not necessarily the right hands, of the wife's clan.[44]

Even before they actively helped raise their Creek children, European American fathers helped provide bicultural attributes. European American fathers did not bring genetic "advantages," as historians once insisted, but they did introduce genes that resulted in phenotypic diversity within Creek communities. As a result the children of intermarriages seemed to have physical features that typified both Creek and American populations. The hues of their hair and skin, the shape of their faces, and their body types often differed from others in the nation. They had, like the Creek daughter of Rachel Pettit, "white hair and a beautiful rosy complextion."[45] Intermarriages between Creeks and African Americans further magnified the physical diversity within southeastern villages. This proved to be the case for Creeks like Mary Ann Battis, whose clan was intermixed with both Africans and European Americans. On one hand, as one observer explained, "Mary Ann's father was white & she is the fairest female I have seen in this nation." On the other hand, a great distinction separated Battis and her other "relations (who are nearly all of them extremely dark people & her mother has some children who have a black father)."[46] Other children of intermarriages appeared to be European Americans. Two of the children of Eliza Hawkins and Creek chief William McIntosh, himself the child of an intermarriage, appeared to one observer to be "completely white."[47] This led some European Americans, such as Senate chairman of Indian affairs Thomas Hart Benton, to believe that the children of intermarriages were really "white men, called half-breeds, because there was a tincture of Indian blood in their veins."[48]

Some European Americans believed they could visually differentiate the children of intermarriages from other Indians. John Bach, for example, described Paddy as "a lad of about sixteen or seventeen years old, from appearance a half-breed."[49] German traveler Philip Georg Friedrich von Reck also believed that physical appearances revealed the mixed parentage of Natives. "Their [Indians] body color is orange, brown and also coppery. White Indians are also seen, although very seldom. The children who have a European father and an Indian mother are always yellow or brown."[50] Other European Americans believed that determining parentage from physical appearances was more difficult. James Stuart, a British traveler, observed that intermarriages slowly changed the appearances of the southeastern Indians. "The great distinction in the appearance of the Indians consists in their being copper-coloured," Stuart wrote. "Their complexion is not red, but somewhat darker than untarnished copper. . . . Their hair is always black, and, in mixture with the whites, remains visible to the third generation." Stuart recognized that intermixture eventually led to the inability to determine ethnic identities but insisted that this transition did not occur quickly. Instead he determined that an Indian appearance remained for several generations after the racial intermixing.[51]

The disagreement over the ability to see evidence of mixed parentage may have resulted from the overreliance on biology, or what nineteenth-century Americans called "blood," in attributing physical appearances. "Mixed" appearances resulted from not only biological factors. Creeks also had to carefully select their clothing, jewelry, and the rest of their costume to fit their desired identities. This knowledge was often learned through personally observing the customs of the cultures. No one seemed to do this more effectively than Alexander McGillivray. Abigail Adams, wife of U.S. president John Adams, met Chief McGillivray during the negotiations of the Treaty of New York in 1790. She observed that McGillivray "dresses in our own fashion, speaks English like a native . . . is not very dark, [and is] much of a gentleman."[52] Adams's confusion resulted, at least in part, from McGillivray's decision to dress like a European American when traveling outside the Creek Nation. Within his native homeland McGillivray also dressed appropriately. As a result Vicente Manuel de Zéspedes described the Creek leader quite differently. The "English quadroon named McGillivray . . . is, in spite of his *purely Indian dress*, an educated man, who writes English with particular elegance. His natural talent, his acquired learning, and his affectation of Indian attire and manners have given him great and universal influence over the Creek and Seminole nations."[53] Zéspedes and Adams both saw McGillivray as a European American but their descriptions differed because the Creek leader manipulated his appearance by selectively choosing his clothes.

McGillivray's apparent conscious decision to alter his appearance, and thus change his identity as he moved between colonial and Indian society, did not always work smoothly. In 1790 McGillivray and several other Creek leaders in New York for a treaty signing were honored by a charitable association called the Tammany Society of the Columbian Order. The organization "received these braves at the Wall Street landing, and escorted them to their lodgings at the City Tavern."[54] At this meeting McGillivray chose an appearance that distinguished him from the other Natives in his company. "McGillivray was dressed in a suit of plain scarlet, the other warriors of the Creeks appeared in their national habit, and as the procession moved up Wall Street the chiefs sang their particular song." Despite his best efforts, McGillivray's appearance did not approximate those of his American hosts. Instead "the Creek chiefs were entertained by the Tammany society, all of the members being in full Indian dress, at which the visitors were much delighted and responded with an Indian dance." With the members of the society costumed in "full Indian dress," McGillivray was the only participant who came to the meeting dressed as an "American."[55] His effort to blend in with his hosts, ironically, led to the opposite result.

Other Creeks who had connections to the deerskin trade similarly chose clothing that defied simple characterization. Traders brought to Creek villages styles, patterns, and fabrics that typified European American costume. Most Creeks used these new items in traditionally Indian manners, but many found ways to appear simultaneously Creek and European American. To increase their ability to blend, these Creeks used fewer permanent tattoos, kept body piercing to a minimum, and learned how to dress in ways that aroused little suspicion in either community.[56] For a few whose appearance seemed white and behavior seemed loyal, their Indian backgrounds could be pushed aside. James Seagrove, for example, claimed that one Creek warrior, who may have been a child of an intermarriage, had overcome his maternal baggage. "The White Lieutenant," he asserted, "possesses nothing of an Indian, but the name. He is a virtuous, good man, and his friendship to our country is not equaled by any in his land."[57]

Most children of intermarriages chose to remain within the world of their mothers and her clan, but the active parenting of European American fathers allowed many Creeks to enter European American society. Sarah Waters and her family exemplified the multiple paths—the ethnic options—that some Creeks could take. The daughter of a Georgia colonel and trader and a Creek mother, Waters grew up among the Creeks just after the American Revolution. She learned to speak "the [Indian] tongue well, it being her mother tongue, and she speaks English well enough for common subjects within the sphere of domestic objects." This allowed her to interpret for her non-English-speaking kin and led Hawkins to choose to use her to inform fellow Creeks about U.S. Indian policy. After her upbringing in a Creek village, she followed the marital path of her mother and married a southern white man. She had "two children by him, a boy and a girl," and allowed "the young man [to be] educated in England, under the direction of his father, and [the son] now resides in Georgia." The daughter remained among the Creeks. Waters, a Creek resident herself, watched as her children explored the ethnic options available to them as they lived in both the American South and the Native southeast.[58]

Several other families bridged the southern frontier. In 1764 Richard Bailey migrated to Creek country. After working as a carpenter and joiner for eight years in Savannah, the English colonist decided to pursue opportunities among the Creeks. Over the next three decades, he married an Indian woman, became a prominent deerskin trader, and fathered at least seven Creek children. By 1797 his actions found him in disrepute. Apparently both Creek and American officials found him equally offensive. Among his many "acts of felloney" was the American claim that he stole African slaves, horses, and property from American citizens, harbored fugitive criminals in his home, and defied colonial authorities by selling liquor to the Creeks.[59] Creeks, like Hopie of Thlothlagalga, also found Bailey's attitudes and actions troubling, telling Hawkins that Bailey "treated some of his town people with contempt, that he had repeatedly declared his determination to live on their lands without their consent."[60]

Even though American officials had reason to punish Bailey as well, legal action came from within Creek society. Efau Haujo, and other Creek leaders, officially banished Bailey and several other "unworthy and unfit" Indian traders for various transgressions. They "are liars and medlars and rogues; they will meddle in public affairs, are constantly circulating reports injurious to our peace, that they have information that mischief is brewing." Bailey's eviction revealed the precarious nature of dual identities on the southeastern frontier and the difficulty of being socialized into two worlds. When his actions deviated from basic Creek norms, they led to censure and the eventual negation of his Creek ethnic option. After thirty-three years of Creek residence, Bailey had few options but to leave his wife and children and return to Georgia.[61]

In the years that followed, Bailey's children explored many of the options available on the southern frontier. Richard Jr. apparently followed his father's example, returning to Georgia soon after his father. He, too, seemed to have little choice. Only one month after his father's eviction, he "had run off with a chief's wife. The woman, if she escapes with her ears, will be safe after the busk, but he will not till the Corn is ripe." Adultery with a prominent Creek woman earned him a temporary eviction, but he further outraged his Native kin with frequent expressions of anti-Indian sentiments. Bailey may have obtained this disregard for Creek customs from his father and from an education that his father helped arrange for him in the 1790 Treaty of New York. In addition to learning reading, writing, literature, and basic mathematics, he also obtained the ethnocentrism so prevalent among colonists. When he returned, he had "so much contempt for the Indian mode of life, that he has got himself into discredit with them [the Creeks]." His informal eviction and ritualized ostracization was the natural culmination of his rejection of his Indian ethnic identity.[62]

Education among American colonists did not lead all of Bailey's Creek children to have "contempt for the Indian mode of life." One of Bailey's other sons, Dixon, accompanied Richard Jr. to school in Philadelphia. He, too, returned to the Creeks with a formal education, but he did so without the same prejudices as his brother. He lived as a planter, owned orchards, and worked in the Indian trade. At the same time, however, he married Sophia Durant, another Creek child of intermarriage, and moved into her village as determined by Creek custom. James and Daniel Bailey, Dixon's twin brothers, also lived among the Creeks until their deaths during the siege of Fort Mims.[63]

Richard's three Creek sisters—Peggy, Polly, and Elizabeth—also explored various options on the southern frontier. Unlike their brothers, they did not have the benefit, or perhaps the burden, of Philadelphia educations. Instead they spent their childhood among their matrilineal kin, learning to dress deerskins, plant corn, and participate in Creek festivals. Although their father never set up a formal Western education for them, he arranged for them to learn to "spin cotton and [taught] the youngest Elizabeth . . . [to] read and write [and be] very industrious." Their embodiment of European American standards supported Hawkins's optimism for the future of the Creek people. "It being demonstrated to me that the Indian women from these two [Elizabeth and Peggy], are capable of and willing to become instrumental in civilising the men."[64] Hawkins accepted the Indian identities of these Creeks, but other Americans perceived them differently. All three Bailey sisters married "white men." Elizabeth married a man named Fletcher, who was killed at Fort Mims, Peggy married Indian trader Josiah Fisher, and Polly married a man named Sizemore and helped him run a ferry in what later became Gainestown, Georgia.[65]

Creek women maintained the upper hand in the socialization of Creek children. Yet, the interests of Creek women and European American fathers frequently overlapped, allowing the fathers to help raise their children. They provided formal and informal education about American culture and mores. When combined with Native upbringings, the socializing efforts of white fathers created bicultural Creeks, or at least Creeks who were comfortable moving in and out of the two societies. They had kin connections to both sides of the frontier, spoke multiple languages, and understood both cultures. They often "looked" like a Creek and like a southerner, and they occasionally altered their dress to suit their desired identity. At times they wore a "blend" of the two costumes and acted in ways that enabled them to live simultaneously in both cultures. As a result these Creeks often had the option of living as Creek Indians, European Americans, or both. They could assert one ethnicity and completely ignore their other, or they could carefully assert the identity that best suited the moment. Quite literally, they could be Creeks in one instance and Americans in another, even as most contemporaries believed this to be impossible.

CHAPTER 5

In Two Worlds

The children of European American fathers and Creek mothers frequently performed essential roles as cultural mediators on the southern frontier. As multilingual speakers of English and Muskogee, and sometimes of other Native and European languages, they had the ability to communicate with both Creeks and European Americans. Linguistic abilities alone, however, did not ensure participation in intercultural affairs. Biculturalism, or at least comfort and acceptance in different communities, often did. Reared to understand and live within two cultures, some of the children of intermarriages instinctively understood the nonspoken implications of the actions and words used by European Americans and Indians, and they could explain the various social expectations and try to prevent the cultural misunderstandings and insults that typified Native–European American relations. Some Creeks with mixed parentage also benefited from their dual identities. Because many Creeks and European Americans believed that the offspring of intermarriages were members of their own communities, these children were encouraged to assist in intercultural affairs. Thus, in the eighteenth and early nineteenth centuries Creek children with European American fathers served as interpreters, messengers, escorts, advisers, and other intermediaries.

The children of intermarriages had more than the ability to become intermediaries. They also often had stakes—psychological as well as economic—in seeing that the worlds of their parents did not conflict. The presence of Creek mothers and European American fathers, for example, created an internal need to create peace between colonists and Creeks. One could only maintain a relationship with the two parents if their peoples could coexist. The parental couple also provided an immediate example of intercultural cooperation, one that pointed to the potential for a new intercultural society. Slafecha Barnett, himself a child of intermarriage, told the Creek's national assembly how intermarriage transformed his people. "When the white people first came among us, the Great Spirit had forbid our mixture—we did mix—and to avoid the pain of separating the husband from his wife, the father from his children, and the brother from his sister, he has continued the course of the mixed blood in our veins. We must remain in this situation, because God is upon the top of us, and directs it to be so." The Creeks, he continued, had contributed to the strength of American society and thus should embrace it. "Gen. Washington acquired a war-name above the rest of the men" he explained, "but the mixture of our blood, and the accession of a part of our strength to his, added not a little to it." If they continued to be divided—whether Creek and Creek or Creek and American—the speaker insisted that they would remain weak. "You all know, my countrymen, who know any thing of the unfortunate history of our country, how slow was his progress when opposed by the strong and undivided arms of our fathers, and how rapid it has been since Whiskey and Malice have divided us—We are all one people."[1] Blending the recent past with Creek traditions, Barnett pointed to the forgotten possibility of intercultural blending.

Not everyone could participate in intercultural affairs on the southern frontier. Not all Natives or European Americans could communicate, let alone mediate, with the "other." Few Creeks, regardless of their paternity, could enter colonial society and comfortably participate in it. Those identified as "African" or "Negro" ran the risk of enslavement when they crossed the cultural divide; others simply struggled to navigate the strange social terrain. They were strangers in an even stranger land. Similarly, few European Americans were welcome or comfortable within Creek villages. Evictions and murders accompanied compromises and exchanges in intercultural dealings. Thus, the southern frontier was an opportunity created by some, exploited by others, and a barrier to most.[2]

Most Creek children of intermarriages never chose to assert their European American identities; nor did they consciously alter their appearances or act contrary to what they believed to be loyalty to their Creek communities. They may have been well prepared to live in and mediate between both worlds, but they resided among their Creek kin as peers. As villagers with extensive obligations to their clan members, the children of intermarriages predominantly identified themselves as Creeks. Yet several Creeks discovered that, regardless of their own actions, they could simultaneously be white southerners and Creek Indians, and that, regardless of their chosen self-identities and residences, they were treated as European Americans in certain circumstances and as Creek Indians in others. Appearances and kinship connections allowed some Creeks to find acceptance in both Creek and American society and to assert dual identities.

Coosaponakeesa, who was frequently referred to by her English name of Mary, discovered the precarious nature of trying to assert two identities in the 1740s.[3] Born to trader Edward Griffin and a female relation of the Creek leader Brims, Coosaponakeesa was raised and educated by her father in South Carolina. Despite this unorthodox upbringing, she never lived far from her Native kin and community. Because her father worked as an Indian trader, she interacted with and learned from both Natives and Europeans from a young age. Her first husband, interpreter Johnny Musgrove, further contributed to her bicultural skills and her comfort within English society. Her identity as Mary, the trusted daughter and then wife of a trader, allowed her access to colonial officials. As Coosaponakeesa, a member of the Wind clan and kinswoman of several prominent village leaders, she moved freely within Creek society. This proved useful when Britain established the colony of Georgia in January 1733. From its inception, Coosaponakeesa placed herself in the center of Governor Oglethorpe's dealings with neighboring Creek Indians. She served as the governor's principal interpreter from 1733 until 1745, and she received financial compensation for her assistance and the prestige that accompanied her position.[4]

Coosaponakeesa married three times. Apparently her ability to participate in the public sphere of colonial Georgia was predicated on her married, and therefore not sexually dangerous, status. Her marriage to Musgrove, himself the child of a Native mother, allowed her to diminish the stigma associated with a powerful woman in the eighteenth century. Once married, she routinely participated as an interpreter, albeit sometimes as her husband's partner. Although her Creek heritage was well known in colonial Georgia, her "civilized" demeanor allowed Governor Oglethorpe to include her in political affairs. At times she was excluded from participation in public affairs, usually when her husband was expected to act on her behalf, but Coosaponakeesa made her skills essential to Oglethorpe's participation on the southern frontier.[5]

Coosaponakeesa's participation in public affairs did not go unchallenged. In 1734, while her husband traveled to England as Oglethorpe's interpreter, she discovered that she had not completely muted her Creek identity within colonial society. In December a drunken Joseph Watson, Johnny's business partner, had an argument with Coosaponakeesa's Creek customers. Watson blamed Coosaponakeesa for the dispute and expressed his anger with violent threats and an errant gunshot. The Creek hunters expressed their outrage, through Coosaponakeesa's interpretation, of course, and threatened violence if their demands were not met. Coosaponakeesa soothed their fears and filed misdemeanor charges against Watson for trying to shoot her. She won her case, but the struggle to maintain her public role did not end there. Watson tried to recover his reputation by pointing to Coosaponakeesa's Indian, and therefore savage, heritage. Watson's strategy backfired. Coosaponakeesa continued to associate with Georgia officials, although under the name Mary, and she increased her trust among the Creeks. A few Georgians called for Watson's release from jail, but most colonists blamed him for threatening to break the precarious peace with the

Creeks. It soon became evident to Georgia's Board of Trustees, and many English colonists, that a drunk Watson caused the uproar and that Coosaponakeesa had smoothed over the unnecessary tensions. In addition, the Creeks made it known to Georgia officials that they "are full of resentment against [Watson] and have petitioned us that Mrs. Musgrove may have the trade." With this request, Coosaponakeesa had solidified her position in the intercultural trade.[6]

After she was widowed in 1735, Coosaponakeesa remarried. Although former servant Jacob Matthews brought little status other than his European heritage to the relationship, the marriage allowed her to both maintain her position as a cultural intermediary and retain her land grants. She continued to help Oglethorpe communicate and negotiate with the Creeks. Once again, while asserting her English identity through marriage and her social affairs, Coosaponakeesa could still convince the Creeks that she remained a kinswoman. As a result "the Wolf, as most other Indian visitors to that town stayed at Mary's place."[7] The Wolf King, who was a relation of Coosaponakeesa, could rely on his kinswoman to fulfill the obligations of clan even though she lived outside of her village. When she visited the Wolf King a few years later, the favor was reciprocated.[8]

Three years after Coosaponakeesa's second husband died, the Creek "interpretess" found another European American husband. This time, in 1743, Coosaponakeesa married Rev. Thomas Bosomworth. The two probably first met when Coosaponakeesa interpreted for Thomas, who was sent to the young colony as a Christian missionary. When the marriage was announced, few Georgians believed it to be true. Coosaponakeesa's marriage signified a rise in status that few had foreseen. Thomas's status combined with Coosaponakeesa's skills to form a powerful combination. For a few years they formed a duo that Georgia authorities could not ignore. Oglethorpe used them to pursue Creek criminals, interpret treaties with the Creeks, and prevent warfare in the region. Together the couple traveled into Creek villages with messages from the governor and the English king, brought back speeches from various Creek leaders, and hosted Creek and American visitors at their home. They occasionally taught Christian missionaries the Muskogee language, and they provided Oglethorpe with most of the knowledge he possessed about the Creeks. For several years the Bosomworths made themselves indispensable to the English colonists.[9]

At times Coosaponakeesa's Creek and European American identities reinforced each other. Many Georgians appreciated that she used her influence among the Creeks to mediate differences between them and prevent hostilities. When Georgians faced enemies other than the Creeks, officials thanked Coosaponakeesa for using "the utmost of her Endeavours in bringing down her Friends and Relations from the Nation to Fight against his Majestys Enemies." Similarly, many Creeks credited her for using her influence among the English colonists to ensure fair trading practices. They recognized that without their kinswoman's assistance the abuses that plagued the deerskin trade might have been much worse. Both Creeks and Americans recognized her influence in both societies, yet they believed that each influence reinforced, rather than contradicted, the other. This was possible as long as the Creeks and Americans refrained from warfare, the Creeks believed that Coosaponakeesa was loyal to her matrilineage, and the Americans believed that she was an English colonist. Influence within the other society was acceptable; membership was not.[10]

Eventually, Coosaponakeesa could not maintain this distinction between influence and membership. In 1745 she repeated her long-standing claim that the Creeks had granted her the rights to three islands—St. Catherine, Sapelo, and Ossabaw. At the same time she asked Georgia for the money due to her as an interpreter. The dispute over these claims extended over the next two decades. English officials asserted that the Creek Indians had no power to cede land to individuals, and that anything to the contrary would be seen as disloyalty to the king. If the Creeks wished to cede land to Mary Bosomworth, a Georgian and a Christian, they needed to act through the proper colonial authority. Because English officials considered Mary to be under their dominion, they proclaimed that she could obtain land only through English law. Thus, in this instance Mary's identity as an Englishwoman hindered her actions on the southern frontier.[11]

Coosaponakeesa began to lose her ability to represent Georgians a year later, in 1746. After a decade of carefully asserting her English identity within Georgia, Coosaponakeesa publicly proclaimed that because she was an Indian woman, the Creeks could deal with her as they wished. By asserting her Creek identity, she provided information that she may have believed essential to her claims, but this act alienated her Georgian allies. They refused to grant her the land or pay the money she claimed Georgia owed her, and they rejected her as a fellow Georgian. Many of the opportunities that were once available to the Bosomworths suddenly disappeared. With Coosaponakeesa's downfall, the once respected reverend resigned his post and became equivalent to an Indian countryman. In the years that followed, the Bosomworths ceased to serve as cultural brokers.[12]

Most Creek children of intermarriages never faced a dramatic denial of their dual identities. Nor did they normally need to cultivate acceptance by Georgian officials in order to participate in intercultural affairs. Instead most of them had their initial foray into the deerskin trade as interpreters and assistants to their European American fathers. Creek children, to some degree, performed many of the same functions for their fathers that Creek wives did for their European American husbands. As the eighteenth century progressed, many of these children became prominent traders on their own, and by the end of the American Revolution they dominated southeastern trade networks.[13]

When the children of intermarriages served as interpreters and traders, it often satisfied the interests of Creek hunters, village leaders, and colonial officials. Not only did these Creek mediators possess the necessary linguistic skills and the bicultural knowledge to mediate social and economic exchanges, but they also benefited from an assumption that their loyalties belonged to the Creeks or European Americans who called upon their services. Creeks and European Americans frequently believed that the children of intermarriages belonged to their own community and therefore could be trusted to favor their own interests or to at least be impartial. They could be what James Seagrove called an "interpreter and a confidential man."[14] Once Creeks and European Americans found the services of a willing intermediary, they frequently had their assumptions confirmed.

European American officials repeatedly insisted that they wanted to find interpreters whom the Creeks found acceptable. Good interpreters limited many of the misunderstandings that plagued frontier relations. Creek leaders, for example, repeatedly complained that some traders negotiated fair exchanges only to alter them unfavorably when they wrote the contracts. The oral contract, they claimed, did not match the written agreement, and the deerskin traders were trying to claim debts that were not owed. As a result, when faithful interpreters emerged, Creek leaders employed them and tried to convince American officials to use them as well. In many instances the Creeks proactively sought out trustworthy interpreters such as Stephen Forrester. In other instances the Creeks turned to individuals such as "James Hutton, who was born and raised in the nation and considered as one of us, [whom] we took as an Interpreter."[15]

The Creeks frequently established formal positions for dependable interpreters. In 1814, for example, U.S. government officials used a Creek man and an Indian countryman to interpret a treaty with several Upper Creek chiefs. The perceived impartiality of the two interpreters, if not their partiality in favor of the Creeks, led Tustunnuggee Thlucco (Big Warrior) and other Upper Creek chiefs to praise the work of "Alexander Cornells, a half-breed, our old and faithful interpreter" and "George Mayfield, . . . a white man, raised in our land." In order to secure their employment as future interpreters, the Creeks provided both men "one mile square" within Creek territory. Each society had something to gain by this arrangement. The Creeks pursued this option, Tustunnuggee Thlucco explained, because it ensured "that you [the U.S. government] may have an interpreter at hand," and at the same time it made sure "that he [Cornells] may continue his usefulness to us."[16] Tustunnuggee Thlucco had other reasons for promoting Cornells. In addition to being a member of a clan, Cornells had proven his loyalty and leadership abilities both as a minor village chief, when he protested incursions of white squatters and settlers, and as a seasoned interpreter.[17] U.S. officials had their own reasons for embracing this arrangement. Benjamin Hawkins, convinced that Cornells's loyalty had been established during the preceding two and a half decades when he served as a paid interpreter and subagent to the Creeks, believed that "half breed Cornells," although "the second chief of the nation," could be trusted to honor his obligations to his father's people. In addition, his father's kinship networks connected him to many of the deerskin traders in the region. In short, Hawkins had no reason to object to the continued use of Cornells as an interpreter and had many reasons to support it.[18]

In the war-filled months that preceded this arrangement, Cornells carefully balanced his dual identities and loyalties. During the Red Stick War, which divided the Creeks, Cornells's acceptance by both Creeks and Americans almost came to an end. For a brief time Hawkins apparently suspected that Cornells was "playing a deep game" of treacherously leaking information to "hostile" Creeks. His suspicions passed, in large part because of the valuable information that Cornells passed to his American allies. Cornells's opposition to the Red Sticks led many Creeks to have similar misgivings. Yet Cornells survived the mistrust, perhaps because of his long-standing history for limiting the intrusiveness of Christian missionaries and for regulating trade and travel through the nation. His loyalty was questioned but never negated. His ability to maintain his dual identities, although almost brought to an end by various suspicions, escaped the war intact. In the years that followed, American officials continued to use him as an interpreter, even while many Creeks looked to him for leadership.[19]

Like Cornells, dozens of other Creek children of European American fathers served as interpreters on the southern frontier. These interpreters facilitated everything from peace treaties to trade relations to missionary work. Colonial authorities—Spanish, French, British, and American—recognized the important roles faithful interpreters performed. Without the assistance of individuals who were well acquainted with the Indians, European American authorities acknowledged the futility of diplomacy and trade and the difficulty of information gathering and traveling.[20] As a result European Americans relied on countless interpreters with European American parentage. William Hambly,

Paddy Carr, John Galphin, Alexander Mayfield, George Lovett, Juan Antonio Sandoval, Juan Garzón, Sam Moniac, and dozens of other children of intermarriages interpreted for the Creeks. Some performed their linguistic functions informally, while others worked professionally for Creek or European American officials. In many instances everyone involved recognized that the interpreters were "born in [the] Creek Nation."[21]

The children of intermarriages became interpreters for reasons of both ability and acceptability. British superintendent of trade John Stuart, in one of many eighteenth-century attempts to define the role and importance of the Indian interpreter, practically reserved the role for the children of intermarriages and white traders. He urged his government to retain "an Intelligent Person . . . in each Nation who shall understand the Language of such Nation, so as to serve occasionally as an Interpreter to deliver Messages sent to, and receive messages from the Indians."[22] Although Stuart did not use the language of race in this job description, his desire for an "intelligent" and multilingual individual who was acceptable to both Indians and the English served to exclude most volunteers from the position. Stuart and other English officials rarely viewed Indians as bright or loyal enough for the position, and few Englishmen without Indian kin or connections had the ability or desire to travel within Indian society. Several decades after Stuart's suggestion, American Solomon Betton offered a more racialist logic for the selection of interpreters. Once again the pool of acceptable participants remained composed almost entirely of the children of intermarriages. Betton suggested that there always be two interpreters present. "One should be an Indian, and the other, a white man," he explained. Only this would "be a Check on the White Interpreter, [and] guard the interest of the Indians."[23] Despite Betton's clear division between "Indian" and "white," in many instances the Creek children of intermarriages served as both the public interpreter and the Creek representative. Several times interpreters who represented the Creeks on one occasion served as the public interpreter on another. The children of intermarriage, in essence, acted as an "Indian" on one occasion and as a "white man" on another.[24]

Most Creek intermediaries did more than translate official information between Muskogee and English or Spanish. They also physically passed information between Creek and European American societies. These messengers carried documents and talks between Creek and European American officials, and they escorted officials as they passed from one society to the other. Creeks with European American fathers often had all of the abilities essential to these tasks. In addition to knowing the paths and roads that traversed the region, they could also move within both Creek and American society, communicate with the linguistically diverse individuals whom they confronted, and be trusted by colonial and Native leaders. Once again, biculturalism provided some Creeks with the skills needed for this mediating function, while their dual identities addressed the competing concerns of both societies.

Timothy Barnard, for example, entered the Creek Nation in the 1760s. He intermarried, became a prominent deerskin trader, and was loyal to the United States during the American Revolution. This endeared him to American officials in the early Republic. In the 1790s he began serving as a paid assistant to the U.S. government. At the same time he worked as an intermediary for several American officials, including several Georgia governors and Indian agent James Seagrove. Seagrove relied on the Indian countryman because "Barnard [was] a man of family and good repute, in Georgia, who has been settled as a trader in the Creek country thirty years, and always a confidential man with their Government."[25] Although Barnard lived among the Indians for decades and had a Creek wife and several Creek children, Seagrove insisted that Barnard never became an Indian and remained a devoted American citizen.

Barnard "confirmed" his loyalty—to both the Creeks and the United States—during the Red Stick War. Like several other Indian countrymen, Barnard sided with the Creek allies of the United States. Throughout the war he provided Hawkins detailed letters about the morale of the "hostile" Red Sticks and "friendly" Creeks, their comparative strengths, their leadership, and their motives.[26] Barnard's loyalty to his Creek wife and her clan, however, also resulted in his use as an intermediary by several Creek leaders. Tustunnuggee Thlucco, Efau Haujo, and other Creek chiefs used Barnard to send messages to American officials in the same way that Seagrove used him years earlier. His residence, actions, and perhaps adoption led these Creek leaders to believe Barnard to be a loyal Creek.[27]

As Barnard became older and physically less able to travel, he increasingly turned to his Creek children to serve as go-betweens on the southern frontier. All of Barnard's children participated as messengers and interpreters. A few bridged European American and Creek society through marriage. Billy Barnard, for example, married Peggy Sullivan, and although they lived among the Creeks, they moved between the two societies. Polly Barnard married Joseph Marshall, himself a Creek child of an intermarriage, and helped him run a ferry on the Flint River. At least three of Barnard's sons helped government officials regulate the southern frontier. During the early nineteenth century, Timpochee, Homanhidge, and Tuccohoppe worked as interpreters and messengers until forced removal took the entire Barnard family west of the Mississippi River and into Indian Territory.[28]

The prominence of Barnard's children on the southern frontier resulted from the desires of several Creek leaders and European American officials. While Barnard's children were still young, Efau Haujo explained to Hawkins that "Mr. Barnard is our old interpreter, and we want one of his sons and his brother to settle out on this side of the Altamaha."[29] Hawkins eagerly complied with Efau Haujo's wishes. In the following years Timpochee followed in his father's footsteps in bridging and blurring the social and cultural divide between Creeks and Americans. He married a Cussetta Indian, lived among her Creek village, and served as a minor chief in several treaty negotiations. Americans, however, continued to believe in the loyalty of their American interpreter. During the Red Stick War, Timpochee supported the Creek allies of the United States, as did his father, and he served as a major in the U.S. Army. When Timpochee signed the 1825 Treaty of Indian Springs as a minor Creek chief, U.S. officials treated it as an act of loyalty. His political influence, Americans believed, resulted from his superior American background, not from his connections within Creek society.[30]

As Timpochee's experience in the U.S. Army revealed, living within the Creek Nation did not preclude him from assisting Americans or even being an American. During the decades prior to removal, Christian missionaries, Indian agents, and various other American travelers benefited from the mediating abilities of the children of intermarriages. Indian agent Hawkins, for example, relied on these Creeks, who seemed "intelligent and [speak] English well enough to be understood," to serve as informants, middlemen, interpreters, escorts, aides, and confidants. Although Hawkins rejected several offers of intermarriages for himself and temporarily banned all marriages between Creeks and Indian agents, he recognized the importance of Creek wives and their children in shaping Native society. Within the Creek Nation, Hawkins established a network of intermarried Creek families to help him extend his "civilization plan." He also used those he called "half-breeds" to teach other Creeks how to spin, plant, or herd. He also relied on loyal Creeks to help maintain law and order within the region. When war broke out in 1813, Hawkins used his connections to obtain information about the hostile Red Sticks and British. When Hawkins needed to travel among the Creeks, he used similar connections to find safe havens and hospitable hosts within nearly all Creek villages. Hawkins believed that many Indian countrymen and their Creek children were debased and untrustworthy, but he embraced those who deemed worthy.[31]

Many European Americans shared the idea that intermarried couples were debased. As stated earlier, some observers decried the lack of character of countrymen simply because they chose to live among the Indians. Who else but the most depraved European Americans, they concluded, would choose the savage life? When European Americans used Indian villages as asylums they simply confirmed this image. More often the claims of depravity occurred when inter-married European Americans seemed to be under the influence of their wives or their clans. In these instances the loyalty and sometimes manhood of the traders were often questioned. Roderick McIntosh, for example, complained to the agent John Stuart that too many traders were out of the control of European American officials. "With respect to the Traders, I can only say that the Nation Swarms with them, that a number of them are notorious Villains, & give me much more trouble than I could expect."[32] The inability of McIntosh to regulate his English countrymen confirmed the depravity of those men who chose to live among the Indians.

Often the identity, and thus the value, of an intermediary was tightly con-nected to reputation of a father. As a result European Americans frequently pointed to the honesty and loyalty of their assistants' and interpreters' fathers. The Creek children of Scottish trader Robert Grierson, for example, discovered that their paternity mattered to American officials. Hawkins, who understood that Creeks viewed fatherhood differently, made sure to refer to Grierson's son, also named Robert, as the "son of the [well-known] Scotchman."[33] Paternity, for this Creek child, continued to shape his identity even though he married a Creek woman named Sinnugee, had six Creek children, and lived according to village and clan norms. In fact, nearly two decades after his father's death, the Creek child was often treated as an Indian countryman rather than a Creek child and life-long resident of Hilibi.[34] European Americans also referred to specific fathers in order to clarify identities of Creek children. In a society fearful of strangers of all ethnicities, unknown Indians were usually deemed dangerous savages. Evidence of European American kin and sobriety often ameliorated these fears. In 1760, for example, Alexander Miln wrote South Carolina gover-nor William Henry Lyttleton to tell him that "a half Breed (David McDonald's Son) who came with his Father died." In this and other cases, Miln referred to David McDonald in order to identify the child. The younger McDonald had not known his father for several decades, but Lyttleton knew his father to be a trusted Scottish trader.[35]

European Americans remained aware of the mothers and residences of many children of intermarriages. Some European Americans indicated the paternal identities of Creeks through such terms as "half-breed," "mestizo," or "half-blood." Such references, although not as persuasive as providing more defini-tive genealogies and character descriptions, often ensured uneasy Americans that the children of intermarriages, and the messages that they carried, could be trusted. [36] In many cases, though, these phrases were insufficient, and the intermediaries struggled to overcome perceptions that they were too Indian. In 1804 Georgia governor John Milledge used a reference to a white father to smooth over the concerns raised by using an "Indian" delivery boy. "This letter will be delivered to you by a half breed Indian who calls himself William Wright son of Joseph Wright, deceased father of the late Mr. Gunn." In addition to his reference to white kin, Milledge also assured the recipient of the letter that the Creek messenger would conform to European American standards of "civility." "I have given Wright a passport and strictly charged him to conduct himself in a proper and sober manner." [37] References to the sobriety of Wright played upon the common stereotype of the drunken Indian. Through claims of sobriety, Milledge minimized the importance of Wright's maternal identity and emphasized the civilizing role of his father.

Hawkins similarly referred to the sobriety of his assistants. In 1797 he "sent . . . a half-breed of the Upper Creeks, to go on with Mr. Robbins and to remain with the surveyors, as an interpreter and asst." Hawkins assured the surveyor that the intermediary could be trusted because "he is sober and of good character." [38] In a different letter written the same day, Hawkins reaffirmed the identity of Len McGee, the other assistant sent to help the surveyor. Hawkins claimed that he "is a prudent, honest, sober and industrious half breed, he speaks the language well it being his mother tongue, and he is willing to be employed about the factory to interpret, to attend to stock, to attend in the store and to do any thing which you may require of him." [39] In short, he was perfectly equipped to help.

In diplomatic affairs the children of intermarriages frequently took advantage of their paternal identities. David Cornell, for example, begged for forgiveness for his waging war against the United States in the years after the Revolution. "I am a son of a white man, Joseph Cornell, interpreter for the United States," he explained. Although the younger Cornell admitted that he "brought in a scalp from Cumberland," he insisted that he should not be treated as a Creek enemy. "The blame ought not, in justice, be laid on me, as I was urged to do it by Captain Olivar, (the Spanish Agent in the nation) and even by the Governor of Pensacola himself." Cornell then promised his personal loyalty and the friendship of the Upper Creeks before reminding Indian agent James Seagrove of his loyal American kin. "I am a younger brother of Ab. Cornell," he wrote, and in the future "shall take his advice." [40] Seagrove accepted Cornell's explanation for the hostilities and embraced his white identity. "I know your father, and have a great regard for him; he always was a friend to the United States, which is his county, and I hope his country will do so too." In addition,

Seagrove urged Cornell to "follow the advice of your cousin Alexander in all things, and you will find me your good friend."[41]

The ability to move between worlds made the children of intermarriages invaluable allies on the southern frontier.[42] Hawkins became so reliant on his assistants that when he found himself without them he was frequently at a loss for what to do. In 1805, for example, his "assistant and interpreter" Alexander Cornells, or Oche Haujo, was found "guilty of an indiscretion in taking a married woman for a night or two from her husband." Under Creek custom Cornells had to wait until the annual busk before he could obtain forgiveness for his participation in an act of adultery. Until then Hawkins worried that "I shall have to meet the Chiefs without his aid, and I know not how I will do without it." Hawkins's reliance transcended his need for linguistic interpretation. Cornells's "high and confidential standing among his own people," Hawkins wrote, "enduces them to consult and rely on him in all difficult cases and he is faithfully attached to the views of government."[43] The agent expressed similar dismay a few years earlier. "Being without an interpreter, I could not avail myself of the information I wished." It was not enough, he inferred, that "one of my guides understood and spoke the Creek tongue." Hawkins also needed someone the Creeks trusted. Hawkins, although a resident among the Creeks for twenty years, understood that he could not fully participate in Creek affairs without the assistance of bicultural assistants.[44]

When Christian missionaries came to Creek villages, they too called upon the services of Hawkins's trusted interpreters. They proved to be essential to the missionary efforts because they knew the territory, the Creek language, and the villages that might be more hospitable to the preachers. Without the safety afforded by Creek escorts and interpreters, the missionaries also knew that they could be evicted from Creek villages or assaulted on the routes that they traveled. Therefore, missionaries rarely traveled alone. In 1807, for example, Moravian preacher Karsten Petersen traveled to the Creek villages that surrounded the Creek Agency in the company of Hawkins and several other "white" escorts: "Mr. Limbaugh, Mr. Barnard, Mr. Lewis, the blacksmith, and a certain Mr. A. Handling, an Irishman, who claimed to be a British Commissioner from East Indian." On a later trip Petersen and his partner Johann Christian Burkard traveled the surrounding areas together. Like many European Americans, they stopped only at the homes of Indian countrymen and bicultural Creeks. Throughout their seven-year stay among the Creeks, 1807 to 1813, these Moravian missionaries did not travel alone and rarely ventured far from the Creek Agency. When they did, they usually ventured to the homes of Indian countrymen and their offspring, and they did so in the company of those they assumed were American escorts.[45] The reliance on Native interpreters who were once European Americans dated back to the sixteenth century when Hernando de Soto relied on the linguistic and diplomatic skills of Juan Ortiz, an adopted captive from Pánfilo de Narváez's 1528 expedition. "This interpreter puts new life into us," he wrote, "for without him I know not what would become of us."[46]

Indian countrymen and their Creek children did more than facilitate safe travels through Creek territory. They also helped missionaries reach the non-English-speaking population. When Burkard decided that he wanted to translate biblical passages into Muskogee, "for several days [he] spent his time with a half-Indian who knew English." Few bilingual Creeks willingly volunteered their services. James Durouzeaux refused to help the Moravians without pay, and "Chief Alec Cornells, half-Indian, interpreter, and a man of considerable intelligence," rarely found the time to "translate a few words into Indian for us to learn." Usually, the missionaries complained, "he was so busy . . . translating for the Colonel [Hawkins] and conducting many conferences with the chiefs . . . that he had no time." The only way to get real information from Cornells was to invite him to dine. In that manner the Moravians obtained assistance with the Muskogee language.[47]

The assistance of Indian countrymen and their Creek children did not necessarily translate into widespread conversions of Creeks. Missionaries had trouble getting villagers, let alone their Creek assistants, interpreters, and hosts, to accept Christianity. They may have been provided with access to Creek society, but the spiritual world of their Native kin remained off-limits. As the descendant of one of the frustrated missionaries recalled, "their slaves heard the Gospel gladly, and large numbers of them were baptized, which was a matter of total indifference to the Creeks." There was an easy explanation for this deaf ear to Christianity. "This new religion which the missionary brought might be good enough for Negroes and Whites—but the Creek religion was vastly superior, and the missionary must not disturb the Creeks in their ancient faith."[48] Still, Christian missionaries could most easily reach the Creek children of Indian countrymen and escaped African American slaves. Finding religious common ground rarely occurred, but its chances increased in families of intermarriage. William Sparks summed up this phenomenon when he observed that "the efforts at civilization seem only to reach the mixed bloods, and these only in proportion to the white blood in their veins."[49]

In large part the perceived correlation between culture change and racial identities resulted from linguistic barriers that most Christian missionaries could not, or chose not to, overcome. Baptist missionary Lee Compere, for example, directed most of his attention to those Creeks who could speak English.

Although Compere eventually learned some of the Creek language, through the assistance of several Creek children of intermarriage, he only interspersed his services with a Muskogee hymn or a translated Lord's Prayer or section of the Bible. Most of his communication with non-English-speaking Indians, whether gathering information or spreading the Christian word, occurred through interpreters. Without their assistance Compere felt useless. He bemoaned when a "day has been spent at home for the want of a suitable interpreter to accompany me in visiting the Indians."[50] Things went slightly better when he obtained a trusting interpreter, but even then Compere regretted that "my preaching was mostly confined to such as understood English excepting when I addressed the Indians through an interpreter." The interpreter, Compere recognized, was essential to frontier preaching.[51]

Fortunately Reverend Compere found a trustworthy assistant and interpreter in John Davis. In 1826 the bilingual Creek became Compere's most important asset when he converted to Christianity and proclaimed his intention to convert other Creek Indians.[52] This act of faith did not convince Compere to let Davis serve as his interpreter. Apparently Davis's African background caused some hesitation in Compere. The Baptist missionary had no choice, however. "There is at present, no white person at the Station but my own family," Compere regretted. Therefore, "to supply the lack of assistance in other respects, I have proposed to allow John Davis, (one of our scholars), five dollars per month to act as interpreter, and to perform other services." A Creek resident, Davis had the ability to escort Compere throughout Creek territory and find some willing listeners. Although Davis had trouble preaching to white audiences in Georgia and Alabama, his African status did not limit his ability to be a broker among fellow Creeks.[53]

With Davis's assistance Compere translated a few hymns, a version of the Lord's Prayer, and sections of the Bible into Muskogee. Nevertheless, Compere discovered that he had little luck counteracting the general attitude of "the chiefs [who] were always opposed to preaching." Creek chiefs, he complained, actively opposed him whenever he entered a Creek village and expressed interest in holding a formal service. Thus, Compere had to make alternative arrangements. At first, he concluded that "I shall be obliged to do it [introduce the gospel] without any form of ceremony, by mingling with the Indians when they assemble in their talk-houses, and so manage to instruct them in the way of familiar conversations."[54] This had its limitations, and Compere wanted to create a stable place of worship. This led him to hold several meetings at Isaac Smith's home, which was "about seventeen miles from us in the midst of a company of white men, and half breeds who can talk English."[55] There Compere found "as good a company of white men, half breeds, and black people, as I expected, which made me feel thankful for such an opportunity of breaking the bread of life." In addition, Compere established the Withington School for acculturating and converting neighboring students. This, too, attracted mostly the Creek children of intermarried European Americans and African Americans. Preaching to an English-speaking audience had its limitations, Compere admitted, but eventually he attracted enough of an audience to support his optimism. When Compere followed the Creeks west in 1828, he had converted, in his words, only a handful of "Indians" but several dozen "Africans and half breeds."[56]

Unlike European American visitors who needed help to survive, many Creek leaders opted to use the Creek children of intermarriage and Indian countrymen as advisers. Creek leaders used their advice, their insights, and their connections to American society while they interpreted treaties or served as messengers. Their effectiveness in negotiating compromises occasionally led to their rise as village leaders, but more often they provided the insights borne of biculturalism. Creek leaders frequently cultivated this advice, and it created the image that the children of intermarriage were assisting, if not controlling, Creek leaders everywhere. This perception led southern author William Gilmore Simms to claim that the "writings [of the Creeks] were prepared by the white men, squatters in the nation." This resulted because "the savages . . . choose white men to be their chiefs and counselors. . . . In this way, a few white men or half breeds, possessed the most unqualified sway over the Indians." Senator Thomas Hart Benton observed something rather similar. The Creeks, he claimed, have become "an oligarchy, governed chiefly by a few white men, called half-breeds." Creeks with European American kin, Benton and Simms proclaimed, held disproportionate influence among the Natives.[57]

European Americans such as Benton and Simms may not have understood the implications of or reasons for the presence of Creek advisers with European American fathers, but their observations exaggerated rather than created this reality. Throughout the long eighteenth century, scores of Indian countrymen and their Creek children advised Creek leaders. Big Warrior would not attend any conference without Indian countryman Kendall Lewis, his son-in-law, by his side, interpreting and advising.[58] Similarly, McGillivray advised Creek leaders throughout the early republic while relying on several other mixed Creeks to assist him assert his own authority. As McGillivray's power increased, he increasingly relied on the children of intermarriages and intermarried European Americans to gather information, send messages, and design effective diplomatic policies.[59] McGillivray, just like other Creek leaders, capitalized on the help of bicultural Creeks and Indian countrymen who understood the two worlds.

The southern frontier also provided the Creek children of intermarriages with various economic opportunities. In addition to the economic opportunities of the deerskin trade, Creeks learned how to profit from the constant stream of Americans who traveled into and through Creek lands. Just as the Creek children of intermarriages profited from interpreting for Christian missionaries and guiding travelers through Creek territory, several took advantage of the common desire of travelers to stay among English-speaking hosts on their journeys through Indian lands. Initially an informal system of inns and homes met this need, but over the course of the eighteenth century this system expanded. By the nineteenth century a system of ferries, tolls, taverns, and inns catered to the travelers. On their journeys through Creek lands, travelers jumped between stops that mirrored the South. They stopped at McGillivray's plantation, Lewis's Tavern, McIntosh's Inn, Crowell's "Old Station," and Walls's Tavern. They moved from cotton plantations that employed African American slaves to small farms filled with livestock to well-stocked European-style inns.[60]

The emergence of such a network occurred gradually. At first travelers took advantage of private homes and the Creek custom of generous hospitality. With the help of a "mustee Creek" guide, for example, naturalist William Bartram traveled through the Creek Nation on the eve of the American Revolution. This "mustee" guided Bartram to several homes occupied by the Creek children of European Americans, Indian countrymen, and white traders. At one stop, a home belonging to a man named Boatswain, Bartram found a model of European American civilization. "It was composed of three oblong uniform frame buildings, and a fourth, four-square, fronting the principal house or common hall, after this manner, encompassing one area. The hall was his lodging-house, large and commodious: the two wings were, one a cook-house, the other a skin or ware-house; and the large square was a vast open pavilion, supporting a canopy of cedar roof." Bartram also recognized the hospitality that Boatswain gave. "We had excellent coffee served up in china ware, by young negro slaves. We had plenty of excellent sugar, honey, choice war corn cakes, venison steaks, and barbecued meat." Bartram's guide ensured that the journey through the Creek villages included stops at several other homes of several Indian traders and Creeks.[61]

After the American Revolution, travelers usually anchored their trip at Hawkins's newly established Creek Agency and then continued by jumping between the residences of Creek children of intermarriages, Indian countrymen, and white traders. In the years that followed, Creeks offered more "safe" places to stop. The completion of the Federal Road in 1804 created a crystallized path for the children of intermarriages to focus their efforts. Secretary of War Henry

Dearborn recognized that Creeks would "derive very considerable advantages from such a Road by keeping Houses of entertainment for travelers & by selling their provisions for ready money."[62] The Treaty of 1805 made these "houses of entertainment" the obligations of the Creek Nation, and several Creek children of intermarriages stepped forward to fulfill this legal burden. Within a couple of years a coordinated system of rest stations were located within a day's travel from each other along the road. In nearly every instance the inns were either owned by a Creek child of an intermarriage or by a white man with a Creek partner. Often these "sleeping partners," as they were called, were the children of intermarriages. This was necessary because the Creeks allowed "no white person to settle in their nation except as their partners, as husbands of Indian women, or in some way or other, closely connected with themselves."[63]

The rest stations served as oases in the midst of what many travelers believed to be a land of savages. They offered what one "gentleman of great respectability" described as a homestead that "in their domestic or household affairs, approaching us so nearly that the difference could hardly be discovered." As a result travelers found more than safe places to spend an evening. They could also dine "at one of the chiefs' houses where the whole business of eating and drinking was done in a stile and manner that might be compared with that of a private gentleman in the best settled states."[64] Adam Hodgson found these oases to be essential, as he relied on the hospitality of several Creek children of intermarriages on his journey in March 1820. After staying at Drury Spain's Inn, where "he gave us some coffee, Indian corn-bread, and bacon," Hodgson set off for the next acceptable resting place. Being that there was "no cabin within a convenient distance" and only the "rude dwellings" of the Indians nearby, Hodgson considered "sleeping in the woods that night." The rest of the trip was more acceptable. After William McIntosh's ferry took him across the Chattahoochee River, he arrived at the Ouchee Bridge, where he "determined to rest the remainder of the day at a stand kept up by a young man from Philadelphia, whose partner is a half-breed. I slept in a log-cabin, without windows; and supped with my host and several unwashed artifiers, and unshaven labourers." As Hodgson continued his journey, he continued to stay at homes owned and run by the children of intermarriages. His hosts eagerly awaited him, his cash, and the other travelers, as they profited from their dual identities and biculturalism on the southern frontier.[65]

During the eighteenth and early nineteenth centuries the Creek children of intermarriages obtained personal benefits and risks through their participation on the southern frontier. Their comfort in different cultures prepared them for traversing dangerous and confusing terrains. They appeared to be members of both communities, they spoke multiple languages, and they understood the unspoken assumptions of both Creek and American societies. As a result they served as interpreters, messengers, advisers, escorts, and hosts, and throughout the eighteenth and early nineteenth centuries they made intercultural interactions possible. Assisting American officials and Creek leaders also resulted in a wide range of economic, social, and spiritual rewards. Many profited from their linguistic skills as paid interpreters or skilled travel guides. Others capitalized on their position on the frontier by running inns, taverns, ferries, and private toll roads. On some occasions they translated their ability to mediate between the two societies into political authority among the Creeks. All these instances forced Creeks to balance carefully their dual identities and loyalties. When Americans or Creeks perceived that an interpreter or messenger had a hostile bias or when they stopped believing they were either a loyal American or fellow Creek, the intermediary could find himself excluded from participating on the frontier. The place of opportunity could turn into a place of hostility.

CHAPTER 6

Tustunnuggee Hutkee and the Limits of Dual Identities

In the eighteenth and early nineteenth centuries many children of intermarriages became village chiefs or took leadership roles in Creek society. These individuals obtained their political and diplomatic authority in traditional ways, but their European American identities provided them opportunities. Their American identities, connections, and loyalties provided various material resources that served as the base of a network of reciprocal relations. They redistributed blankets, livestock, cash, and food. In return, Creeks listened to the children of intermarriages and often offered their support. In short, the children of intermarriages often became political leaders because they were able to turn their connections to European American society into benefits for their fellow Creeks. Thus, for much of the eighteenth and early nineteenth century, political authority in the southeast had both American and Native roots.

The experiences of one man, known as William McIntosh Jr. among the Americans and Tustunnuggee Hutkee among the Creeks, illuminates the intertwined nature of political authority in the early American southeast. McIntosh served as a Creek warrior in the Red Stick War of 1813–14 and in the First Seminole War. In both instances McIntosh fought as a Creek Indian but allied himself with the United States. These military exploits earned McIntosh a reputation among the Creeks and Americans for martial valor and courage. McIntosh turned this to his advantage and translated his reputation into diplomatic authority among the Creeks. His rise to power, as well as his fall from grace, directly resulted from his dual identity and his bicultural backgrounds. McIntosh's ascendancy did not perfectly replicate the paths taken by earlier and subsequent mixed leaders. However, the reasons behind it help explain the routes that other children of intermarriages took. The ability to be—or at least to be recognized as—both a clanned Creek Indian and a fellow European American helped individuals such as Mary Musgrove Matthews Bosomworth, Alexander McGillivray, James McQueen, and William Weatherford obtain authority among the Creeks.

William McIntosh's authority did not rest squarely on the shoulders of Creek society. Rather, the roots of his authority were on both sides of the frontier. One could not disconnect William McIntosh from Tustunnuggee Hutkee. McIntosh's dual identity as both a southerner and a Creek Indian combined to legitimize his position as a powerful Creek leader. Patriarchal American society provided Tustunnuggee Hutkee with the material resources necessary to expand his authority among the Creeks because it believed that McIntosh embodied European American culture and thus was naturally the most "civilized" and trustworthy Native. This, in turn, allowed McIntosh to obtain more authority and thus confirm the assumptions of the neighboring Americans. Through his access to money, livestock, and slaves, McIntosh created an extensive network of reciprocal relations and obtained the domestic allegiances of hundreds of Creeks and several Creek villages. In this manner the celebrated war chief expanded his military authority into the domestic sphere and became one of the most influential pre-removal Creek leaders.

Just before dawn broke on Saturday, April 30, 1825, nearly four hundred Creek warriors surrounded the plantation of William McIntosh, a traitor in their eyes for having signed the controversial Treaty of Indian Springs the previous February. They torched the main house, and when McIntosh fled outside to escape the flames, he was struck by the volley of dozens of rifles. Etome Tustunnuggee, a Creek leader who had helped orchestrate the Treaty of Indian Springs, met a similar fate. After killing the two men and burning the house, the assailants sacked McIntosh's property. Two witnesses later recalled that the "banditi were busily engaged, from the commencement of the horrid scene until a late houre of the morning, in plundering and destroying every thing valuable, as well [as] the property of the white men who were present at the property of the general." The warriors even tore "a frock off a young Indian female" and left "several small children stark naked." As the sun set, the attackers dispersed, and under the cover of darkness, the dead were buried. In addition to the high cost in human lives, a once-thriving plantation had been reduced to ashes; its slaves, cattle, hogs, and horses were either miles away or had been slain.[1]

During the ensuing months the emotional rhetoric that characterized the initial response of U.S. officials to the McIntosh murder turned to a more rational discussion of political legitimacy and a radical reconsideration of the events that culminated in his death. Although Americans never reached consensus over the validity of the treaty, many rejected the idea that McIntosh was slain by an angry mob. In addition, they stopped believing that the massacre was "the signal for a ferocious Indian war" that might burst "upon us like a thunderbolt."[2] Instead, after the rhetoric cooled, authorities increasingly recognized that McIntosh was rightfully executed by a Creek police authority known as the Law Menders for an offense against Creek law. The *Niles Weekly Register* epitomized the new interpretation when it reported in May 1825 that "McIntosh was not murdered; but rather that he has been duly executed, according to the known laws and usages of the nation to which he belonged."[3] The article pointed to a law, one that McIntosh had rigorously supported when it was agreed upon by the Creek National Council, that called for the execution of any Creek leader who ceded land to the United States. As a result the United States reluctantly voided the Treaty of Indian Springs, which McIntosh had orchestrated in February 1825 and which ceded all the Creek lands within Georgia to the United States. Despite this change in both the public's perception and official policy, land-hungry Georgians continued to proclaim the treaty's legitimacy, and hundreds of Creeks—mostly supporters of McIntosh—removed west as stipulated by the treaty.[4]

The federal government's investigation into the execution exposed more than the political factionalism among the Creek Indians; it also revealed that McIntosh was not the man that federal and state authorities believed him to be. He was not a white southerner who obtained the allegiance of the Creek Nation because of his "advanced" cultural traits, martial valor, and "white heritage."[5] Despite a military rank awarded by the United States, he was not empowered by the Creeks just because he was commissioned as a general. Nor was he a "civilized Indian" who naturally led the "full-blooded" savage nation. In Creek society McIntosh went by the name Tustunnuggee Hutkee, and his leadership abilities depended on his clan connections, military exploits, and extensive network of reciprocal relationships. He had authority, especially among the Lower Creeks, but he never possessed absolute authority. Tustunnuggee Hutkee competed for authority with several other Creek leaders—of various ethnic backgrounds—and he lived within a range of tribal norms and regulations. When the Creek Law Menders justified their killing of Tustunnuggee Hutkee, they stressed the slain leader's Creek ethnic identity and the purpose and legality of the act. The execution "was not intended as hostilities against the whites." Instead, "it was only a fulfillment of their own laws which General McIntosh himself had signed, and declared in the square at Broken Arrow during the late treaty at that place." McIntosh had merely broken his agreement "that if any Indian chief should sign a treaty of any lands to the whites, he should certainly suffer death." In this statement the Law Menders identified McIntosh as one of the legitimate leaders of the Creek Nation and accepted his identity as a Creek Indian. Creeks and white Americans saw McIntosh rather differently.[6]

Recent historians have expanded on the Law Menders' justification of McIntosh's death. They begin by explaining how McIntosh's leadership in the treaty negotiations violated a Creek law that prohibited the signing away of lands to the United States. The egregious details of this crime furthered the outrage within Creek society. Several tribal delegations that had opposed the proposed treaty had left the negotiations before they were concluded; others refused to sign. Although fifty-two Creeks signed the document, only six were headmen, and only McIntosh was a member of the Creek National Council. Nevertheless, through the treaty McIntosh agreed to cede more than 6,700 square miles of tribal land in return for an immediate payment of $10,000, with $190,000 to be paid over the next fourteen years. This transferred almost all of the Creek holdings in Georgia, with the only exceptions being for those lands "improved" by McIntosh and some of his supporters. McIntosh retained much of the land he personally controlled, obtained cash incentives to sign and enforce the treaty, and otherwise contradicted the desire of most Creek leaders. In short, judged historian Michael D. Green, the Treaty of Indians Springs was "fraudulent by the standards of any society, concluded in violation of the clearly expressed orders of both interested governments [and] riddled with bribery, chicanery, and deceit."[7]

Yet the path that led to the execution of McIntosh is helpful in understanding a more important issue, the nature of authority on the southern frontier. Children of intermarriages, especially those who served as cultural brokers on the early American frontier, played important roles, and McIntosh is an example of this aspect of frontier society. Scholars, who have recently given these individuals a tremendous amount of attention, have tended to assert either that individuals who bridged two conflicting cultures necessarily lived on the margins of Indian and European American society or that they should be understood solely within the matrilineal Indian context in which they lived.[8]

Both these constructive approaches to cultural brokers fall short of fully explaining the rise and fall of William McIntosh. On one hand, tensions clearly emerged when individuals, regardless of their backgrounds, try to appease two competing groups. McIntosh's treasonous actions largely resulted from his inability to please and meet the expectations of two different societies. Caught between the demands of two worlds, McIntosh found himself in a no-win situation. This explanation, however effective it may be in explaining his downfall, cannot address how individuals like McIntosh could maintain their positions of authority for so long or obtain them in inherently Native ways. Even the most acculturated children of intermarriages were treated as the children of their mother's clan, and their connections to the marketplace provided access to desired materials and information. Yet by highlighting the importance of Native identities, scholars have overlooked the importance of having ties to European American society. McIntosh maintained and fostered these connections throughout his life. Without understanding these connections, we cannot comprehend either his rise or his fall from power.

It is necessary to explore why European Americans and Creeks originally arrived at such radically different understandings of McIntosh and the events that resulted in his death in order to create a more complete understanding of how McIntosh obtained, and then lost, authority in the early nineteenth century. His rise and fall from power illuminates the importance of addressing the interrelation between the two worlds in which he lived. As the child of a Creek woman and a member of the Wind clan, McIntosh undeniably lived and died by the rules of Creek society. Creeks expected McIntosh to distribute his wealth; moreover, his status as a warrior dictated his status as a man.

McIntosh was born into the privileged world of his mother's family. Senoia, McIntosh's mother, belonged to the Wind clan and enjoyed connections to several powerful relatives. Several sources refer to her as a "princess," largely because of the appearance that her brothers exerted near royal influence. Other sources refer to her as a *heniha*, or spokesperson, mistakenly assuming that she would share the appellation of her brother Chief Howard Heniha of the Chehaw town. Behind the misperceptions that led to calling her a *heniha* or a princess, Senoia and her brothers were born into the world of a politically connected mother and clan. In addition to Howard Heniha, two other brothers, Tuskena-hah and Tomoc Mico, held leadership positions within their respective villages. Tomoc Mico even served as a Law Mender prior to McIntosh's execution. When McIntosh was a child, these powerful maternal uncles would have trained him in the manly arts of hunting, warfare, and diplomacy. They likely taught him how to use a bow and arrow, stalk prey, and use a rifle. They also would have led by example. They taught the virtue of reciprocity, the obligations of clan, and the power of oratory.[9]

For many years as a young adult, McIntosh fulfilled the expectations of his Native kin by redistributing money, cattle, food, and other trade goods. In return, many Creeks reciprocated McIntosh's generosity by extending him authority and occasionally agreeing to his often controversial decisions.[10] At the same time McIntosh benefited from the realities that he was the child of a Scottish man with kinship connections that permeated southern society, that he was an individual who practiced what were perceived to be various white southern cultural traits, and that he was comfortable within his father's world. He participated in the marketplace, spoke English, owned slaves, herded cattle, and consistently proved his loyalty to U.S. officials. He may have been Creek in the eyes of fellow Creeks, but his paternity and cultural practices resulted in a different image in the eyes of white society. Like several other children of intermarriages, McIntosh lived within two worlds simultaneously. Rather than being contradictory, however, his two identities reinforced one another.

McIntosh's Creek residence and matrilineal ties did not negate his acceptance in white Georgian society. Instead, many European Americans assumed McIntosh had been incorporated into American culture. McIntosh's sense of ease within American society and among Americans reinforced the image that he was a southerner living among the Indians. Because "McIntosh lived a life reflecting both his white, Scottish ancestry and his Indian blood," he could move in and out of American society without much trouble. In 1818 he traveled to Augusta, Georgia, to attend a formal dinner thrown in honor of his courageous military service in the War of 1812 and the First Seminole War. Writer William Gilmore Simms believed that "the very intimacy which the Creek Chief possessed among the whites" confirmed his father's socializing influence and McIntosh's southern identity. [11] A description published in the *Niles Weekly Register* supported this impression. It reported that "we have seen him in the bosom of the forest, surrounded by a band of wild and ungovernable savages— we have seen him too, in the drawing room in the civilized walks of life, receiving that meed of approbation which his services so justly merit. In each situation we found him the same, easy and unconstrained in his address, and uniform in his conduct." [12] Thomas McKenney, chief administrator of Indian affairs from 1816 to 1830, believed that "having been thrown into the society of the more polished of our people, and having been the associate of our officers in the wars on our southern borders, [McIntosh] had acquired all the manners and much of the polish of a gentleman." McIntosh, socialized by both his Scottish father and Creek mother, understood the importance of acting appropriately in each society, and he had the upbringing to do so. [13]

McIntosh's actions within Creek society reaffirmed his standing as a well-bred southerner. He helped institute innovations within Creek society that made it appear more "civilized" to Americans. In addition to pushing for a centralized form of government and justice, McIntosh also promoted slaveholding, cattle and hog herding, cotton agriculture, English-style schools, Western ideas of land ownership and economics, and patrilineal descent. These actions led Secretary of War James Barbour to call McIntosh "a steady friend of the United States, and of Civilization." Although a majority of the Creeks never approached or accepted the standards of "civilization" that McIntosh adopted, a faction of Creek Indians readily incorporated these new conceptions of gender, land, work, economics, government, and authority. In some circles McIntosh received credited for these changes. [14]

McIntosh practiced what he promoted. He lived a lifestyle that Americans recognized as part of antebellum southern civilization. A planter, merchant, and soldier, McIntosh owned two plantations—Acorn Town (Lockchau Talofau) and Indian Springs. He operated two ferries, and he established an inn and tavern on his plantation at Acorn Town and another inn at Indian Springs. He even built a 118-mile toll road through Creek territory, which both added to his personal coffers and further ensured the use of his network of ferries, inns, and taverns. McIntosh also grew cotton, owned more than one hundred slaves, herded more than eight hundred head of cattle, raised dozens of hogs and horses, farmed on enclosed land, and sent his children to American schools. McIntosh could write and read English. He fought alongside American soldiers in the War of 1812 and the First Seminole War, and in doing so he convinced many Americans that his word could be trusted as that of a man of honor. Through his successful exploits, McIntosh rose from a major to a colonel to a brigadier general of the U.S. Army. This reputation led Woodward to write that "McIntosh, though raised among savages, was a General; yes, he was one of God's make of Generals." In sum, McIntosh's Creek residence did not hinder his reputation within American society; if anything, his actions among the Creeks made him increasingly appear to be American.[15]

His reputation as a "civilized Creek" and a "southern gentleman" increased as dozens of Americans stayed as his guests on his plantations. Travelers frequently took advantage of his hospitality on their journeys through Creek society, often on their way to New Orleans. Some went to Indian Springs to enjoy the "Great Medicine Water," while at the same time enjoy the comforts of civilization in the wilderness.[16] McIntosh used these moments to further his image as a white man among the Indians. In 1797 Francis Baily came upon McIntosh's "habitation," which he described as "a poor sorry place, little better than an Indian hut." Despite its image, Baily noticed that McIntosh "appeared to have every thing which such a country affords in the greatest abundance about him." More importantly, McIntosh drew a distinction between himself and his Native neighbors and told Baily "that the Indians (who are a lazy, indolent race, in respect to husbandry) were such incessant beggars, that he was not only prevented from bettering his situation, but oftentimes reduced to great straits himself."[17] Within a decade, McIntosh offered accommodations more in line with European American expectations. Adam Hodgson met McIntosh while in New York and accepted an invitation to "stop by" if he ever happened to be in the Creek Nation. When Hodgson visited in 1820, McIntosh's two-story plantation house (estimated to be worth $1,500 in 1824) exceeded his expectations.[18] Hundreds of other travelers paid to stay at McIntosh's inns and frequented his tavern on their western journeys, for he offered these short-term guests all of the comforts of "civilization." The plantation's comfort convinced American officials such as Indian agent David Mitchell to choose it as a place for negotiations in 1820. The inn at Indian Springs boasted thirty-four rooms, a dining room that routinely featured piano playing, elaborate etchings on the walls, and waters blessed with "medicinal powers." In the aftermath of McIntosh's execution, the U.S. government estimated that his destroyed property on one of his two residences was worth more than $10,000, although McIntosh's family believed its worth to be much greater.[19]

McIntosh's identity as a Georgian did not rest solely on his actions. He also looked the part, confirming the belief of some Americans that the redness of Indians was but a temporary condition. Indeed, McIntosh physically resembled many of his European American neighbors. Thomas McKenney, chief administrator of Indian affairs from 1816 to 1830, described McIntosh as "the handsome Creek who looked like a swarthy-skinned Scots Highland chief." Another American asserted that he had "a mild, gentle face, more expressive of humor than of boldness."[20] Others were more confused by his appearance. Southern author William Gilmore Simms claimed that "McIntosh, in the general expression of his countenance, its color, &c. appears to me, less to resemble the Indian, than some of the bright mulattoes whom we hourly encounter in our streets."[21] Simms, like other Americans, could not categorize McIntosh as an Indian based on his appearance because the Creek leader's appearance was puzzling. Furthering the confusion, McIntosh adapted his clothing, often referred to as "a blend of European and Indians styles," to his circumstances. Whether in tribal councils or in Augusta, Savannah, or Pensacola, McIntosh understood that his dress reflected his identity, and when McIntosh traveled in American society, he hardly conformed to American expectations of the Indian.[22]

In the years that preceded his execution, McIntosh epitomized the connections between intermarriage and the incorporation of Native Americans into European American society. During his tour of several Creek villages in 1819, Ebenezer H. Cummins explained the American conception of the "temporary Indian" and the potential for intermarriage. "Amalgamation with the whites . . . is the only means, supported by experience, to preserve to the country the blood of her aboriginal sons. And this amalgamation, of the savage and civilized races, has produced, in some of the oldest states, men of the first eminence in the union." Cummins pointed directly to the McIntosh family to support his argument. "In the very neighbourhood of the country of which we have been treating, is a rising family of the name of M'Intosh, commonly called halfbreeds, possessed of many of the higher virtues, and particularly distinguished in military achievements." As proof of the McIntosh family's acceptance by Georgians, Cummins pointed to "a son of the late governor of Georgia, General David B. Mitchell, [who] recently married Miss M'Intosh, an accomplished girl . . . though descended of an Indian mother." As Cummins saw it, McIntosh confirmed the potential for Creeks to be incorporated with Georgians. "The truth is, after the missionary system, and the system of taming by the arts, shall have failed in the benevolent purpose of rescuing the savage from heathenism and extinction," he wrote "amalgamation will have preserved precious streams of Indian blood, coursing the veins of many generous loyal citizens." Cummins believed McIntosh to be partly Indian in his "blood," but fully American in his identity. Intermarriages, Cummins claimed, cemented social connections because they created an intricate, multicultural web of kinship.[23]

By 1825 McIntosh had such a network, one that was created by both his own actions and the actions of his kinsmen and kinswomen. Under the Creek custom of polygamy, McIntosh's father, Captain McIntosh, married two Creek women and sired children with both. When Captain McIntosh permanently left the Creeks and returned to Georgia, he remarried. With Barbara, his Scottish-American wife, Captain William provided young William with an extensive non-Native kin network. Through his father's lineage, young McIntosh became cousin to Georgia governor George M. Troup, and half-brother to Georgia legislator William R. McIntosh and to John McIntosh, who worked at the Savannah port as collector for the Treasury Department.[24] Not surprisingly, Troup refused to accept that his cousin was rightfully executed in 1825. Instead he blamed the U.S. agent to the Creeks, John Crowell, the "most depraved of our own Color," for the murder.[25]

Although McIntosh had extensive kinship ties within American society by virtue of his father's marriages, he also arranged marriages for himself and his children to further his personal ties to American and Indian societies. Following his father's polygamous example, McIntosh married Susannah Coe (a Creek), Peggy (a Cherokee), and Eliza Grierson (a child of a Creek-American intermarriage). With connections to the most powerful neighbors—Native and American—McIntosh expanded the kin network that was provided to him at birth. McIntosh's children also married prominent Creeks, Cherokees, and Americans. One daughter married trader Thomas Spalding, and as Cummings observed, another married the son of Indian agent and Georgia governor David B. Mitchell. A third daughter married Samuel Hawkins, the federal interpreter for Creeks. In this way McIntosh ties extended to the prominent families and clans in the region and to the power structure of the United States, Georgia, and neighboring Native villages. These ties strengthened McIntosh's American identity and later provided him access to the resources that supported his network of reciprocation.[26]

McIntosh's marriages to Native women did not diminish his European American identity among southerners. In the years prior to his execution, McIntosh's "full-blooded" Creek wife and Cherokee wife were often ignored within American society much like most of the "left-handed" or "Winchester" marriages of the Indian traders. In the eyes of Americans these "marriages of convenience" did not have the same force of law as those with "white" wives. Because intermarriages abided by the standards of Native society, as opposed to European American mores, most Americans considered the Indian participants such as Susannah Coe and Peggy to be merely "wenches" and dismissed their relationships with McIntosh as "casual marriages."[27] At the other extreme, Americans validated McIntosh's connection with Eliza, the "more civilized" daughter of Samuel Hawkins. Brigadier General Alexander Ware could call Eliza, unlike McIntosh's other wives, "an Indian rising above what is commonly found in females of that Nation." American observers, such as Ware, rarely mentioned the other wives; Eliza had their full attention. Even McIntosh's polygamy seemingly avoided censure in American society. In short, American attitudes toward William (and his children) often typified the attitude toward other "half-breeds"; they were deemed to be "semi-civilized," "white" Americans who lived among the Creeks, if not as Creeks.[28]

Because Americans identified McIntosh as one of their own, they eagerly accepted him as a spokesperson for the Creeks. Although McIntosh initially obtained prominence within Creek society on the terms of the Native community—he was a war chief—U.S. officials helped McIntosh expand his power by providing him three crucial advantages in his claims to authority within Creek society. First, they chose to make treaties with McIntosh instead of holding councils with his opposition, a group that usually represented a majority of the Creek people. Second, officials frequently selected McIntosh as a linchpin in the distribution of the annuity and the other "spoils" of land cessions and war. Third, the authorities paid McIntosh for his allegiance with land, trade monopolies, and other valuable resources. These advantages allowed McIntosh to support a network of reciprocal obligations with a sizable core of Creek followers. In each case an understanding of McIntosh's American identity shaped the decisions of the officials. At the same time a self-aware McIntosh actively asserted his appearance and loyalty to cultivate American favor and then translate it into authority among tribal members. Although McIntosh never represented a majority of the Creeks, the advantages he received allowed him to expand his authority without the full consent of the Creek people. Many Creeks opposed his actions and even tried to remove him from power, but McIntosh's network of reciprocal relations allowed him to continue to exert authority into the 1820s.

The faith that European Americans had in McIntosh often led them to ignore legitimate divisions and dissent within Creek society. On several occasions U.S. officials chose to meet with McIntosh rather than his opposition. Throughout the Creek's pre-removal history European Americans chose primarily to make treaties with "friendly Indians," "peace parties," or Creek factions who readily agreed to their demands. This, along with the belief that acculturated Indians were naturally more civilized, enabled officials to assume that the children of European American men and Indian women logically ruled the Natives. At the same time, their opposition, in spite of widespread support among the Natives, could be ignored so American policy could be pursued. The self-serving results of treating with allies who readily agreed to demands made the decision to recognize them as tribal leaders even easier. In McIntosh's case the terms of several treaties provided the resources that, once distributed, would further increase his personal authority within Creek society.[29]

As early as 1805, U.S. officials provided the means for McIntosh to begin creating an extensive network of obligations within Creek society. That year, in the Treaty of Washington, McIntosh helped orchestrate the cession of the land between the Oconee and Ocmulgee rivers to the U.S. government and provide the Americans access to the Federal Road, a road from the Ocmulgee to Mobile, Alabama. In the process he protected his personal interests and his network of reciprocal obligations. The treaty mandated that "the Creek chiefs will have boats kept at the several rivers for the conveyance of men and horses, and houses of entertainment established at suitable places on said path for the accommodation of travelers." Naturally McIntosh enjoyed the advantages of this legal "obligation."[30] He arranged to build an inn and tavern along the road and received the right to run ferries across the Chattahoochee River. He also used the annuity that resulted from this treaty, $20,000 in money and goods, to expand his personal authority. Throughout the next decade McIntosh helped distribute these goods, as well as access to the deerskin trade, as part of his personal network of reciprocal obligations. In the process (as he would continue to do in the future) McIntosh also used these resources to enhance his appearance as a European American among the Creeks.

During the War of 1812 McIntosh opposed the Red Sticks, a nativist and anti-American movement that comprised a majority of the Creeks. Instead he allied himself with Andrew Jackson against the majority of his fellow Creeks. Jackson was impressed with the Creek leader, writing that "Major M'Intosh (the Cowetan) who joined my army with part of his tribe, greatly distinguished himself."[31]

McIntosh's martial valor, a trait cherished in the antebellum South, endeared him to the southern general. So did McIntosh's civilized demeanor. McIntosh even shared, perhaps even internalized, Jackson's paternalistic rhetoric in descriptions of Indian and American societies. Just before his execution, McIntosh appealed to the Georgia legislature for assistance in words that paralleled Jackson's. "You have torn us up by the roots, but still you are our brothers and friends. You have promised to replant us in a better soil, and to watch over us and nurse us."[32] McIntosh—like so many other acculturated Creeks with European lineages—so deviated from Jackson's conception of "real Indians" that Jackson readily accepted his support and trusted his intentions. McIntosh's self-association with the Creeks did not matter; Jackson saw him as a leader of the Creeks but identified him as an American.[33]

Jackson's perception of McIntosh did not prohibit their diplomatic dealings. If anything, McIntosh's American identity allowed Jackson to trust him. In 1814 McIntosh wrote to Jackson about hostilities committed by Georgians against "friendly" Creek towns in response to an attack by "hostile" Creeks. Jackson was incensed. Confident in the accuracy of McIntosh's reports, the general ridiculed the acts as "base" and "cowardly." Although Little Prince and other Creek leaders protested the American misdeeds, only McIntosh's complaints found the receptive ears of the government. Jackson and McIntosh convinced Georgia officials, who initially insisted that the Georgians had justly attacked hostile villages, to apprehend those who commanded the expedition. In addition, Indian agent David Mitchell paid McIntosh to compensate for the loss. Unknown to the Georgians involved, these actions furthered the prestige McIntosh enjoyed within Creek society—he had the power to obtain justice from American sources.[34]

McIntosh's decision to oppose the Red Sticks alienated him from many other Creeks. The protection afforded by the United States military allowed him to narrowly escape the ire of the Red Sticks, who at one point called for his death. This would not be the last time that McIntosh would arouse the mistrust of the Creek majority. On multiple occasions factions of Creek leaders unsuccessfully tried to remove McIntosh from his positions of authority. As much as they deemed him "too much attached to the interest of the white people," McIntosh's access to the desired material resources and the personal networks that he created combined to permit him to maintain his position as one of several powerful Creek men.[35]

The terms of peace imposed by the United States in 1814, even as they devastated the Creek Nation as a whole, helped McIntosh retain the loyalty of many of the Creeks who supported him. The U.S. government recognized that the war left the Creeks "reduced to extreme want," and since they did not have any "means of subsistence," it agreed to "furnish gratuitously the necessaries of life, until the crops of corn can be considered competent to yield the nation a supply." The famine that followed the war provided McIntosh with an opportunity to become essential to the nation when he arranged to assist coordinating the "obligation" of distributing the food. McIntosh, even as he placed the Creeks in the precarious position of dependence, held the power to ease the famine. Many Creeks, even some who had opposed McIntosh and the U.S. government during the earlier war, rewarded their leader with reluctant support.[36]

Not only did McIntosh obtain his resources through treaties and trade monopolies, but his appearance as a "civilized" resident among the Indians endeared him to Benjamin Hawkins. In the latter years of his service, Hawkins used McIntosh to distribute the annuity, as well as a wide array of tools, animals, crops, and various other supplies.[37] Hawkins targeted McIntosh for his assistance because the Creek man represented the ultimate aims of Hawkins's "civilization plan." Hawkins tried to teach the Creeks to follow McIntosh's example and become farmers, weavers, and independent yeoman citizens. Hawkins also entrusted McIntosh with authority because the Creek leader had shown his loyalty to the United States, especially when he opposed Tecumseh and the nativist Red Stick Creek faction in 1813 and when he arranged the arrest and execution of Creek warriors who disturbed travel on the Federal Road in 1812 and 1813.[38] Not surprisingly, McIntosh remained loyal to Hawkins during the Red Stick War and further strengthened his bond with a significant distributor of resources.

McIntosh became even more powerful after Hawkins's death in 1816. David Mitchell, who became McIntosh's in-law in August 1818, was appointed the new Indian agent, and he used his alliance with McIntosh throughout his administration. The Creek leader had so much control over the annuity during these five years that one observer stated, "in certain matters [McIntosh] was in fact the agent."[39] During Mitchell's stay among the Creeks the U.S. government paid lucrative annuities, which amounted to more than $80,000 in goods in 1817 and 1818. McIntosh, and his allied chiefs, assisted with the distribution, but little money changed hands. They gave gifts of food, looms, clothing, guns, powder, thread, ribbons, and livestock, and their authority grew in return. McIntosh primarily profited from the annuity through its utility in creating his network of personal obligations. In the process McIntosh infused American goods into Creek villages in unprecedented volume. Moreover, under Mitchell, McIntosh and other fellow Creeks received more than $85,000 to reimburse them for the property that was destroyed during the Red Stick War.[40]

McIntosh further attracted resources from the national government by leading a group of Creek warriors against the Seminoles in Florida. In 1818 General Jackson rewarded McIntosh for his efforts in the First Seminole War by authorizing him to redistribute cattle that were redeemed in Florida. "During the . . . campaign as you have been advised," Jackson wrote, "large droves of cattle were captured from the Enemy. They proved a seasonable supply to my army. The cows, calves & younger cattle however were generally preserved, and by my orders delivered to General McIntosh for an equal distribution among the Chiefs & Warriors of the Nation."[41] McIntosh repaid his supporters with cattle and reinforced his network of reciprocal obligations. A treaty signed earlier that year provided McIntosh with even more resources to redistribute. Formally the treaty exchanged two tracts of Creek land for $20,000 and a ten-year annuity of $10,000. In the process, however, McIntosh arranged to have "non-Creek traders" removed from Creek villages. This had profitable benefits for McIntosh, as most of the traders who remained worked under his auspices. McIntosh not only became a distributor of the annuity but also protected his trade monopoly. Control of the deerskin trade and the annuities provided him with the resources necessary to extend his claims to power.[42]

In the years that followed the First Seminole War, McIntosh arranged with Mitchell to have the Creek warriors in his brigade paid for their participation. Within two years McIntosh received more than $30,000 to distribute among his 1,500 warriors and arranged direct payments for himself and his field and staff officers that amounted to more than $3,500. General Jackson also promoted six Creeks who served under Jackson, two to colonel, two to lieutenant colonel, and two to major. Not surprisingly, several of the signers of the Treaty of Indian Springs had earlier thanked McIntosh for receiving payment for their service against the Seminoles. Furthermore, after McIntosh helped remove hundreds of Seminoles in 1819, U.S. officials thanked McIntosh with even more resources for distribution.[43]

McIntosh's ability to extend his authority throughout the Creek Nation reached a peak in 1821. That year, at the first Treaty of Indian Springs, McIntosh arranged for special land cessions for himself. He obtained 1,000 acres at Indian Springs and 640 acres around his plantation on the west bank of the Ocmulgee River. He also directly received, for distribution among his supporters, half of the $400,000 the Creeks were to get for their land. In addition to these favors, McIntosh convinced American officials to pay him another $40,000 to compensate him for his support and personal efforts in arranging earlier treaties. McIntosh may have received plenty of resources to distribute among his clan and supporters, but his power remained closely watched and limited by his Creek opponents.[44]

McIntosh's extensive network of authority did not last. Without an autonomous source of supplies to distribute, McIntosh depended on his connections to American society to obtain the needed resources. In 1821, when John Crowell replaced Mitchell as agent to the Creeks, McIntosh's access to these goods disappeared. McIntosh's actions, which had always been contentious, appeared even more suspect now that he could not participate as much as he had earlier in Creek patterns of reciprocation. Unlike Mitchell, Crowell made all annuity payments in cash and thus eliminated McIntosh's main source of authority. According to Samuel Hawkins, who was executed two days after McIntosh for signing the Treaty of Indian Springs, Crowell used this to augment his own needs. He paid the annuity "in fifty and hundred dollar bills to the principal chiefs, to be divided by them to their respective towns; the Big Warrior told the agent, at the time, that the money could not be fairly divided, for the want of smaller bills, and requested the agent the next time he paid them off to bring small bills." Crowell responded by telling them to travel to Fort Mitchell where "his brother [Thomas] had goods, and that he had given him a license and that they might buy what goods they wanted." In addition, Crowell "cautioned the chiefs against counterfeiters, and said there were a great many counterfeit bills and many suspicious persons about, but that the change that his brother had was genuine." When the chiefs arrived at Thomas's store, "and asked him to change their money; he told them . . . that he would give to the chiefs of the towns each five dollars in cash, but that the balance of the money must be laid out in goods. Some of the chiefs agreed to do so; but others refused, and went off." Thomas Crowell even reportedly overcharged for his goods, demanding "fifty cents per yard, of the same description of goods that General McIntosh had furnished the nation at twenty-five cents per yard only a few months ago." Despite the alleged higher prices and frustrations felt by some, John Crowell successfully cut McIntosh and the traders who supported him out of the annuity loop. Nonetheless, Crowell's critics and McIntosh's supporters (who should be treated with skepticism) claimed that the new Creek agent replaced one corrupt system with another. In any case McIntosh's personal network weakened, and by 1825 the Law Menders could execute him without threatening Creek customs or their survival.[45]

McIntosh tried to maintain his position of authority under Crowell, but their personal animosity toward one another made this difficult. Crowell tried to remove traders such as George Stinson, who married maternal relations of McIntosh's and helped distribute goods to kin and neighbors. In addition he tried to limit McIntosh's access to the resources that supported his authority.[46] The only way for McIntosh to obtain power was to get a new source of goods to distribute or to get rid of Crowell. This desperation logically culminated in the 1825 Treaty of Indian Springs. McIntosh may have lost some of his authority among the Creeks—he was at best the fifth most powerful Creek leader—but several Americans officials still had faith in his ability to enforce such an act. Although many Creek leaders arrived at Indian Springs without prior information on the American demands, McIntosh and American officials had prearranged all the treaty's details. They also had contingency plans if the Creek leader could not obtain the full support of the other chiefs. McIntosh and the Americans knew that the treaty was a foregone conclusion long before the formal negotiations began. When most of the Creek representatives left the meeting in protest of the terms, McIntosh, fifty-one Creek followers of various ranks, and the U.S. officials signed the treaty anyway.[47]

During the years that preceded his death, McIntosh used his network of reciprocal relationships to become, in the hyperbolic words of Adam Hodgson, "the Most popular and influential person in the nation."[48] Many Americans believed this to be the case. McIntosh, however, never ruled the Creeks totally. His authority, like that of all Creek leaders, was precarious and rested on his ability to convince others to follow him rather than his ability to force them to accept his decisions. Even at its height, McIntosh's authority was contested, not blindly heeded, throughout parts of the Creek Nation. At his death, his influence covered only the villages that immediately surrounded his home. Residents of only eight of the fifty-six Creek towns signed the 1825 Treaty of Indian Springs, and nearly all the other signers of the treaty had directly received aid from McIntosh in the preceding years. In late 1825 Chilly McIntosh could claim only Broken Arrow, Coweta, Talladego, and Hilibi as Creek towns loyal to his father's legacy.[49]

Recent chroniclers of McIntosh have stressed his taking of bribes, his "selling out" of Native culture, his accommodation to American culture, his acquiescence to American diplomatic demands, and his infamous role in the forced removal of the Creek people. Yet none of these indictments should diminish McIntosh's standing as a Creek. His actions, no matter how unscrupulous, self-serving, or devious, never erased his identity. Crowell, perhaps McIntosh's strongest contemporary critic, pointed to the slain leader's esteemed status when he explained the illegitimacy of the 1825 Treaty of Indian Springs. "With the exception of McIntosh, and perhaps two others, the signatures to this treaty are either chiefs of low grade, or not chiefs at all."[50] Little Prince, who both sided with and opposed McIntosh, agreed with Crowell's assessment of McIntosh's identity. "We are Creeks. We have a great many Chiefs and headmen, but be they ever so great they must abide by the laws. We have guns & Ropes and if any of our people break there laws those Guns & Ropes are to be their end. These laws are not made for any particular person but for all."[51] McIntosh may have become a vilified Creek, but his identity as a Creek should not be doubted.

McIntosh obtained power within the legitimate structure of Creek society. Some of his decisions and actions may have been unwanted, perhaps even unwarranted, but his rise to power had roots within the Creek social structure, not from its margins. McIntosh obtained his prominence within Creek society because of his ability to balance carefully two identities—that of a Creek and that of an American—and his ability to translate the advantages provided by his European American identity into sources of power in Creek society. Throughout his life he strategically asserted the identity that would best suit the circumstances. He cultivated kin connections within Indian and American society, arranging marriages for himself and his children. Early in his career he actively placed himself as a confidant and assistant to both Creek leaders and U.S. officials. He chose his friends carefully, arranged treaties to his benefit, and decided to accommodate the demands of American officials. Yet neither the Creeks nor McIntosh could fully determine the distribution of authority on the Georgia frontier. Americans helped legitimize this Creek leader because of their perception of McIntosh's American identity. Thus on the early American frontier McIntosh obtained power and authority from Creek and American sources. His rise to power in the first two decades of the 1800s signified the opportunities afforded to individuals who could reconcile Native and European American identities. In the end, however, his execution signified the difficulty involved in doing just that.

McIntosh was not the only individual to use his biculturalism to obtain authority on the southern frontier. Some were more successful in their ability to maintain two seemingly irreconcilable identities. Dozens of interpreters used their dual identities to obtain positions of prominence within the Creek Nation. Usually this occurred without conflict. The most notable leaders, those who tried to assert centralized power among the Creeks, usually overextended their authority. Those who appeared too willing to accept American demands faced the disapproval of the Creek majority, while those who resisted American desires too strongly faced the ire of American officials. Most children of intermarriages who became leaders, however, were able to maintain their dual identities for years before their downfall or death. Mary Musgrove Matthews Bosomworth served as Governor James Oglethorpe's interpreter for over a decade until she proclaimed herself "Queen" of the Creeks. Her delicate balance of dual loyalties came to a crashing halt in 1743, when American officials felt that her loyalty was in doubt. She ceased to be an American among the Creeks; she was a Creek woman. Alexander McGillivray had better success. He maintained his position among the Creeks until his death. Always perceived by European Americans as his Loyalist father's child, McGillivray was able to use this to his benefit while negotiating with the British and Spanish. Antipathy within the young United States created opposition to his rule, but his biculturalism still allowed him to appear to be a legitimate, if not desirable, leader of the Creeks. His identity among the Creeks was quite different. He was accepted as a Creek leader, and they rewarded his ability to play the European powers off each other with their increased loyalty.[52] At the other extreme, William Augustus Bowles maintained dual identities when he traveled among the Creeks, but rather that earning the support of any European power, he was condemned as a dangerous British leader among the Indians.[53]

CHAPTER 7

The Insistence of Race

In the years surrounding McIntosh's execution, European Americans increasingly embraced a racial definition of whiteness. Although a debate raged over the ability of Indians to Americanize, many Americans became certain of the immutability of the identities of Indian countrymen and the whiteness of their Creek children. This change had two significant ramifications. First, a series of conflicts occurred as a result of disagreements over the identities of Indian countrymen and their Creek children. Even as the children of intermarriages continued to interpret, mediate, and otherwise soothe intercultural frictions, they also became the sources of conflict. Sometimes they created tensions; at other times they were the central topics of the tensions. Second, the change allowed some Indian countrymen and their Creek children to reject their Creek residences and become free white members of southern society. As the reality of Indian removal became more imminent, some Creeks, whether adopted Indian countrymen or the children of Creek mothers, claimed their white heritage, muted their Creek backgrounds, occupied eastern lands, and otherwise avoided going west with the rest of their villages. Their racial ambiguity provided an option unavailable and undesirable to the majority of Creeks.

This volume began with the case of Ambrose Brissert, the man mistakenly arrested as a spy because he was "dressed like an Indian" in Pensacola. If you recall, the Spanish magistrates had to accept the Creek identity of that English-born man, albeit reluctantly, because his Creek kin and Fus-hatchee neighbors insisted upon it. The Creeks were willing to fight, or at least willing to use threats of violence, to protect their kin and their right to determine who was and who was not a Creek. Not surprisingly, Brissert was not the only resident of a Creek village who had his identity questioned or misunderstood in the early American southeast. Throughout the pre-removal era, dozens of Indian countrymen and their Creek children were the focus of cultural misunderstandings. In each case racial logic prevented European Americans from grasping the structure of Creek society and the identities of its members.

For Indian countrymen the belief in the immutability of the white race affected the European American understanding and treatment of marriages between Indian countrymen and Creek women. When George Galphin married a Creek woman, for example, Indian agent David Taitt continued to refer to "Galphins Indian Wench & *her* Children."[1] Rather than accept the emerging Native identity of Galphin and his choice to cross the cultural divide, Taitt viewed him through the lens of southern masculinity. Galphin had not succumbed to Native culture; he was subduing it. The Indian women remained passive entities in the arrangement, simply allowing themselves to be used by European American men.[2] The perception of Indian women as wenches paralleled the larger problem of seeing exterior motives for all Creek behavior. Just as Taitt believed that Galphin was using his Creek wife, not following Creek customs or becoming a Creek himself, Taitt and other European American leaders consistently assumed that Native diplomacy was the extension of their foreign enemies. For example, Spaniard Luis de Unzaga repeatedly claimed that only interference by the United States could lead to hostilities between the Spaniards and Creeks.[3] Englishman Henry Ellis similarly blamed the Creeks' May 16, 1760, attack on resident traders in Oakfuskee on the French, who desired to create a "Rupture between those Indians and us." In the process Ellis ignored the unruly behavior of traders and the diplomatic designs of Handsome Fellow, the leader of the assault.[4] By denying Creeks the ability to make choices on their own terms, these instances helped European Americans minimize the sovereignty of Creek villages.

European Americans maintained their belief that Indian countrymen and their Creek children who were on the warpath were still fellow European Americans—albeit dangerous ones. They usually dismissed as "disguises" the ritual skin paints, tattoos, and costumes used by Creek warriors when they were worn by individuals who otherwise "appeared white." During the American Revolution, for example, East Florida governor Patrick Tonyn "hear[d] by people that come from Georgia [that] there were about thirty Indians with a number of white people painted and dressed like Indians to the number of about seventy" that attacked Tybee Island. Tonyn continued to consider the soldiers as "disguised Americans" even after reports indicated they scalped their victims. Rather than use the eighteenth-century language of cultural reversion and claim that the white men were becoming Indians in the most stereotypical way, the governor simply stated that through scalping and "other signs of the most savage barbarity . . . the white people exceeded the ferocity of the Indians." The power of race, as well as the unconscious need to prevent European Americans from becoming Indians, convinced Governor Tonyn that Indian clothing and loyalties were mere costumes and ruses. Tonyn and other European Americans were fooled by the appearances of these "white" Indians and thus called them Indian generals and leaders.[5] American officials such as Lewis Cass concluded that "Every British trader admitted into the Indian Country is in fact a British Agent. They systematically seize every opportunity of poisoning the minds of the Indians."[6] Similar confusion and frustrations arose when the children of intermarriages, such as Josiah Francis, chose to oppose the United States in the War of 1812 or the Red Stick War. Their racial background prevented them from fully embracing the Red Stick cause. In the words of one unconvinced observer, this was the case for Francis, who only "pretends to be a prophet."[7]

When European Americans accepted the possibility that white men could turn Indian or at least take on Indian loyalties, they often had rather self-serving reasons. During the First Seminole War in 1819, for example, one U.S. Congressman refused to accept that there were English-born Creek warriors, but his insistence stemmed from a desire to punish the race traitors. "These Englishmen [have] 'joined a savage nation, who observe no rules, and give no quarter.'" Thus, he concluded, "we have a right to treat them precisely as we might treat the savages who they have joined, and that we would have a right to put the savages to death upon a principle of retaliation." By letting Indian countrymen become Indians, and "savages" at that, Americans justified tactics of war that were usually reserved for the racial "other" and withheld from European American enemies.[8]

European Americans rarely contemplated the identities, racial or otherwise, of Indian countrymen and their Creek children. Discussions of sovereignty and legal jurisdiction, however, occasionally made such discussions necessary. After the War of 1812, for example, the United States offered to compensate loyal Creek warriors with individual plots of recently ceded land. The status of the Indian countrymen needed to be known. Colonel Gilbert Russell, who was charged with distributing the lands, explained: "There are about ten white men who have long resided within the limits of the Creek Confederacy, and have been viewed as adopted Citizens there of—they not only took an active part with the United States throughout the war, but they and their families suffered greatly in the loss of lives and property." The issue came down to a single question. "In what light," he asked the secretary of state, "ought the Indian Country-men to be viewed—whether as Indians or Citizens of the United States?" After apparently not receiving a response, Russell followed the racial logic of treating the Indian countrymen as Americans. He denied the Indian countrymen the plots of land due to them as Indian men and therefore made hundreds of additional acres of Creek lands available for white Alabamans.[9]

In many instances Indian countrymen used their ambiguous identities to their advantage. In 1815 and 1816 several Indian countrymen petitioned for compensation in regards to an "act to authorize the payment for property lost, captured, or destroyed by the enemy, while in the military service of the United States."[10] They made their appeals, even though they understood that they had fought in Indian regiments, "not in that kind of military service which has been formally recognized." Such actions, they admitted, were "not included within the express provisions of the law," but they insisted that "they are unquestionably within its principle & spirit." In addition the petitioners asked that the children of intermarriages be considered as well. "One of [the petitioners], it is true, was an Indian of the half blood: but your petitioners most respectfully suggest to your honourable body whether a difference of colour can afford any claim to higher consideration from the justice of the American people."[11] Once again, members of the U.S. House of Representatives adhered to a racial identity to justify their actions. Following the same rules that governed the compensation for citizens on the frontier, the government paid the claimants with money deducted from the Creek annuity.[12]

Creek leaders widely condemned those Creeks who received land and gifts from the U.S. government, but they usually did so with language indicative of a censure of a fellow Creek. They did not deny their Creek identities or accept them as Americans. They insisted that William McIntosh, one of the Creeks rewarded in 1818 for his service against the Seminoles, "has caused much blood to be spilt, for which we denounce him to the whole nation."[13] Matters became more confusing when the compensation went to the Creek families of those who were killed during the war. As much as the claimants may have been considered European Americans, Hawkins, upon the urging of Creek representatives, insisted that the property follow matrilineal lines and remain with their "woman and children."[14]

Just as the question of legal reimbursement brought the issue of identity to the forefront, so did matters of frontier justice. When one Creek woman with a European father engaged in the Indian trade without a license, American officials had to decide if any law had been broken. "If Mrs. [Sophia] Durant is an American Citizen," Secretary of War Henry Dearborn told Benjamin Hawkins, "have her arrested and punished as principal by the Law regulating intercourse with the Indians. . . . If she is an Indian, which I presume not the case, we have no control over her."[15] Dearborn wanted Durant to be an American; if she were a Creek, he recognized that he had no formal authority over her. At the same time, the Creeks insisted on punishing Indian countrymen and the children of intermarriages when they were guilty of transgressions. For example, after a series of depredations committed by Creek war parties that included at least one Indian countrymen and several children of intermarriages, the White Lieutenant explained to James Seagrove that it was the duty of the

Creeks to find just punishment. "I hope you are a man, and we are men, and can punish our bad people ourselves; and the day shall come that we will do it."[16] In short, issues of vengeance and justice led both Creeks and European Americans to define Indian countrymen and the children of intermarriages as members of their own communities.

The conflict over Creek identities and the connections to sovereignty became explicit in the 1824 trial of George Stinson. Stinson was an Indian countryman who faced prosecution in Savannah for trading among the Creeks without a license. John Crowell, the U.S. Indian agent among the Creeks, recognized the high stakes of the trial. "Have white men who take with an Indian Woman a right to become traders without a licence[?] If they have there will be no licenced traders. For this plain reason, they will all have Indian wives for the sake of being irresponsible to the laws regulating trade & intercourse with the Indian tribes, and will keep Shops of Whiskey in stead of useful goods for the Indians."[17] Indians, he believed, could not be trusted to protect themselves. During the trial Stinson admitted to his occupation as a trader but "contended that the Creek Indians were a Sovereign & independent Nation and were competent to naturalise . . . a citizen of that Nation with full powers and authority to do all & very act which Indians themselves could do, consequently the case . . . did not come within the purview of the laws regulating trade & intercourse with the Indian Tribes."[18] Stinson presented witnesses that testified to his adoption, his Creek family, and the practice of not licensing Indian countrymen. Rather than challenging the prosecution's facts, Stinson tried to turn the trial into one about the Creeks' sovereignty.

Stinson's legal strategy suited Crowell and the district attorney fine. The district attorney "produced the Treaty of Fort Jackson . . . which expressly declares that the Creek Indians shall not admit among them, any persons or traders except [those who] derive their authority from the . . . U[nited] States." This, he asserted, meant that the Creeks could not accept Stinson, or anyone else who had not been officially sanctioned by U.S. officials, as a trader. Before the jury deliberated, Judge Jeremiah Cuyler nearly sunk Stinson's case. "In his charge to this Jury, [he] stated explicitly that the Indian Tribes within the limits of the U[nited] States were not sovereign & independent . . . [and] he was Surprised to hear Gentleman [like Stinson and his attorney] at this day contend for such doctrine." With these words the judge did more than explicitly contradict Stinson's claim that a sovereign Creek nation could regulate its own borders. By calling Stinson a "Gentleman," he also implicitly characterized Stinson as a white American. Furthermore, the judge stated that "it was very clear that the Def[endan]t. had violated the laws of Congress."[19] Although the judge and

Indian agent refused to accept the adoption of Stinson or the sovereignty of the Creek Nation, the members of the jury apparently could. They found Stinson, as a Creek man, not guilty.[20]

Quite similarly, Creeks and Americans conflicted over matters of jurisdiction when Indian countrymen and their Creek children committed crimes. One "Mr. Lawrence," for example, fled Georgia "with a price of four hundred guineas on his head and . . . settled among the Creeks." After the bounty did not immediately secure his return, his actions within Creek country further aroused the concerns of European American society. When he and a band of Tallapoosa Creek Indians tried to steal slaves from a frontier community and sell them elsewhere in Georgia, colonial authorities took notice.[21] After an extensive correspondence dedicated to finding Lawrence, West Florida governor Vicente Folch sent a small militia detachment into the Creek Nation. When they found him at the house of Charles Weatherford, an Indian countryman himself, the posse extracted "justice." After the execution Alexander McGillivray wrote to Folch saying that such actions needed to end. Too often, he claimed, colonists entered Creek villages to administer instant justice. McGillivray agreed that Lawrence should have been punished, but he demanded that in the future Creeks be punished by Creeks.[22]

In each instance the question of identity did not rest on biology alone. Crowell may have brought the charges against Stinson in order to limit the power of McIntosh rather than assert the sovereignty of the United States over the Creeks. For the jury in Savannah the acquittal may have resulted from the intricacies of local politics rather than the strengths of the respective legal cases.[23] Yet the issues of sovereignty and identity could not be separated from each other. Creeks continued to maintain that they had the right to maintain their borders and to determine who was and who was not a Creek.[24]

The ambiguity of the identities of Indian countrymen and their Creek children became most evident during Indian removal, the process by which most Creeks were forced west of the Mississippi River in the initial decades of the nineteenth century. After years of taking advantage of their ambiguous identities, the relocation of the Creeks west of the Mississippi River provided one last opportunity for Indian countrymen and their children to choose their racial and national identification. They could either find a way to remain east of the Mississippi by asserting their European American heritage, or they could choose to maintain their Creek identity and move west. In essence, then, Indian removal caused an identity crisis for many Creeks. The children of intermarriages, who often defined themselves by their ability to move seamlessly between Creek and southern societies, lost this ability when the geographic space that they occupied disappeared. Yet the children of intermarriage could grasp one last bicultural moment during the process of removal. Because of their cultural backgrounds and appearances, they experienced an ethnic moment where they needed to prioritize one ethnic identity and abandon the other. They could no longer be both Creeks and Americans. By choosing their residence they necessarily chose a single ethnic identity and a range of cultural norms that accompanied it. Most members of the Creek Confederacy—regardless of their racial heritage—decided to follow their Creek identity and found themselves on a westward trajectory. At the same time, however, dozens of Indian countrymen and many of their Creek children opted to remain within the United States as American citizens.

This reality matched the often-ignored rhetoric of American politicians. Throughout the removal debates American officials widely asserted that removal was a choice for the southeastern Indians, not an inevitability. Southeastern Indians, especially those who could "pass" for white Americans, could stay east of the Mississippi River and live as American citizens. Those who could not were to move themselves or be removed by the U.S. military.[25] The rhetoric of removal made it clear that one did not need European American ancestry in order to stay. Andrew Jackson explained: "My white children in Alabama have extended their law over your country. If you remain in it, you must be subject to that law. If you remove across the Mississippi, you will be subject to your own laws."[26] Yet, President Jackson and others understood that staying in Alabama or Georgia meant more than accepting American law; it also meant accepting American conceptions such as race, property and family. In 1833 J. Terhune explained this reality: "If you prefer an Indian woman, to a white lady for a wife buy your land, and support her, (if you live in Georgia) as other Georgians do. But if you prefer being an Indian, and of receiving Indian privaleges, go to Arkensaw where the Indians have a right to grant your privaleges."[27] Terhune, in essence, reminded a minority of the southeastern Indians that they could choose their identities and thus their residences.[28]

Even though most Creeks had neither the desire nor ability to claim their American citizenship, some Creeks established this reality long before forced removal was an immediate threat. In some cases, such as the Creeks' eviction of trader Richard Bailey and his son, individuals had no choice but to move "back" into European American society. More often, however, the decision was made as it was perceived to be the best available option. Yet unlike the pessimistic rhetoric expressed by some scholars and nineteenth-century European Americans, American society welcomed Indian countrymen and Creeks "back" into its fold. Despite years of living in Creek villages, Indian countrymen could mute their decisions to live among the Natives and return to the land and ethnic identities of their birth. Similarly, the children of intermarriages could often claim the rights afforded to them as the children of European American fathers.

The transformation of William Weatherford from a hostile anti-American Creek warrior to a respectable southern gentleman may be the most remarkable example. In the aftermath of the Red Stick War in 1814, Weatherford saw the United States force his Creek brethren to cede thousands of acres within Georgia. Americans justified their aggressive actions as punishment for the Creeks' hostility to the United States and their savage alliance with the British in the correlating War of 1812. Rather than moving off the ceded lands, Weatherford remained on his plantation and soon found himself living among newly arrived American settlers.[29]

Weatherford, a Creek child of Indian trader Charles Weatherford and Sehoy (Marchland Tate), was a prominent nativist leader in the Red Stick War. Like many Creek children of intermarriages, Weatherford owned several African American slaves, a plantation, a racetrack, and dozens of cattle.[30] Unlike many acculturated Creeks, however, Weatherford followed the interests of his nativist matrilineage and opposed U.S. interests in the Red Stick War. Although his mixed ethnic background was well known within American society, Weatherford became known as a "hostile Creek."[31] His participation (if not leadership) in perpetrating the bloody "massacre of Fort Mims" in 1813 led to widespread condemnation of him in American society. His association with the killing of nearly four hundred "friendly" white Americans, Creek Indians, and African slaves seemingly confirmed to white Americans the influence of his Creek mother and his "savage" upbringing. Indeed, his actions made him known by his Indian names, Lamochatee and Red Eagle—and less and less as a Weatherford. He embodied all the attributes expected of ethnic Indians in the early nineteenth century.[32]

After the Battle of Horseshoe Bend in 1814, Jackson demanded that the "hostile Creeks" surrender their now infamous "half-breed leader."[33] Rather than leave his Native countrymen and family in an unenviable situation, Weatherford opted to "surrender himself voluntarily." He snuck into Jackson's camp and went to see the American general. His surrender startled Jackson, who "asked him how he dared to appear in his presence, after acting such a part as his did at Fort Mims?" Weatherford replied, "I am in your power, Do with me what you please." Although Jackson still saw Weatherford as a potential enemy, he apparently saw the "civilized" nature of the Creek leader. Rather than lock Weatherford in chains, demand retribution for his hostile leadership against Fort Mims, or even try him for war crimes, Jackson merely warned the Creek leader and gave him the "liberty to return to his own camp." After this meeting Old Hickory knew that "Weatherford was no savage and much more than an ordinary man by nature, and [Jackson] treated him very kindly indeed."[34]

General Jackson offered Weatherford more than just the ability to return to his Creek village. In the midst of warning Weatherford not "to try the fate of arms once more," Jackson asserted that "if you really wish for peace, stay where you are, and I will protect you." This olive branch revealed Jackson's paternalism toward loyal Indians while also reflecting his desire to bring acculturated Indians into American society and out of Native society. Weatherford accepted this offer of protection and replied that his fight was gone. "There *was* a time, when I *had a chance.* I have none, *now*—even *hope* is ended! Once I could animate my warriors; but I cannot animate the dead. Their bones are bleaching on the plains of Tallshatches, Talladega, and Emuckfau; and I have not surrendered myself without reflection."[35] With these dramatic words, the Creek man signified the death of his Native identity. His struggle to maintain a dual identity was over.

In the following decade Weatherford lived immersed in American society. Once known for being "the leader of the butchery at fort Mims," the Creek warrior now lived as a southern "gentleman" among the white settlements near Montgomery, Alabama.[36] Weatherford married Mary Stiggins, a white woman, in 1817, with General Sam Dale serving as a groomsman. Dale had fought the hostile Creeks only a few years earlier but had come to respect Weatherford as his friend. Weatherford justified asserting an American identity and abandoning his matrilineage because he had no viable options; he reportedly told Dale that "his old comrades, the hostiles, ate his cattle from starvation; the peace party ate them from revenge; and the squatters because be was a d—d Red Skin." By returning to American society, however, he muted his Indian identity and lived as his father's son.[37]

In subsequent years Weatherford continuously struggled to maintain his recently asserted ethnic identity of a white American and lose the infamy he earned at Fort Mims. As he succeeded in his endeavor to claim a civilized white identity, he altered the perception of his role at Fort Mims. Contemporaries tried to insert elements of "civility" into his actions by proclaiming that he ordered that women and children be spared during the assault. Others minimized Weatherford's role in the attack by stating that Weatherford "was no chief, but had much influence with the Indians." He was not an Indian, they wrote, but only a misguided adviser.[38] Not all Americans accepted Weatherford into the

ranks of civilized society. His past actions at Fort Mims prevented total abso-
lution or acceptance. One obituary for "Witherford the Prophet," for example,
rejoiced that the "celebrated Savage Warrior is at length vanquished; the dis-
troyer is conquore[d]; the hand which so profusely dealt death and dissolation
among 'the whites' is now motionless." His racial identity, intricately connected
to the perception of his recent past, left him on the fringe of his chosen society.
Nevertheless, Weatherford spent the last ten years of his life among his American
friends and white kinsmen. [39]

Weatherford was not the only Indian countryman who "returned" to American society. In the century that preceded removal, dozens of intermarried Indian traders discovered that their lives among the Indians did not negate their
European American identities. In fact, throughout the early American period
Indian countrymen routinely left the Creek Nation and "returned" to their
lives in European American society. Anti-Indian sentiment occasionally tar-
nished the reputations of Indian countrymen and their Creek children within
European American society, but it did not negate their European American
identities. The children of intermarriages usually remained with their Creek
mothers and matrilineages, but the option of proclaiming their American identities remained intact until the 1820s. They too could mute, if not totally negate,
their Native American pasts and live under the laws that regulated free, white
southerners. [40]

Forced removal, however, intensified the division between Creek and American society and provided one last moment where Creeks could assert their ethnic option. For some, this meant dramatic transformations. Both George Stiggins and Thomas Woodward, for example, lived in two worlds in their youth.
They frequently traveled between the societies of their mixed parents, conversed
with Creeks and Americans, and maintained dual identities. [41] Andrew Jackson, who frequently expressed derision for acculturated "half-breeds," never
accepted Woodward's dual identity. Instead, in 1818 he ridiculed Woodward as "a
damned long Indian looking son-of-a-bitch." Just over a decade later, however,
Woodward became known more for his role as one of Alabama's "founding
fathers." By remaining in Alabama, Woodward established himself as one of
the state's patriarchs. [42]

Stiggins underwent a similar transformation. Although he spent his later
years as a gentleman and a respected member of southern society, the former
trader could never fully reject his Creek ethnic identity. He could only mute
it. [43] This problem was compounded by his decision to write a narrative of
Creek history, a history he observed as a participant. After years of asserting
a Creek identity and living among the Creeks, he could not erase his personal

involvement from his descriptions of Creek history. His "membership" among the Creeks—essential to his claims to historical authenticity—also proved to be a liability. In his "Narrative of the Creek Nation as written by a member of the Tribe," Stiggins primarily referred to Creek Indians in the third person but occasionally inserted the first-person perspective. In his "traditional history and genealogy of *my* woe-worn and pitiable country," Stiggins described "*their* settlements" and "other applicable surnames given to distinguish *their* grade."[44] He even indicted the character of the Creek Indians—of whom he once considered himself a member. "*They*," Stiggins wrote "appreciate a good character very little either in themselves or anyone else in the common scenes of life." Stiggins many have physically rejected his Creek identity by opting out of forced removal, but he could not easily erase the psychological connections to his Creek past.[45]

Not surprisingly, several Indian countrymen refused to obey the dictates of forced removal. Barrent Dubois married one of the daughters of Creek leader Big Warrior and then spent the early decades of the nineteenth century as an agent and interpreter for the U.S. government. Described by Albert J. Pickett as an "intelligent New Englander . . . who had long lived among the Tooka-batchas," Dubois decided that removal west did not suit him. He belonged in American society. When his wife and adopted family moved west in 1836, Dubois reclaimed his white heritage and remained in Alabama. There he integrated himself back into American society with little fanfare. In the eyes of American officials, nothing could be more normal. Dubois had "returned" to the land of his birth and proclaimed the virtues of American civilization.[46]

For the children of intermarriages, the decision to reject removal usually meant abandoning family members and fellow villagers. Mary Ann Battis, for example, abandoned her parents and siblings when they moved west in 1828. Rather than joining her Creek kin on their journey into Indian Territory, Battis found asylum at the Asbury Methodist Mission. Her decision to stay was compounded by the mixed Indian, black, and white lineages of her family. Battis, whose fair appearance and Christian education allowed her to integrate herself into white society, asserted an option that her siblings apparently did not have. Because they rejected American cultural norms and were seen as "extremely dark," they could stay in Alabama only as colored Americans. Mary Ann, therefore, watched as removal separated her from her family. While Mary Ann's kin went west, she successfully had "her habits and views confirmed by a residence amongst the Whites [in Milledgeville, Georgia]." There her Christian education provided a means of opting out of forced removal.[47]

Battis was not the only Creek who used religion as a means to stay among the

Americans. Several Creeks used baptisms to assert their acculturated identity. In 1825 Indian countryman [William?] Hardridge arranged for the baptisms of himself, his Creek wife, and their children. In mid-December he took them to the Asbury Mission, and as a family they religiously embraced their American identities. Other Creeks used their baptismal names to help assert their acculturated American identities and mute their Native pasts. Through baptism Joseph Marshall became Joseph Soule, Jesse Brown became Jesse Lee, Thomas Carr became Thomas Coke, and John Winelett became John Wesley. In each case a new name accompanied a new American identity and residence. All four of these baptized Creeks opted for integrating themselves into American society rather than removing with Creek society.[48]

The ethnic options asserted by Creeks during the 1820s and 1830s continued within the oral traditions of the rural white South. Generations after forced removal erased the "Indian" option within the region, several southerners "discovered" that their ancestors included "full-blooded" Creek women. This recognition occurred alongside many fraudulent claims by Americans who claimed to be Creeks in order obtain Creek lands. Their connection to Native families, however, had not prohibited their participation in southern white culture. Their Indian pasts did not make them part of "colored society." For the two or three generations after removal, they lived as white southerners.[49]

Perhaps the most prominent Creek who turned American was Alabama politician Robert Jemison Jr. Jemison descended from a prominent intermarried couple. His mother directly descended from Samuel Mims, the Creek leader whose home temporarily protected hundreds of African slaves, Creeks, and Americans during the Red Stick War. Although Samuel Mims and most of the residents of Fort Mims were killed in 1814, Jemison's mother had not been at the fort and after the battle merged into American society. Robert Jemison Jr. served in the Alabama House of Representatives, the Alabama Secession Convention, and the Senate of the Confederate States of America. He established a stately cotton plantation where he built his "Cherokee Mansion," a name choice that reveals his continued consciousness of his Indian past while also obscuring his Creek heritage. In addition to his economic and political forays in southern society, Jemison also helped found a Methodist church in Tuscaloosa, Alabama. Apparently, Creek lineage or "Indian blood" had not inhibited the rise of the Jemison family. Ironically, in the years following the American Civil War some of the Alabama land once inhabited by the Creeks was renamed Jemison county.[50]

The children of intermarriages usually left unexplored or unfulfilled the option of integrating into American society. Most Creeks found the option of "becoming American" to be a fate worse than forced removal. Integration into American society was frequently more undesirable than it was unobtainable. The ethnocentric implications of accepting "American terms" aside, most Creeks found the idea of separating from their clans and villages to be a social death. Their identities were wrapped up in the social obligations determined by clan ties. Losing these ties was not merely perceived as disruptive by most Creeks; it was considered devastating. Not surprisingly, in the 1930s dozens of interviewed Creeks recalled their white and mixed ancestors who took the "Trail of Tears."[51] These Creeks followed their matrilineal families and moved west. Removal tore some of the children of intermarriages away from their European American spouses and children, while forcing others to abandon their mills, taverns, inns, ferries, farmlands, and homes. In this regard they faced the same disruptions as fellow Creeks. Unlike other Creeks, however, the children of intermarriages frequently had to abandon their American identities when they moved west. The decision to go to Indian Territory, although never an easy decision, was compounded by the dual identities of many Creeks.[52]

Many Creeks, who had once moved in and out of Creek and European American society, recognized that moving west was their only option. Chilly McIntosh, for example, led a group of Creeks to Indian Territory west of the Mississippi in 1828. In the short time after his father's death, Chilly vigorously asserted both his and his father's Creek identity. In his attempts to vindicate his father and avenge his death, Chilly in no uncertain words distanced himself from his American identity. By following his Creek identity and his father's vision, he left behind fertile farmlands, as well as a lucrative inn, a tavern, two ferries, and his kin connections within American society. He received moderate financial compensation for his losses from the U.S. government, and he maintained some of his political power within Indian Territory. Nevertheless, his journey west minimized the authority borne of biculturalism on the southern frontier. When his journey ended in Indian Territory, Chilly McIntosh no longer had any traces of his European American past.[53]

Indian countrymen, many of whom were elderly when Indian removal forced them to choose their ethnic identity, also embraced their Creek identities by moving west. Kendall Lewis, who escaped a murder accusation by coming to the Creeks almost three decades earlier, followed his Creek wife's family west to Arkansas in late 1828. In the process he confirmed to some American observers that ever since "he took an Indian wife . . . [he] has been identified with the Creek Indians."[54] Although it became well known that Lewis married the daughter of Big Warrior, a prominent Creek chief, for most of his life American observers had treated him as if he were merely a resident of a Creek village. Decades after Lewis joined the Creeks, one American wrote that "Colonel Kendall Lewis an intelligent and worthy old gentleman, has lived longer among the Creek Indians than any *white man* now alive, and is perhaps more familiar with the history and localities of the creek country . . . than any other." This estimation of Lewis's identity slighted the fact that Lewis had a Creek wife and several Native children, lived in a Creek village for over four decades, and served as a Creek diplomat on several occasions. Lewis was considered a "white man" and an outsider to Creek society, despite his marriage, political position, and loyalty.[55] Before removal took him west, Lewis had successfully used his identity as a "white man" to attract American travelers to his tavern, and on several occasions travelers commented on his "gentlemanly" ways and "civilized" demeanor. Margaret Hunter Hall wrote, "The Indian chiefs allow white men to establish taverns in their territory for the accommodation of travelers. We are this night at a most excellent one kept by a man of the name of Lewis, who has a squaw to wife." Similarly the Moravian missionaries, Johann Christian Burkard and Karsten Petersen, believed that Lewis was a fellow white American when they used him as a guide through the Creek Nation. On April 15, 1811, they expressed thanks in their diary that "a white man, a blacksmith from Georgia named Lewis act[ed] as my guide." William Potts expressed a similar impression in his diary, when he wrote that "Lewis is a white man, but has an Indian wife."[56] Only his decision to follow the dictates of his Creek identity and family forced the recognition that he "had adopted the life of the Indians."[57]

In the 1820s and 1830s the children of intermarriage did not passively accept forced removal as a foregone conclusion. Nor did they face the dualistic choice of either staying and resisting or leaving and living. Instead, the destruction of the southern frontier provided the children of intermarriages with the additional option of staying and amalgamating into American society. They could opt to assert their white ethnic identities and mute their Indian pasts. They could assert the aspects of their bicultural backgrounds that best suited a life as a white American among "fellow" Americans. This decision was rarely simple or smooth. Both options frequently separated husbands from wives, parents from children, and American kin from Creek kin.

The U.S. policy of forced removal ended the ability to assert simultaneously Creek and American identities. Although mixed-race cultural brokers continued to shape Indian-white relations in Indian Territory, biculturalism no longer fostered dual identities. As the nineteenth century progressed, Creeks and white Americans became more insistent that races were immutable categories. One-drop rules, previously reserved for those with African heritage, extended to

Indian communities. Creeks, who previously incorporated white Americans in the same manner that they accepted Native outsiders, increasingly viewed white spouses as unwanted cultural intruders. In the middle of the nineteenth century, white men could no longer turn Indian because neither the Creeks nor the Americans believed this to be possible. The shared ideology of race precluded this possibility.

Epilogue

Race, Clan, and Creek

In the early nineteenth century, as racial divisions increasingly became an accepted reality on the southern frontier, the Creeks told a story that explained the origins of race in terms that seemingly violated their nonracial worldview. "Some people once came to a very small pool of water to bathe. The man who entered . . . first came out clean and his descendants, the white people, have the same appearance. He had, however, dirtied the water a little and so the next man was not quite so clean, and his descendants are the Indians. By this time the water was very dirty and so the last man came out black and his people are the negroes."[1] Even as the tradition embraced the importance and inevitability of biological differences between Indians, Africans, and Europeans, it still adhered to the Creek's nonracial worldview. Rather than permanent and primordial divisions separating humankind, the tradition pointed to the historical and perhaps recent emergence of racial difference. Underneath the range of skin colors, the explanation inferred, people were essentially the same; only an accident created racial differences.

Creeks and Southerners, much like the oral tradition, urges us to be more careful with the language and logic of race in writing about early American Indian history. This process is a difficult one. The language of *half-breed* and *mestizo* litter available English, Spanish, and French primary sources, and the logic of race frequently shaped the behavior of the European Americans who left most of the records. Native sources recorded in the past century also use the language of blood quantum, implying partial Indianness for people whose actions were consistently Creek. Yet Creeks in the eighteenth and early nineteenth centuries held a nonracial understanding of the boundary between themselves and outsiders. Although Creeks never issued a proclamation that conveniently defined this boundary, their behavior throughout the long eighteenth century demonstrates that they did not believe that a racialized boundary existed. Race and the language of blood may have become central components of Creek and Indian identities in subsequent years, but this was not always the case. Creeks—of various villages, clans, and cultural dispositions—routinely adopted, incorporated, and accepted the Creek identities of African, European American, and

Native newcomers. The issue of village and clan membership was simply not a biological one.

The emergence of race began during the decades that preceded removal, but it did not yet threaten to eliminate the importance of clan and village allegiances. Even the Red Stick War (1813–14), which corresponded with Tecumseh's efforts to create a pan-Indian alliance throughout the Great Lakes and Ohio River Valley, demonstrated the internal tensions regarding race and identity within Creek society. On one hand, as several scholars have demonstrated, the Redsticks employed rhetoric that pointed to the creation of a racial division between white Americans and red Creeks. For example, they declared that all non-Creeks "should immediately remove [from Creek lands], otherwise they should by them be considered as *whites* and *enemies.*"[2] By implying "whites" were naturally outsiders and therefore "enemies," the Redsticks connected biology and tribal identities in a way that contradicted earlier ideas about ethnic and racial inclusivity. This racial logic also appeared during the 1813 assault on Fort Mims, an assault that at least according to one warrior resulted because "the Master of Breath has ordered us not to kill any but white people and half breeds."[3]

At the same time, though, several American observers watched as the Redsticks warned the Creek children of intermarriages to choose their cultural paths. They could no longer embrace both their maternal ties to Indian society and their paternal ties to European American society. "As to the half Breeds," an observer reported, "the revolutionists have no quarrel with them. If they fall into the new order of things; it will be well. They will remain unmolested:- but if they take part with white men; they will meet with the fate of white men."[4] As much as the rhetoric of race characterized this claim, it also pointed to continued importance of clan ties, tribal loyalties, and the ability to choose one's identity. White paternity did not eliminate one's place in Creek society; allegiance to the United States did. As a result some children of intermarriages felt the need to prove their Creekness by publicly rejecting their European American heritage. In June 1813, for example, "the brother, brother in marriage & son of Sam Macnac actually burnt his houses and destroyed much of his property."[5] Perhaps this need to prove one's loyalty helped convince several children of intermarriages to become prominent Redstick leaders.

After the war the struggle to define Creek boundaries and otherwise limit the power of clan-based identities continued. In many instances Creeks found ways to preserve clan identities even as they acknowledged paternity and race. In addition to limiting the entrance of *white* visitors into their villages, the Creek National Council restricted marriages and treated European American husbands with new suspicion. A few Creek women married white men, but these relationships increasingly came under regulations designed to protect Creek sovereignty. In some instances the laws violated Creek property norms by protecting the interests of paternal children over maternal ties. An 1818 law, for example, declared "that if a *white* man takes an Indian woman, and have Children by her, and he goes out of the Nation, he shall leave all his property with his Children for their support." The rationale for the widely publicized law was clear; white fathers would no longer be able to deprive Creeks of their property. In following years clans resorted to prenuptial agreements to protect female property from white husbands.[6] The prenuptials, like the 1818 law, reserved their restrictions for *white* husbands. The tensions between race and clan remained.

Despite these developments, race and identity never became as firmly linked in pre-removal Creek society as they did in the antebellum white South. In the late nineteenth and twentieth centuries the logic of race infringed on the traditional terrain of clan and village ties. The continued use of African slaves, American laws regarding blood quantum, the desire to protect limited resources, a series of pan-Indian movements, the out-migration of Creeks from reserved lands and into urban areas, and the continued immersion of Creeks into an increasingly race-based American society all resulted in the erection of new barriers to village, clan, and tribal membership. Some Creeks began to pay more attention to paternal relations and to view the children of European American–Creek intermarriages with suspicion. Census takers recorded the color of skin and physical traits, while village councils increasingly defined membership through blood percentages rather than clan ties.

By the twentieth century the oral tradition that described the accidental creation of race could no longer account for the increased importance of race. Physical differences explained too much for it to be simply the result of a meaningless accident. As a result another more elaborate tradition emerged as the dominant explanation. "Man was made; but when he stood up before his Master he was *white*! The Great Spirit was sorry; he saw that the being he had made was pale and weak." His next attempt, the tradition explains, went even more poorly. "When the second being rose up, and stood before him, he was *black*! The Great Spirit liked the black man less than the white, and he shoved him aside to make room for another trial." With that, the Indian was created, "and the red man pleased him." The Great Spirit then attached appropriate cultural attributes to each race. Because "I made you first," the Spirit gave the white man the first choice. "The white man opened the boxes, looked in, and said, 'I will take this.' It was filled with pens, and ink, and paper, and compasses." With literacy firmly attached to white society, the Spirit told the Indian to choose next, because "the red man is my favorite." He picked the box "filled with tomahawks, knives, war clubs . . . and such things as are useful in war and hunting." The "negro" was stuck with "axes and hoes, with buckets to carry water in, and long whips for driving oxen, which meant that the negro must work for both the red and white man." In short, Indians, Africans, and Europeans had separate creations, and they acted according to the cultural dictates of the Great Spirit. Creek society embraced the connections between culture, race, and identity, and perhaps as this tradition concluded, "it has been so ever since."[7]

Abbreviations

ADAH	Alabama Department of Archives and History, Montgomery
AGI	Achivo General de Indias, Seville, Spain
ASPFR	*American State Papers, Class I: Foreign Relations*, 6 vols. (Washington DC: Gales & Seaton, 1833–59)
ASPIA	*American State Papers, Class II: Indian Affairs*, 2 vols. (Washington DC: Gales & Seaton, 1832–34)
ASPMA	*American State Papers, Class V: Military Affairs*, 7 vols. (Washington DC: Gales & Seaton, 1832–61)
CA	Creek Agency
CIL	"Creek Indian Letters, Talks, and Treaties, 1705–1839," ed. Louise F. Hays, typescript, GDAH
CRG	Allen D. Candler, Kenneth Coleman, and Milton Ready, eds., *The Colonial Records of the State of Georgia*, 32 vols. (Atlanta: Franklin Printing & Publishing, 1904–16)
DM	Draper Manuscripts Collection
EFP	East Florida Papers
FHQ	*Florida Historical Quarterly*
GDAH	Georgia Department of Archives and History, Atlanta
GHQ	*Georgia Historical Quarterly*
GHS	Georgia Historical Society, Savannah
GLB	Governors Letter Books
HL	Henry E. Huntington Library, San Marino, California
IPHC	Grant Foreman, Indian Pioneer History Collection, Oklahoma Historical Society, Oklahoma City
LBH	C. L. Grant, ed., *Letters, Journals and Writings of Benjamin Hawkins*, 2 vols. (Savannah: Beehive Press, 1980)
LC	Lockey Collection
LR	Letters Received
LS	Letters Sent
M	Microcopy
NA	National Archives, Washington DC
OIA	Office of Indian Affairs

PC   Papeles Procedentes de Cuba

PKY   P. K. Yonge Library of Florida History, University of Florida Library, Gainesville

PLP   Panton, Leslie and Company Papers, University of West Florida, Pensacola, Microfilm

PRO CO   Public Records Office, Colonial Office

SD   Santo Domingo Papers

SN   George Stiggins, "A Historical Narrative of the Genealogy tradition, and downfall of the Ispocoga or Creek tribe of Indians, written by one of the tribe," ADAH

UGA   University of Georgia, Hargrett Rare Book and Manuscript Library, Athens

WD   War Department

WMQ   *William and Mary Quarterly*, 3rd series

Notes

INTRODUCTION

1. Arturo O'Neill to Luis de Unzaga, February 16, 1783, LC, PKY; Alexander McGillivray to O'Neill, March 10, 1783, LC, PKY.

2. Spellings of Creek towns and names vary from source to source. For sake of consistency I have followed the spellings used in John R. Swanton, *Early History of the Creek Indians and Their Neighbors* (Washington DC: Government Printing Office, 1922); John R. Swanton, "Social Organization and Social Usages of the Indians of the Creek Confederacy," in *Forty Second Annual Report of the Bureau of American Ethnology to the Secretary of the Smithsonian Institution* (Washington DC: Government Printing Office, 1928); John R. Swanton, *The Indians of the Southeastern United States* (Washington DC: Government Printing Office, 1946); John R. Swanton, *Indian Tribes of the Lower Mississippi Valley and Adjacent Coast of the Gulf of Mexico* (Washington DC: Government Printing Office, 1911).

3. O'Neill to Unzaga, February 15, 1783; O'Neill to Unzaga, February 16, 1783; O'Neill to Unzaga, May 20, 1783; Unzaga to O'Neill, July 10, 1783; O'Neill to Unzaga, August 21, 1783; all in LC, PKY.

4. This book uses the term "European American" to encompass a variety of non-Native, non-African peoples. It includes primarily the English, French, Scots, Irish, Spanish, and their descendents in the United States.

5. Claudio Saunt, *A New Order of Things: Property, Power, and the Transformation of the Creek Indians, 1733–1816* (New York: Cambridge University Press, 1999), 2; Jean Chaudhuri and Joyotpaul Chaudhuri, *A Sacred Path: The Way of the Muscogee Creeks* (Los Angeles: UCLA American Indian Studies Center, 2001), 141, 143–48; Stephen Aron, "Pigs and Hunters: 'Rights in the Woods' on the Trans-Appalachian Frontier," in *Contact Points: Frontiers from the Mohawk Valley to the Mississippi, 1750–1830*, ed. Andrew R. L. Cayton and Fredrika J. Teute (Chapel Hill: University of North Carolina Press, 1998), 189.

6. James H. Merrell, "'The Cast of His Countenance': Reading Andrew Montour," in *Through a Glass Darkly: Reflections on Personal Identity in Early America*, ed. Ronald Hoffman, Mechal Sobel, and Fredrika J. Teute (Chapel Hill: University of North Carolina Press, 1997), 39. See also James H. Merrell, *Into the American Woods: Negotiators on the Pennsylvania Frontier* (New York: W. W. Norton, 1999), 73–77.

7. Theda Perdue, *"Mixed Blood" Indians: Racial Construction in the Early South* (Athens: University of Georgia Press, 2003); Theda Perdue, *Cherokee Women: Gender*

and Culture Change, 1700–1835 (Lincoln: University of Nebraska Press, 1998); James Taylor Carson, *Searching for the Bright Path: The Mississippi Choctaws from Prehistory to Removal* (Lincoln: University of Nebraska Press, 1999).

8. A few important works on cultural brokers include Daniel K. Richter, "Cultural Brokers and Intercultural Politics: New York–Iroquois Relations, 1664–1701," *Journal of American History* 75 (June 1988): 40–67; Nancy L. Hagedorn, "'A Friend to Go between Them': The Interpreter as Cultural Broker during Anglo-Iroquois Councils, 1740–70," *Ethnohistory* 35 (Winter 1988): 60–80; Margaret Connell Szasz, ed., *Between Indian and White Worlds: The Cultural Broker* (Norman: University of Oklahoma Press, 1994), 3–20; Frances E. Karttunen, *Between Worlds: Interpreters, Guides and Survivors* (New Brunswick: Rutgers University Press, 1994); Nancy Shoemaker, *Negotiators of Change: Historical Perspectives on Native American Women* (New York: Routledge, 1995); Elizabeth Vibert, *Trader's Tales: Narratives of Cultural Encounters in the Columbian Plateau* (Norman: University of Oklahoma Press, 1997).

9. For interpretations that employ similar definitions of identity, see Michele Gillespie, "The Sexual Politics of Race and Gender: Mary Musgrove and the Georgia Trustees," in *The Devil's Lane: Sex and Race in the Early South*, ed. Catherine Clinton and Michele Gillespie (New York: Oxford University Press, 1997), 187–201; and Michael D. Green, "Mary Musgrove: Creating a New World," in *Sifters: Native American Women's Lives*, ed. Theda Perdue (New York: Oxford University Press, 2001), 29–47. George Chapman argued several years ago that Chief William McIntosh lived in two worlds, but he did not explore how these connections reinforced each other. Chapman, *Chief William McIntosh: A Man of Two Worlds* (Atlanta: Cherokee, 1988).

10. Circe Strum carefully explores the complexities of modern Indian identity in *Blood Politics: Race, Culture, and Identity in the Cherokee Nation of Oklahoma* (Berkeley: University of California Press, 2002).

11. For introductions to the historical connections between race and Indian identity see M. Annette Jaimes, "Some Kind of Indian: On Race, Eugenics, and Mixed Bloods," in *American Mixed Race: The Culture of Microdiversity*, ed. Naomi Zack (Lanham MD: Rowman & Littlefield, 1995), 133–53; Karen I. Blu, "Region and Recognition: Southern Indians, Anthropologics, and Presumed Biology," in *Anthropologists and Indians in the New South*, ed. Rachel A. Bonney and J. Anthony Paredes (Tuscaloosa: University of Alabama Press, 2001), 71–85.

12. O'Neill to Josef de Ezpeleta, October 19, 1783, LC, PKY.

13. Daniel F. Littlefield Jr., *Africans and Creeks: From the Colonial Period to the Civil War* (Westport CT: Greenwood Press, 1979); Theda Perdue, *Slavery and the Evolution of Cherokee Society* (Knoxville: University of Tennessee Press, 1979); Jack D. Forbes, *Africans and Native Americans: The Language of Race and the Evolution of Red-Black Peoples* (Urbana: University of Illinois Press, 1993); Kathryn E. Holland Braund, "The Creek Indians, Blacks and Slavery," *Journal of Southern History* 57 (November 1991): 601–36; William G. McLoughlin, "Red Indians, Black Slavery and White Racism: America's Slaveholding Indians," *American Quarterly* 26 (October

1974): 367–85; Katja May, *African Americans and Native Americans in the Creek and Cherokee Nations, 1830s to 1920s* (New York: Garland, 1996).

14. Forbes, *Africans and Native Americans*, esp. 233–34; W. David Baird, "Are There 'Real' Indians in Oklahoma? Historical Perceptions of the Five Civilized Tribes," *Chronicles of Oklahoma* 68 (Spring 1990): 20; William T. Hagan, "Full Blood, Mixed Blood, Generic, and Ersatz: The Problem of Indian Identity," *Arizona and the West* 27 (Winter 1985): 309–26.

15. Andrew Juan Rosa, "El Que No Tiene Dingo, Tiene Mandingo: The Inadequacy of the 'Mestizo' as a Theoretical Construct in the Field of Latin American Studies—The Problem and Solution," *Journal of Black Studies* 27 (November 1996): 278–91; Forbes, *Africans and Native Americans*, 100–101, 103, 125–30.

16. Only a few scholars have employed the term *métis* for individuals of mixed ancestry in the southeast. For example, see Joel W. Martin, *Sacred Revolt: The Muskogee's Struggle for a New World* (Boston: Beacon Press, 1991), 79–84; Robbie Ethridge, *Creek Country: The Creek Indians and Their World* (Chapel Hill: University of North Carolina Press, 2003); Daniel Richter, *Facing East from Indian Country: A Native History of Early America* (Cambridge: Harvard University Press, 2001), 183, 230, 232. A good overview of the *Métis* can be found in Jacqueline Peterson and Jennifer S. H. Brown, eds., *The New Peoples: Being and Becoming Métis in North America* (Lincoln: University of Nebraska Press, 1985).

17. Colin G. Calloway, "Neither White nor Red: White Renegades on the American Indian Frontier," *Western Historical Quarterly* 17 (January 1986): 53.

1. THE INVITATION WITHIN

1. James H. Merrell, *The Indians' New World: Catawbas and Their Neighbors from European Contact through the Era of Removal* (New York: W. W. Norton, 1989); Patricia Kay Galloway, *Choctaw Genesis, 1500–1700* (Lincoln: University of Nebraska Press, 1995); Martin, *Sacred Revolt*. For a countering view, see Neal Salisbury, "The Indians' Old World," *WMQ* 53 (July 1996): 435–58.

2. Randolph J. Widmer, "The Structure of Southeastern Chiefdoms," in *The Forgotten Centuries: Indians and Europeans in the American South, 1521–1704*, ed. Charles M. Hudson and Charmen Chaves Tesser (Athens: University of Georgia Press, 1994), 125–55; Charles M. Hudson, "The Hernando de Soto Expedition, 1539–1543," in Hudson and Tesser, *Forgotten Centuries*, 74–103; Marvin T. Smith, "Aboriginal Depopulation in the Postcontact Southeast," in Hudson and Tesser, *Forgotten Centuries*, 257–76.

3. Alfred Crosby, "Virgin Soil Epidemics as a Factor in the Aboriginal Depopulation in America," *WMQ* 33 (April 1976): 289–99.

4. Henry F. Dobyns, *Their Number Become Thinned: Native American Population Dynamics in Eastern North America* (Knoxville: University of Tennessee Press, 1983), 328–35; Jerald T. Milanich, *Florida Indians and the Invasion from Europe* (Gainesville: University Press of Florida, 1995). Some depopulation preceded European contact.

George R. Milner, "Epidemic Disease in the Post-Contact Southeast: A Reappraisal," *Mid-Continental Journal of Archaeology* 5 (Spring 1980): 3–17.

5. Marvin Smith, *Archaeology of Aboriginal Culture Change in the Interior Southeast* (Gainesville: University Press of Florida, 1987), 86–112; Charles M. Hudson, Marvin T. Smith, Charles De Pratter, and Emilia Kelley, "The Tristán de Luna Expedition, 1559–1561," *Southeastern Archaeology* 8 (Summer 1989): 31–45.

6. Vernon James Knight, "The Formation of the Creeks," in Hudson and Tesser, *Forgotten Centuries*, 373–92; Allan Gallay, *The Indian Slave Trade: The Rise of the English Empire in the American South* (New Haven: Yale University Press, 2002), esp. 23–69.

7. See Joshua Aaron Piker, "'Peculiarly Connected': The Creek Town of Oakfuskee and the Study of Colonial American Communities, 1708–1785" (PhD diss., Cornell University, 1998).

8. J. Leitch Wright Jr., *Creeks and Seminoles: The Destruction and Regeneration of the Muscogulge People* (Lincoln: University of Nebraska Press, 1986), 5; Swanton, "Social Organization," 46–47.

9. Lee Compere to Albert James Pickett, April 6, 1848, Pickett Manuscripts, ADAH.

10. Albert James Pickett, *History of Alabama and Incidentally of Georgia and Mississippi, from the Earliest Period* (Charleston: Walker & James, 1851), 89, 128–33; Pickett to Thomas H. Hobbs, November 24, 1857, Pickett Manuscripts, ADAH; Trustee Memorial to the King asking for payment of the passage and expenses of this visiting Indian chiefs from Georgia, August 21, 1734, PRO CO, 5/670; copy of a letter written by Oglethorpe on his return from Georgia, June 27, 1733, Joseph Vallence Bevan Papers, GHS. See also Francis Le Jau to the Secretary, May 10, 1715, in *The Carolina Chronicle of Dr. Francis Le Jau, 1706–1717*, ed. Frank J. Klingberd (Berkeley: University of California Press, 1956), 152; James Glen to the Duke of New Castle, December 1, 1748, Letter Book of James Glen, HL; [Henry Ellis] to Lieut. Col. Bouquet, June 24, 1757, Lord Loudoun Papers, HL; Thomas Brown to Thomas Townshend, June 1, 1783, PRO CO, 5/82; Albert S. Gatschet, *A Migration Legend of the Creek Indians, with a Linguistic, Historic and Ethnographic Introduction*, vol. 1 (1884; reprint, New York: AMS Press, 1969), 118.

11. Glen to Lords Commissioner, October 2, 1750, Letter Book of James Glen, HL.

12. Interview with Sam J. Haynes, February 18, 1938, IPHC, 40:12992. See also Interview with Louis Graham, May 28, 1937, IPHC, 35:6038; Interview with Billie Spencer, November 13, 1937, IPHC, 14:12142.

13. See John R. Swanton, *Myths and Tales of the Southeastern Indians* (1929; reprint, Norman: University of Oklahoma Press, 1995), 10–17, 95, 118–20, 134–38, 178–80, 240–41.

14. Margaret Ervin Austill, "Life of Margaret Ervin Austill," *Alabama Historical Quarterly* 6 (Spring 1944): 92–98; Eunice Barber, "Narrative of the Tragic Death of Darius Barber," in *The Garland Library of Narratives of North American Indian Captivities*, ed. Wilcomb E. Washburn (New York: Garland, 1977), 36:17–18. See

also "The Captivity of Jane Brown and Her Family," in Washburn, *Garland Library of Narratives*, 64:1–15; "Shocking Murder by the Savages of Mr. Darius Barber's Family, in Georgia, on the 26th of January," in Washburn, *Garland Library of Narratives*, 36:26; James Adair, *Adair's History of the American Indians*, ed. Samuel Cole Williams (1775; reprint, New York: Promontory Press, 1930), 417.

15. Barber, "Narrative of the Tragic Death," 36:17–18. See also Manuel de Montiano to the King, July 20, 1747, LC, PKY; Thomas S. Abler, "Scalping, Torture, Cannibalism and Rape: An Ethnohistorical Study of Conflicting Values in War," *Anthropologica* 34 (1992): 3–20. See also Daniel Richter, "War and Culture: The Iroquois Experience," *WMQ* 40 (October 1983): 530–34.

16. Thomas M. Ellis to Pickett, August 26, 1847, Pickett Manuscripts, ADAH. See also Charles J. Kappler, ed., *Indian Treaties, 1778–1883* (Washington DC: Government Printing Office, 1904), 49, 59, 86, 156, 266.

17. T. E., "Account of the Creek Indians, by a Gentleman who has Resided Among Them," *European Magazine*, June 1793, 408.

18. Barber, "Narrative of the Tragic Death," 36:21.

19. John Bartram to Peter Collinson, September 30, 1763, in *The Correspondence of John Bartram, 1734–1777*, ed. Edmund Berkeley and Dorothy Smith Berkeley (Gainesville: University Press of Florida, 1992), 609.

20. "Von Reck's Journal," in *Von Reck's Voyage: Drawings and Journal of Philip Georg Friedrich von Reck*, ed. Kristian Hvidt (Savannah: Beehive Press, 1980), 47. See also John Drayton, *A View of South-Carolina, As Respects Her Natural and Civil Concerns* (Charleston SC: W. P. Young, 1802), 55.

21. Speech of George Washington, December 8, 1795, ASPFR, 1:27. Benjamin Hawkins to J[onathan] Halsted, October 10, 1809, Rhees Collection, HL; Stephen Bull to Henry Laurens, March 14, 1776, in *The Papers of Henry Laurens*, ed. Philip M. Hamer, George C. Rogers Jr., and Maude E. Lyles, 13 vols. (Columbia: University of South Carolina Press, 1988), 11:163–64.

22. Henry Hamilton, January 26, 1779, in *Henry Hamilton and George Rogers Clark in the American Revolution with the Unpublished Journal of Lieut. Gov. Henry Hamilton*, ed. John D. Barnhart (Crawfordsville IN: R. E. Banta, 1951), 169.

23. John Walton Caughey, *McGillivray of the Creeks* (Norman: University of Oklahoma, 1938), 325, n. 319; "Captivity of Jane Brown and Her Family," in Washburn, *Garland Library of Narratives*, 64:1–15; Le Jau to Secretary, April 22, 1708, in Klingberd, *Carolina Chronicle*, 37; Le Jau to Secretary, September 15, 1708, in Klingberd, *Carolina Chronicle*, 41; Le Jau to Secretary, October 10, 1713, in Klingberd, *Carolina Chronicle*, 134. For an example of the attempts to return escaped slaves, see Common Council Ratification of Treaty of Friendship and Commerce between James Oglethorpe and the Chief Men of the Lower Creek Nation, October 18, 1733, PRO CO, 5/67.

24. James W. Covington, "Migration of the Seminoles into Florida, 1700–1820," *FHQ* 46 (April 1967): 340–57; Charles H. Fairbanks, "The Ethno-Archeology of the

Florida Seminole," in *Tacachale: Essays on the Indians of Florida and Southeastern Georgia in the Historic Period*, ed. Jerald Milanich and Samuel Proctor (Gainesville: University Press of Florida, 1978, 1994), 163–77; Wright, *Creeks and Seminoles*, 5–6, 36; Richard A. Sattler, "Remnants, Renegades, and Runaway Seminole Ethnogenesis Reconsidered," in *History, Power, and Identity: Ethnogenesis in the Americas, 1492–1992*, ed. Jonathan David Hill (Iowa City: University of Iowa Press, 1996), 36–69.

25. Kathryn E. Holland Braund, *Deerskins and Duffels: Creek Indian Trade with Anglo-America, 1685–1815* (Lincoln: University of Nebraska Press, 1993), 186.

26. Adair, *History of the American Indians*, 285. For a look at Creek population trends, see Peter Wood, "The Changing Population of the Colonial South," in *Powhatan's Mantle: Indians in the Colonial Southeast*, ed. Peter H. Wood, Gregory A. Waselkov, and M. Thomas Hatley (Lincoln: University of Nebraska Press, 1989), 56–61; J. Anthony Paredes and Kenneth J. Plante, "A Reexamination of Creek Indian Population Trends: 1738–1832," *American Indian Culture and Research Journal* 6, no. 4 (1982): 5–9.

27. Adair, *History of the American Indians*, 285.

28. SN, ADAH, 55; Braund, *Deerskins and Duffels*, 5–10, 13.

29. Wright, *Creeks and Seminoles*, 3.

30. Gatschet, *Migration Legend*, 9. The persistence of non-Muskogee ethnic identities has been posited as an explanation for Creek factionalism. See Wright, *Creeks and Seminoles*; Pickett, *History of Alabama*, 81; D. W. Eakins, "Some Information Respecting the Creeks, or Muscogees," in *Information Respecting the History, Condition and Prospects of the Indian Tribes of the United States: Collected and Prepared Under the Direction of the Bureau of Indian Affairs, Per Act of Congress of March 3d, 1847*, ed. Henry R. Schoolcraft, 5 vols. (Philadelphia: Lippincott, Grambo, 1853), 1:266; SN, ADAH, 11–13.

31. Paul Wilhelm, *Travels in North America, 1822–1824*, trans. W. Robert Nitske, ed. Savoie Lottinville (Norman: University of Oklahoma Press, 1973), 135.

32. Interview with Turner Tiger, January 1, 1938, IPHC, 91:12193. See James Oglethorpe to Board of Trustees, March 12, 1733, in *General Oglethorpe's Georgia: Colonial Letters, 1733–1743*, ed. Mills Lane, 2 vols. (Savannah: Beehive Press, 1975), 1:7.

33. President and Assistants to Benjamin Martyn, April 15, 1748, in *CRG*, 24:235.

34. Bernard Romans, *A Concise Natural History of East and West Florida*, ed. Rembert W. Patrick (1775; reprint, Gainesville: University of Florida Press, 1962), 89–90.

35. T. E., "Account of the Creek Indians," 407.

36. SN, ADAH, 5.

37. For a discussion of the centrality of Creek clans, see Alexander Spoehr, *Changing Kinship Systems: A Study in the Acculturation of the Creek, Cherokee, and Choctaw* (Chicago: Field Museum of Natural History, 1947).

38. SN, ADAH, 55.

39. Lyman Draper, August 16, 1886; Tus-te-nuck-o-chee, August 22, 1883; J. G.

Vore to Draper, December 15, 1881, all in Tecumseh Papers, DM. John Sugden, *Tecumseh: A Life* (New York: Henry Holt, 1998), 15, 240.

40. Hawkins to Cusituh Micco, [1799], Benjamin Hawkins Papers, North Carolina Department of Archives and History, Raleigh; Hawkins to McGillivray, March 6, 1790, LC, PKY; Jonathan Milledge to Hawkins, December 31, 1802, GLB, GDAH; A Report on Creek Indian Affairs by Mr. Bevan, October 22, 1825, in ASPIA, 2:784–861.

41. History Notebook, vol. 1, Pickett Manuscripts, ADAH. See Statement of Middleton, December 21, 1791, AGI, C:1436, PKY.

42. Efau Haujo, May 28, 1798, in LBH, 1:187; Braund, "Creek Indians," 612–13, 621.

43. McGillivray to Arturo Miró, March 24, 1784, LC, PKY.

44. Wright, *Creeks and Seminoles*, 27; Martin, *Sacred Revolt*, 34–42.

45. Carl Mauelshagen and Gerald H. Davis, eds. and trans., *Partners in the Lord's Work: The Diary of Two Moravian Missionaries in the Creek Indian Country, 1807–1813* (Atlanta: Georgia State College, 1969), 61.

46. *The Missionary* (Mount Zion GA), April 13, 1823.

47. Wright, *Creeks and Seminoles*, 29.

48. Martin, *Sacred Revolt*, 43. See also Interview with Louis Dunson, March 25, 1937, IPHC, 26:5482.

49. Michael D. Green, "The Creek Confederacy in the American Revolution: Cautious Participants," in *Anglo-Spanish Confrontation on the Gulf Coast during the American Revolution*, ed. William S. Coker and Robert R. Rea (Pensacola FL: Gulf Coast History and Humanities Conference, 1982), 54–75. Creeks also divided their loyalties in the French and Indian War, the Seven Years War, the War of 1812, the Seminole Wars, and the American Civil War. See Christine Schultz White and Benton R. White, *Now the Wolf Has Come: The Creek Nation in the Civil War* (College Station: Texas A&M University Press, 1996).

50. Wright, *Creek and Seminoles*, 3, 7, 10; Braund, *Deerskins and Duffels*, 6; James Oglethorpe to Board of Trustees, March 12, 1733, in Lane, *General Oglethorpe's Georgia*, 1:7.

2. "THIS ASYLUM OF LIBERTY"

1. Caleb Swan, "Position and State of Manners and Arts in the Creek, or Muscogee Nation in 1791," in Schoolcraft, *Information Respecting the History,*5:263.

2. Swan, "Position and State of Manners," 5:263.

3. Swan to Knox, April 29, 1795, in Swan, "Position and State of Manners," 5:252. See also 5:262–63, 268–69, 272–74.

4. Swan, "Position and State of Manners," 5:260–61.

5. Swan, "Position and State of Manners," 5:272. See also Swanton, "Social Organization," 384.

6. Louis Milfort, *Memoirs; or, A Quick Glance at My Various Travels and My Sojourn in the Creek Nation*, ed. and trans. Ben C. McCary (1802; reprint, Kennesaw GA: Continental Book, 1959), 72.

7. Hawkins, January 3, 1797, in *LBH*, 1:33–34.

8. Thompson Woodward to J. J. Hooper, November 3, 1858, in Thomas Simpson Woodward, *Woodward's Reminiscences of the Creek, or Muscogee Indians, Contained in Letters to Friends in Georgia and Alabama* (Montgomery AL: Barrett & Wimbish, 1859), 115; *LBH*; SN, ADAH.

9. Enoch Parsons to Lewis Carr, September 7, 1832, OIA, CA, LR, M234, 223:307–8; Parsons to Andrew Jackson, September 21, 1833, OIA, CA, LR, M234, 223:1030–40. See Jeanne Robey Felldin and Charlotte Magee Tucker, *1832 Census of Creek Indians taken by Parsons and Abbot* (Tomball TX: Genealogical Publications, 1978).

10. Hawkins, December 21, 1796, in *LBH*, 25; J. D. Driesbach to Lyman Draper, July 1784, DM.

11. This number represents a conservative estimate drawn from the records of Spanish, British, and American traders, diplomats, missionaries, and travelers. It favors participants in the deerskin trade over those who sought refuge and those who maintained their European American connections over those who "turned Indian." At least five hundred of these newcomers are referred to by name within the historical records.

12. For alternative explanations of Indian countrymen, see James Axtell, "The White Indians of Colonial America," *WMQ* 32 (January 1975): 55–88; and Calloway, "Neither White nor Red," 43–66.

13. Hawkins, "A Sketch of the Creek Country in the Years 1789 and 1799," in *LBH*, 1:305; Woodward to J. J. Hooper, November 3, 1858, in Woodward, *Reminiscences*, 115.

14. Woodward to Pickett, April 25, 1858, in Woodward, *Reminiscences*, 41; Hawkins to Price, June 8, 1798, in *LBH*, 1:200–201.

15. Deposition of James Ore, June 16, 1792, in *ASPIA*, 1:274.

16. Barber, "Narrative of the Tragic Death," 36:19.

17. Hawkins, "Sketch of the Creek Country," in *LBH*, 1:301. For examples of the successful redemption of captives, see Deposition of James Ore, June 16, 1792, in *ASPIA*, 1:274; Andrew Pickens to Thomas Pinckney, October 6, 1787, Andrew Pickens Papers, HL; James Hoggarth to McGillivray, May 25, 1792, in Caughey, *McGillivray of the Creeks*, 324–25; George Matthews to Col. Milton, January 3, 1798, GLB, GDAH; Matthews to James Seagrove, January 3, 1793, January 1, 1794, GLB, GDAH; William M. Willett, *A Narrative of The Military Actions of Colonel Marinus Willett, Taken Chiefly From His Own Manuscript* (New York: G. & C. & H. Carvill, 1831), 111. Elsewhere this was not the case. See Axtell, "White Indians of Colonial America," 55–88.

18. Pickett, *History of Alabama*, 323–26. See Extract of a letter from Frederic in Georgia, in *South Carolina Gazette*, August 15, 1743; Knox Mellon Jr., "Christian Priber's Cherokee Kingdom of Paradise," *GHQ* 57 (Fall 1973): 319–31.

19. The economic and political sources of unrest within the lower interior South have been well documented. See Rachel N. Klein, *Unification of a Slave State: The Rise of the Planter Class in the South Carolina Backcountry, 1760–1808* (Chapel Hill: University of North Carolina Press, 1990).

20. David Dobson, *Scottish Emigration to Colonial America, 1607–1785* (Athens: University of Georgia Press, 1994), 103–22, 153–67; Edward J. Cashin, *Lachlan Mc-Gillivray, Indian Trader: The Shaping of the Southern Colonial Frontier* (Athens: University of Georgia Press, 1992), 16–17; Ferenc Morton Szasz, *Scots in the North American West, 1790–1917* (Norman: University of Oklahoma Press, 2000), 52; see also 49–77. William S. Coker and Thomas D. Watson emphasized the Scottish connection to the South's largest trading company by describing the group as "Scotsmen All." See Coker and Watson, *Indian Traders of the Southeastern Spanish Borderlands: Panton, Leslie & Company and John Forbes & Company, 1783–1847* (Pensacola: University of West Florida, 1986), 15–30. To a lesser degree Creek costumes were also shaped by repeated gifts of clothing from Spaniards in Cuba. See Pierce Sinnot to Stuart, March 2, 1768, Gage Papers, American Series.

21. Notes taken from the lips of Dr. Thomas G. Holmes in relation to various expeditions made by Captain Blue, Col. Benton & others in 1814–1813, Pickett Manuscripts, ADAH; Woodward to Hooper, October 31, 1858, in Woodward, *Reminiscences*, 88; Extract of a Letter from Capt. Jackson of the Loyal Refugees to Colonel John Stuart, July 7, 1778, PRO CO, 5/79; Cashin, *Lachlan McGillivray*, 37–41; David Taitt to Stuart, March 16, 1772, PRO CO, 5/73.

22. Stuart, Observations on the Plan for the Future Management of Indian Affairs Humbly Submitted to the Lords Commissioners of Trade and Plantations, December 1, 1763, PRO CO, 323/19. See also Stuart to Thomas Gage, March 14, 1766, December 19, 1766, Gage Papers, American Series.

23. Richard White, *The Roots of Dependency: Subsistence, Environment, and Social Changes among the Choctaws, Pawnees, and Navajos* (Lincoln: University of Nebraska Press, 1983), 69–96; Braund, *Deerskins and Duffels*, 30, 121–38.

24. Wilbur R. Jacobs, ed., *Indians on the Southern Colonial Frontier: The Edmond Atkin Report and Plan of 1755* (Columbia: University of South Carolina Press, 1954), 39.

25. Reply of the Indians to the talk delivered this 27th day of June 1802 at Jack Wards, June 27, 1802, WD, LR, M271, 1:148–50. See also James Habersham to George Galphin, October 16, 1772, James Habersham Papers, GDAH; Thomas McKenney to John Crowell, September 23, 1824, LS, OIA, M21, 1:200; To the Mico's Head-Men and Warriors of the Creek Nation, the Governor of Georgia sends Greeting, May 26, 1760, Henry Ellis Papers, GHS.

26. Kathryn E. Holland Braund, "Guardians of Tradition and Handmaidens to Change: Women's Roles in Creek Economic and Social Life during the Eighteenth Century," *American Indian Quarterly* 13 (Summer 1990): 251; Braund, *Deerskins and Duffels*, 78–79; Clara Sue Kidwell, "Indian Women as Cultural Mediators," *Ethnohistory* 39 (Spring 1992): 97–107.

27. Thomas Bosomworth in the Coweta Town in the Creek Nation, October 11, 1752, in *Documents Relating to Indian Affairs, May 21, 1750–August 7, 1754*, ed. William L. McDowell Jr. (Columbia: South Carolina Archives Department, 1958),

2:306. See Glen to Duke of New Castle, December 1, 1748, in Letter Book of James Glen, HL; James Stuart, *Three Years in North America*, 2 vols. (Edinburgh: Robert Cadell, 1833), 2:134.

28. Reply of the Indians to the talk delivered this 27th day of June 1802 at Jack Wards, June 27, 1802, WD, LR, M271, 1:148–50.

29. Hawkins to Price, May 29, 1798, in *LBH*, 1:195.

30. John Lawson, *A New Voyage to Carolina*, ed. Hugh Talmage Heffler (Chapel Hill: University of North Carolina Press, 1975), 191–92.

31. William Bartram, *The Travels of William Bartram*, ed. Mark Van Doren (New York: Dover, 1955), 170.

32. Not surprisingly, most of the sources that originally pointed to the supremacy of the Wind clan came from men who married into the clan and used their "royal" connections to ameliorate any decline in social status that would have been associated with a marriage to a Creek woman. For example, see Milfort, *Memoirs*, 8, 135; O'Neill to José de Ezpeleta, October 19, 1793, LC, PKY; White Lieutenant and David Cornell, etc., to Seagrove, June 14, 1793, in *ASPIA*, 1:378–79, 381, 396; SN, ADAH, 56; Woodward to Pickett, June 21, 1858, in Woodward, *Reminiscences*, 61.

33. McGillivray to Hallowing King of the Cowetas, April 14, 1786, in CIL, 101.

34. Report of Joseph Vallence Beven to George M. Troup, October 22, 1823, in *ASPIA*, 2:793.

35. John F. D. Smythe, *Tour in the United States of America*, 2 vols. (1784; reprint, London: New York Times & Arno Press, 1968), 1:190–91. See also Richard A. Sattler, "Women's Status among the Muskogee and Cherokee," in *Women and Power in Native North America*, ed. Laura F. Klein and Lillian A. Ackerman (Norman: University of Oklahoma Press, 1995), 218; Swanton, "Social Organization," 346–56, 384.

36. Saunt, *New Order of Things*, 254–59, 266–69; Martin, *Sacred Revolt*, 133–68; Claudio Saunt, "Domestick . . . Quiet Being Broke: Gender Conflict among Creek Indians in the Eighteenth Century," in Cayton and Teute, *Contact Points*, 151–74.

37. Extract of a Report of Totummee Hayo and Robert Walton to Agent of Indian Affairs, November 4, 1799, LC, PKY. Similar punishments were also used for certain sexual transgressions. See Thomas Eyre to Robert Eyre, December 4, 1740, in Lane, *General Oglethorpe's Georgia*, 2:502–4.

38. Lawson, *New Voyage to Carolina*, 46, 190; Herbert Moller, "Sex Composition and Correlated Culture Patterns of Colonial America," *WMQ* 2 (April 1945): 131; Affidavit of James Maxwell, June 12, 1751, in McDowell, *Documents Relating to Indian Affairs*, 2:70; Abstract of a letter from David Taitt, September 21, 1772, PRO CO, 5/74; Lawson, *New Voyage to Carolina*, 190; Bartram, *Travels*, 170, Swan, "Position and State of Manners," 5:254, 268.

39. Abraham Steiner, January 22, 1804, in "The Moravians' Plan for a Mission among the Creek Indians, 1803–1804," ed. Carl Mauelshagen and Gerald H. Davis, *GHQ* 51 (September 1967): 363. For adultery and its punishment, see Swanton, *Indians of the Southeastern United States*, 701–3; Romans, *Concise Natural History*, 98.

40. Jean-Bernard Bossu, *Travels in the Interior of North America, 1751–1762*, ed. Seymour Feiler (Norman: University of Oklahoma Press, 1962), 131–32; Adam Hodgson to [?], April 3, 1820, in Adam Hodgson, *Letters from North America, Written During a Tour in the United States and Canada* (London: Hurst, Robinson, 1824), 2:130; Hawkins to Thomas Jefferson, July 11, 1803, in LBH, 2:455; Thomas Eyre to Robert Eyre, December 4, 1740, in Lane, *General Oglethorpe's Georgia*, 2:502–4; SN, ADAH, 43–45; John Pope, *A Tour Through the Southern and Western Territories of the United States of North-America; the Spanish Dominions on the River Mississippi, and the Floridas; the Countries of the Creek Nations; and Many Uninhabited Parts* (Richmond VA: John Dixon, 1792), 56–57; Stuart, *Three Years in North America*, 2:159–60.

41. Thomas Jones to Trustees, October 23, 1741, in CRG, 23:123–24.

42. Oglethorpe to Trustees, February 12, 1743, in Lane, *General Oglethorpe's Georgia*, 2:660.

43. Joseph Fitzwalter to Oglethorpe, July 5, 1735, in CRG, 20:426; Fitzwalter to Oglethorpe, January 16, 1735, in CRG, 20:163.

44. Philip H. Riaford to Pickett, February 8, 1850; Thomas M. Ellis to Pickett, August 26, 1847; Notes taken from the lips of Abram Mordecai an old jew 92 years of age who had lived 60 years among the Creek Indians, all in Pickett Manuscripts, ADAH.

45. Augustus Loomis, *Scenes in the Indian Country* (Philadelphia: Presbyterian Board of Publication, 1818), 201.

46. Lawson, *New Voyage to Carolina*, 192.

47. Loomis, *Scenes in the Indian Country*, 200–201.

48. Patrick Tonyn to Thomas Townshend, May 15, 1783, in *Documents of the American Revolution, 1770–1783*, ed. Kenneth G. Davies, 21 vols. (Dublin: Irish University Press, 1972–79), 21:168.

49. Stuart to George Germain, August 23, 1776, PRO CO, 5/77.

50. Frank Moore, *Diary of the American Revolution*, 5 vols. (New York: Scribner, 1854), 5:228. See also Michael D. Green, "Alexander McGillivray," in *American Indian Leaders: Studies in Diversity*, ed. R. David Edmunds (Lincoln: University of Nebraska Press, 1980), 42.

51. Tonyn to Taitt, [?] 1776, in Davies, *Documents of the American Revolution*, 12:108.

52. June 6, 1776, in *The Moravians in Georgia*, ed. Adelaide L. Fries, 6 vols. (Baltimore: Genealogical Publishing, 1967), 3:1065. See also O'Neill to Luis de Unzaga, February 16, 1783, LC, PKY; Rev. Jas. Creswell to William H. Drayton, July 27, 1776, in *Documentary History of the American Revolution*, ed. R. W. Gibbes, 3 vols. (New York: D. Appleton, 1853), 3:30.

53. Jefferson to William Phillips, July 22, 1779, in *The Papers of Thomas Jefferson*, ed. Julian P. Boyd, 21 vols. (Princeton: Princeton University Press, 1952), 3:46.

54. John Martin to Friends and Brothers [in the Creek Nation], January 11, 1782,

in "Official Letters of Governor John Martin," GHQ 1 (December 1917): 282. See also Anthony Wayne to Nathaniel Greene, February 1, 1782, in *Sources of American Independence: Selected Manuscripts from the Collections of the William L. Clements Library*, ed. Howard Peckham, 2 vols. (Chicago: University of Chicago Press: 1978), 2:378–79, and Wayne to Greene, April 1, 1782, 2:394–95.

55. SN, ADAH, 151.

56. Swan, "Position and State of Manners," 263.

57. "Founder of This City: Sketch of Earliest Inhabitant of the Capital City—Pen Pictoryre of 'Old Mordecai' by Col. Pickett.—Something about the First Man Who Planted Cotton in Alabama," January 21, 1904, in *Montgomery Evening Times*, Pickett Manuscripts, ADAH.

58. Alexander Semple to Samuel Elbert, May 18, 1785, LC, PKY. Revolutionary soldiers also fled to Indian villages. See McGillivray to Vincent Emanual de Zéspedes, February 6, 1789, LC, PKY.

59. Loomis, *Scenes in the Indian Country*, 201; "Schneider's Report of His Journey," in *Early Travels in the Tennessee Country*, ed. Samuel Cole Williams, ed. (Johnson City TN: Watuga Press, 1938), 246. See Gage to Earl of Halifax, April 27, 1765, in *The Correspondence of General Thomas Gage with the Secretaries of State, 1763–1775*, ed. Clarence Edwin Carter, 2 vols. (New Haven: Yale University Press, 1931), 1:56; Milfort, *Memoirs*, 135; Congress at Pensacola, in *Mississippi Provincial Archives, 1763–1766, English Dominion*, ed. Dunbar Rowland (Nashville: Press of Brandon Printing, 1911), 1:193.

60. Timothy Pickering to William Eaton, November 26, 1795, in Eaton Collection, HL; Phillippe De Rigaud de Vaudreuil to Rouille, April 28, 1751, in *Mississippi Provincial Archives, French Dominion*, ed. Dunbar Rowland and Albert Godfrey Sanders, 5 vols. (Jackson: Press of the Mississippi Department of Archives and History, 1927–84), 5:71; Memoir of D'Artaguett to Pontchartrain on Present Condition of Louisiana, May 12, 1712, in Rowland and Sanders, *Mississippi Provincial Archives*, 5:60; Price to Tench Frances, January 11, 1796, OIA, Records of the Creek Trading House, M4.

61. "Journal of David Taitt's Travels from Pensacola, West Florida, to the through the Country of the Upper and the Lower Creeks, 1772," in *Travels in the American Colonies*, ed. Newton D. Mereness, 497–582 (New York: Macmillan, 1916), 512; see also 527.

62. Woodward to E. Hanrick, December 9, 1857, in Woodward, *Reminiscences*, 7–10. See also Diego De Vegas to O'Neill, May 8, 1788, PLP; O'Neill to Estevan Miro, June 19, 1788, PLP.

63. Samuel Quincy to Peter Gordon, March 3, 1735, in Lane, *General Oglethorpe's Georgia*, 1:129–30.

64. February 24, 1743, in *Journal of William Stephens, 1671–1753*, ed. E. Merton Coulter, 2 vols. (Athens: University of Georgia Press, 1958–59), 1:175.

65. Personal communication, John Moore, University of Florida, 1995. Jan Vansina

explores oral traditions in *Oral Tradition as History* (Madison: University of Wisconsin Press, 1985).

66. James Wright, December [?], 1771, in CRG, 28, pt 2:840–44.

67. May 11, 1811, in Mauelshagen and Davis, *Partners in the Lord's Work*, 48.

68. William Young to Patrick Tonyn, November 5, 1784, LC, PKY.

69. July 11, 1744, August 4, 1744, July 1, 1745, in Coulter, *Journal of William Stephens*, 122–23, 131–32, 222.

70. Thomas C. Hunter to William Wyatt Bibb, November 1, 1818, in *The Territorial Papers of the United States*, ed. Clarence Edwin Carter, 28 vols. (Washington DC: United States Printing Office, 1934–49), 18:452. See Stephen Forrester to Juan Nepomuleno de Quesada, December 3, 1792, PLP; Hawkins, [?] 1803, in LBH, 2:457; Carlos Howard to Henry O'Neill, May 23, 1785, LC, PKY.

71. John Cunningham to Israel Pickens, November 21, 1822, Alabama Governor (1821–25, PICKENS) Reward Files, 1822–24, ADAH.

72. McKenney to John Innerarity, July 11, 1818, PLP.

73. Traylor Russell, "Kendall Lewis: Citizen of Four Nations—United States—Creek—Republic of Mexico—Republic of Texas" (typescript, University of Georgia Library, March 15, 1969).

74. Hawkins to Lewis, September 4, 1815; Hawkins to Lewis, February 16, 1814; Thomas Ellis to Pickett, August 26, 1847; all in Pickett Manuscripts, ADAH. "Payroll of the general, field, and staff officers of General William McIntosh's brigade of Creek Warriors, lately in the service of the United States," January 14, 1820, in ASPMA, 2:119; Commissioners to General Edmund P. Gaines, July 3, 1825, in ASPIA, 2:834; Major Butler to the Commissioners, July 4, 1825, 2:834–35.

75. J. Leitch Wright Jr., *William Augustus Bowles: Director General of the Creek Nation* (Athens: University of Georgia Press, 1967), 6, 36–37; Hawkins to Various Creek Chiefs, December 10, 1799, in LBH, 1:279. See Saunt, *New Order of Things*, 86–88.

76. Hawkins to Samuel Dexter, July 26, 1800, in LBH, 2:342.

77. "Substance of a voluntary declaration made by Sundry of Bowles Banditti at St. Augustine 21 Nov. 1788 and which Since been Confirmed by them and the others now prisoners on Oath," November 21, 1788, PLP; Zéspedes to José de Ezpeleta, November 24, 1788, LC, PKY; Thomas Forbes to Governor Halkett [Pensacola], March 6, 1802, PLP; O'Neill to Estevan Miró, January 3, 1789, PLP; George Handley to Zéspedes, November 25, 1788, in "Force Transcripts, Georgia Records Council Correspondence, 1782–1789," ed. Louise Frederick Hays (typescript, GDAH).

78. History Notebook, vol. 2, Pickett Manuscripts, ADAH.

3. KIN AND STRANGERS

1. Andrew Jackson to Colonel William Moore, November 15, 1833, in *Correspondence of Andrew Jackson*, ed. John Spencer Bassett, 7 vols. (Washington DC: Carnegie

Institute, 1926–27) 5:225; Andrew Jackson to Rachel Jackson, December 19, 1813, in Bassett, *Correspondence of Andrew Jackson*, 1:400–401.

2. Andrew Jackson to Rachel Jackson, January 28, 1814, in Bassett, *Correspondence of Andrew Jackson*, 1:447, December 7, 1823, 3:215–16, December 28, 1823, 3:220, March 27, 1824, 3:241; Rachel Jackson to Andrew Jackson, March 21, 1814, in Bassett, *Correspondence of Andrew Jackson*, 1:482; Andrew Jackson to Rachel Jackson, December 29, 1813, Huntington Manuscripts, HL; Andrew Jackson to Rachel [(Donelson) Richards] Jackson, March 4, 1814, Huntington Manuscripts, HL.

3. James Parton, *Life of Andrew Jackson* (New York: Mason Brothers, 1860) 1:440; Michael Paul Rogin, *Fathers and Children: Andrew Jackson and the Subjugation of the American Indian* (New York: Vintage Books, 1975), 11; Robert V. Remini, *The Legacy of Andrew Jackson: Essays on Democracy, Indian Removal, and Slavery* (Baton Rouge: Louisiana State University Press, 1988), 46–57.

4. Bernard W. Sheehan, *The Seeds of Extinction: Jeffersonian Philanthropy and the American Indian* (New York: W. W. Norton, 1973), 4.

5. Robert F. Berkhofer Jr., *The White Man's Indian: Images of the American Indian from Columbus to the Present* (New York: Vintage Press, 1978), 41. See also Karen Ordahl Kupperman, *Indians and English: Facing Off in Early America* (Ithaca NY: Cornell University Press, 2000); Karen Ordahl Kupperman, *Settling with the Indians: The Meeting of English and Indian Cultures in America, 1580–1640* (Totowa NJ: Rowman & Littlefield, 1980), 35.

6. Winthrop D. Jordan, "American Chiaroscuro: The Status and Definition of Mulattoes in the British Colonies," WMQ 19 (April 1962): 183–200. See also the essays in "Constructing Race: Differentiating Peoples in the Early Modern World," special issue of the WMQ 54 (January 1997).

7. Saunt, *New Order of Things*, 139–204.

8. Daniel H. Usner Jr., *Indians, Settlers and Slaves in a Frontier Exchange Economy: The Lower Mississippi Valley before 1783* (Chapel Hill: University of North Carolina Press, 1992), 16–17, 56–59, 244–75.

9. Ebenezer H. Cummins, *Summary Geography of Alabama, One of the United States* (Philadelphia: William Brown, 1819), 22; *Niles Weekly Register*, December 5, 1818; Stuart, *Three Years in North America*, 2:150; John C. Calhoun to Henry Clay, January 15, 1820, in *The Papers of John C. Calhoun*, ed. Robert L. Meriwether, 17 vols. (Columbia: University of South Carolina Press, 1959–86), 4:576.

10. "Removal of the Indians," *Baptist Missionary Magazine* 10 (December 1830): 362–64. Almost the same exact words were used in "Report from the War Department, December 5, 1818," *Niles Weekly Register*, December 1818, 26.

11. John Mason to James Madison, January 18, 1818, Superintendent of Indian Trade, LS, M16, D:201.

12. W. David Baird, "Are There 'Real' Indians in Oklahoma? Historical Perceptions of the Five Civilized Tribes," *Chronicles of Oklahoma* 68 (Spring 1990): 4–23.

13. Dorothy Downs, "British Influences on Creek and Seminole Men's Clothing,

1733–1858," *Florida Anthropologist* 33 (June 1980): 46–65; Braund, *Deerskins and Duffels*, 124–25.

14. Bartram, *Travels*, 393–94. For example, see Adair, *History of the American Indians*, 33.

15. Berkhofer, *White Man's Indian*, 33–54, 113–44, 186–94; Sheehan, *Seeds of Extinction*, 3–118; Reginald Horsman, *Race and Manifest Destiny: The Origins of American Racial Anglo-Saxonism* (Cambridge: Harvard University Press, 1981), 205–6. The degree to which "early modern conceptions of difference" or human variations can be equated with "race," if not a form of "proto-race," has been overstated by many scholars. See Joyce E. Chaplin, "Natural Philosophy and an Early Racial Idiom in North America: Comparing English and Indian Bodies," *WMQ* 54 (January 1997): 229–31.

16. John F. Meginness, *Biography of Frances Slocum, the Lost Sister of Wyoming* (New York: Arno Press, 1974), 196.

17. Lacque Le Moyne, *Narrative of Le Moyne, An Artist who Accompanied the French Expedition to Florida Under Laudonniére, 1564* (Boston: James R. Osgood, 1875), 10; Lawson, *New Voyage to Carolina*, 192; Clark Wissler, *Indians of the United States* (New York: Anchor Books, 1966), 276–81.

18. Berkhofer, *White Man's Indian*, 27; David Rich Lewis, *Neither Wolf nor Dog: American Indians, Environment, and Agrarian Change* (New York: Oxford University Press, 1994), 3–21.

19. William Gilmore Simms, "The Broken Arrow: An Authentic Passage from Unwritten American History," *Ladies Companion*, January 1844, 117.

20. Roy Pearce and J. H. Miller, eds., *Savages of America: A Study of the Indian and the Idea of Civilization* (Baltimore: Johns Hopkins University Press, 1965); Gregory Nobles, "Breaking into the Backcountry: New Approaches to the Early American Frontier, 1750–1800," *WMQ* 46 (October 1989): 641–70.

21. Isaac McCoy, *History of Baptist Indian Missions: Embracing Remarks on the Former and Present Condition of the Aboriginal Tribes; Their Settlements within the Indian Territory, and their Future Prospects* (New York: H. & S. Raynor, 1840), 19.

22. For an intriguing look at the debate over the origins of the "red Indian," see Nancy Shoemaker, "How Indians Got to be Red," *American Historical Review* 102 (June 1997): 625–44.

23. Jefferson to Hawkins, February 18, 1803, in *The Works of Thomas Jefferson*, ed. Paul Leicester Ford, 12 vols. (New York: G. P. Putnam's Sons, 1892–99), 7:214; Ivan Hannaford, *Race: The History of an Idea in the West* (Washington DC: Woodrow Wilson Center Press, 1996), 233; Faye V. Harrison, "The Persistent Power of 'Race' in the Cultural and Political Economy of Racism," *Annual Review of Anthropology* 24 (1995): 47–74. Big Warrior would later use quite similar language. In the future, he stated, "our Children might be raised with your Children, and become one people and that you might settle down and be our protector." [Big Warrior] to Jackson, October 3, 1815, Ayer Collection, Newberry Library.

24. Jacques Fontaine, *Memoirs of a Huguenot Family*, trans. Ann Maury (New York: Putnam, 1872), 350.

25. Mark Catesby, *The Natural History of Carolina, Florida, and the Bahama Islands: Containing the Figures of Birds, Beasts, Fishes, Serpents, Insects, and Plants*, 2 vols. (London: Benjamin White, 1771), 1:viii.

26. John Archdale, *A New Description of That Fertile and Pleasant Province of Carolina: With a Brief Account of its Discovery, Settling, and the Government Thereof to this Time. With Several Remarkable Passages of Divine Providence during my Time* (London: John Wyat, 1707), 7.

27. Philip Thicknesse, *Memoirs and Anecdotes of Philip Thicknesse, Late Lieutenant Governor of Land Guard Fort, and Unfortunately Father to George Touchet, Baron Audley* ([London?]: author, 1788), 46.

28. Lee Compere, "Extracts from Mr. Compere's Journal," *Baptist Missionary Magazine* 7 (1827): 85–88; 143–44, 181–84, 321–25; 8 (June 1829): 198; 12 (1833): 183; Circular, May 18, 1821, LS, WD, M15, E:101.

29. Thomas Ashe, "Carolina or a Description of the Present State of that Country, Thomas Ashe, 1682," in *Narratives of Early Carolina, 1650–1708*, ed. Alexander S. Salley, 138–59 (New York: Scribner's Sons, 1911), 156.

30. Samuel Urlsperger, *Detailed Report of the Salzburger Emigrants Who Settled in America, 1733–1734* (Athens: University of Georgia Press, 1968), 143.

31. European Americans also used hair as a means of demarcating Indians from Americans. See Karl Bernhard, *Travels through North America, During the years 1825 and 1826*, 2 vols. (Philadelphia: Carey, Lea & Carey, 1828), 2:24; Catesby, *Natural History of Carolina*, 1:viii; Romans, *Concise Natural History*, 112; Stuart, *Three Years in North America*, 2:161.

32. Pickett, *History of Alabama*, 1:75.

33. Hvidt, *Von Reck's Voyage*, 45.

34. Jefferson quoted in Daniel Boorstin, *The Lost World of Thomas Jefferson* (Chicago: University of Chicago Press, 1948), 84. See also Reverend James Madison to Jefferson, December 28, 1786, in Boyd, *Papers of Thomas Jefferson*, 10:543.

35. Extract of a letter from Gentleman at Augusta in Georgia, dated the 17th Instant, *South Carolina Gazette*, June 25, 1753.

36. Swanton, *Indians of the Southeastern United States*, 808.

37. "A Short Description of the Province of South Carolina: With an Account of the Air, Weather, and Diseases, at Charlestown, Written in the Year 1763," in *Historical Collections of South Carolina*, ed. B. R. Carroll, 2 vols. (New York: Harper & Brothers, 1836), 2:516.

38. Swanton, *Indian Tribes of the Lower Mississippi Valley*, 51.

39. "Survey of West Florida, 1768," in *Colonial Captivities, Marches, and Journeys*, ed. Isabel M. Calder (New York: Macmillan, 1935), 229.

40. Thomas Campbell, "Thomas Campbell to Lord Deane Gordon: An Account of the Creek Indian Nation, 1764," *FHQ* 8 (January 1930): 162; Thomas Eyre to

Robert Eyre, December 4, 1740, in Lane, *General Oglethorpe's Georgia*, 2:504; Adam Hodgson to [?], April 3, 1820, in Hodgson, *Letters from North America*, 130; "Short Description of South Carolina," in Carroll, *Historical Collections of South* Carolina, 2:515; Romans, *Concise Natural History*, 98.

41. Lawson, *New Voyage to Carolina*, 190.

42. January 26, 1744, in Coulter, *Journal of William Stephens*, 64.

43. SN, ADAH, 144; Caughey, *McGillivray of the Creeks*, 118, n. 62; Talk of Part of the Creek Indians to the Georgia Legislature, August 3, 1786, in Caughey, *McGillivray of the Creeks*, 124.

44. List of Indians to be invited to Pensacola, [Winter 1793–94], LC, PKY; Le Moyne, *Narrative of Le Moyne*, 10.

45. Barber, "Narrative of the Tragic Death," 7. See also Milford, *Memoirs*, 31, 67; Patrick Tonyn to Taitt, [?] 1776, in Davies, *Documents of the American Revolution*, 12:108; Rev. Jas. Creswell to W. H. Drayton, July 27, 1776, in Gibbes, *Documentary History of the American Revolution*, 3:30.

46. Manuel de Montiano to the King, July 20, 1747, SD, reel 46, legajo 866, 534, PKY; "Captivity of Jane Brown and Her Family," in Washburn, *Garland Library of Narratives*, 64:1–15; Barber, "Shocking Murder by the Savages," in Washburn, *Garland Library of Narratives*, 36:26.

47. Interview with George Looney, June 28, 1937, IPHC, 55:6500a; Swanton, "Social Organization," 112–13.

48. Jean-Bernard Bossu to the Marquis de l'Estrade, November 7, 1751, in Bossu, *Travels in the Interior of North America*, 65. Tattoos were used throughout the southeast. See Swanton, *Indian Tribes of the Lower Mississippi Valley*, 56–57.

49. "True Relation of the Vicissitudes that Attended the Governor Don Hernando de Soto," in *Narratives of the Career of Hernando de Soto in the Conquest of Florida*, ed. and trans. Edward G. Bourne, 2 vols. (New York: Allerton Book, 1973), 1:26.

50. Pickett, *History of Alabama*, 56; emphasis added.

51. Barber, "Narrative of the Tragic Death," 36:7. Axtell writes that the initiation process turned "whites" into "Indians." "Symbolically purged of their whiteness by their Indian baptism, the initiates were dressed in new Indian clothes and decorated with feathers, jewelry, and paint." Such an interpretation overstates the importance of race in Creek society. Non-Creek Indians had to be initiated into Creek society just as white Americans were. Paint and other markings did not "purge" "whiteness"; they made Creeks out of all outsiders. See James Axtell, *The European and the Indian: Essays in the Ethnohistory of Colonial North America* (New York: Oxford Press, 1981), 187.

52. Leslie Hall, *Land and Allegiance in Revolutionary Georgia* (Athens: University of Georgia Press, 2002); Peter W. Bardaglio, *Reconstructing the Household: Families, Sex, and the Law in the Nineteenth-Century South* (Chapel Hill: University of North Carolina Press, 1995); Bertram Wyatt-Brown, *Southern Honor: Ethics and Violence in the Old South* (New York: Oxford University Press, 1982).

53. John S. Bassett, ed., *The Writings of Colonial William Byrd* (New York: Doubleday, Page, 1901), 8–9.

54. O'Neill to Marques de Sonora, July 11, 1787, in Caughey, *McGillivray of the Creeks*, 157. See also Lawson, *New Voyage to Carolina*, 246; *South Carolina Gazette*, April 14, 1732; March 30, 1757, in Fontaine, *Memoirs of a Huguenot Family*, 349. For other proponents of Indian-European intermarriages, see J. H. Johnston, "Documentary Evidence of the Relations of Negroes and Indians," *Journal of Negro History* 14 (January 1929), 21–43; James Silk Buckingham, *Slave States in America*, 2 vols. (1842; reprint, New York: Negro Universities Press, 1968), 1:77; James Oglethorpe to Harmon Verelst, April 24, 1736, in CRG, 21:216; Joseph Fitzwalter to James Oglethorpe, July 5, 1735, 20:426; Glen to the Board of Trade, October 25. 1753, PRO CO, 5/350; Edmund Atkin's Report to the Lord's Commissioners, May 30, 1755, Lord Loudoun Papers, HL.

55. Jefferson to Hawkins, February 18, 1803, in Ford, *Works of Thomas Jefferson*, 7:214.

56. Sheehan posits that "civilization" and "intermixing" were two disparate alternatives for "solving the problem of Indian-white relations." It seems that he sees too great a difference between the two. Sheehan, *Seeds of Extinction*, 174–75.

57. *South Carolina Gazette*, April 14, 1732.

58. Meigs cited in William G. McLoughlin, *Cherokees and Missionaries, 1789–1839* (Norman: University of Oklahoma Press, 1984), 69. See also Francis Le Jau to Secretary, August 30, 1712, in Klingberd, *Carolina Chronicle*, 121; *State of the British and French Colonies in North America with Respect to Number of People, Forts, Indians, Trade and Other Advantages* (London: A. Millar, 1755), 18.

59. Hawkins to Matthew Hopkins, March 17, 1799, in LBH, 1:243.

60. O'Neill to José de Gálvez, July 11, 1787, LC, PKY.

61. An Account of the Names and Families among the Indians together with a Hint of Their Native Government to Ralph Izard, Esquire, April 15, 1708, in *Nairne's Muskhogean Journals: The 1708 Expedition to the Mississippi River*, ed. Alexander Moore (Jackson: University Press of Mississippi, 1988), 61; J. B. Brebner, "Subsidized Intermarriage with the Indians," *Canadian Historical Review* 6 (March 1925): 33–63.

62. J. Hector St. John Crevecoeur, *Letters from an American Farmer* (New York: E. P. Dutton, 1957), 208–9.

63. See *Strictures Addressed to James Madison on the Celebrated Report of William H. Crawford Recommending the Intermarriage of Americans with Indian Tribes* (Philadelphia: Jesper Harding, 1824).

64. Identity is both a "presentation of self" and an "understanding of others." See the essays in Hoffman, Sobel, and Teute, *Through a Glass Darkly*; Michael Zuckerman, "Fabrication of Identity in Early America," WMQ 34 (April 1977): 184–214; Elaine K. Ginsberg, ed., *Passing and the Fictions of Identity* (Durham: Duke University Press, 1996).

4. PARENTING AND PRACTICE

1. Hawkins, February 16, 1797, in *LBH*, 1:47.

2. Hawkins to Jefferson, July 11, 1803, in *LBH*, 2:455.

3. Glen to Board of Trade, October 25, 1753, PRO CO, 5/350.

4. Creek Chiefs to Mitchell, November 22, 1819, David B. Mitchell Papers, Newberry Library.

5. Stuart, *Three Years in North America*, 159. Modern scholars have repeatedly asserted that Creeks with white fathers disproportionately behaved in ways associated with colonial society. See Saunt, *New Order of Things*, 2. Various European Americans shared this perception in the eighteenth century. See Estevan Miró to Gálvez, August 1, 1784, LC, PKY; McKenney to Barbour, December 27, 1826, OIA, LS, M21, 3:274.

6. J. N. B. Hewitt, "Notes on the Creek Indians," in Smithsonian Institution, *Bureau of American Ethnology Bulletin*, no. 123, ed. J. R. Swanton (Washington DC: United States Government Printing Office, 1939), 145.

7. See also Swanton, *Early History of the Creek Indians*, 373; Swanton, "Social Organization," 346–56, 384.

8. See Brenda E. Stevenson, *Life in Black and White: Family and Community in the Slave South* (New York: Oxford University Press, 1996), 95–139.

9. Mary Griffith usually entered the historical record with the surname of one of her three husbands—Musgrove, Matthews, or Bosomworth. However, she was named Coosaponakeesa at birth and was baptized Mary Griffith. Doris Debrman Fisher, "Mary Musgrove: Creek Englishwoman" (PhD, Emory University, 1990), 51. See also George White, *Historical Collections of Georgia Containing the Most Interesting Facts, Traditions, Biographical Sketches, Anecdotes, Etc., Relating To Its History and Antiquities From Its First Settlement to the Present Time; Compiled From Original Records and Official Documents* (New York: Pudney & Russell, 1855), 21.

10. Oglethorpe to Board of Trustees, June 1, 1736, in Lane, *General Oglethorpe's Georgia*, 1:276. See December 2, 1737, in Nehemiah Curnock, ed., *The Journal of the Reverend John Wesley, A. M.*, 2 vols. (London: Robert Culley, 1955–56), 1:409; John Wesley to Dr. Bray's Associates, February 26, 1737, in *The Letters of the Rev. John Wesley, A. M.*, ed. John Telford, 8 vols. (London: Epworth Press, 1931), 1:224.

11. *Gentleman's Magazine*, August 1, 1793; George White, *Historical Collections of Georgia*, 154.

12. Caughey, *McGillivray of the Creeks*, 15.

13. Stuart to Lord Germain, October 6, 1777, in Davies, *Documents of the American Revolution*, 14:194; McGillivray to Miró, August 20, 1788, McGillivray to Benjamin James, August 10, 1792, both in LC, PKY.

14. Swan, "Position and State of Manners," 5:252.

15. Extract from the *Pennsylvania Packet and Daily Advertiser*, January 18, 1790, in Caughey, *McGillivray of the Creeks*, 278.

16. Royal Cedula, December 13, 1783, EFP, PKY, b44, e4.

17. Mitchell to Calhoun, February 3, 1818, in Carter, *Territorial Papers of the United States*, 18:244.

18. Benjamin Griffith, "Lt. David Moniac, Creek Indian, First Minority Graduate at West Point," *Alabama Historical Quarterly* 43 (Summer 1981): 104; "David Tate to Cadet David Moniac," *Alabama Historical Quarterly* 19 (Fall and Winter 1957): 407–8.

19. Woodward to Pickett, August 12, 1858, Woodward, *Reminiscences*, 73; Hawkins to William Eustis, August 27, 1809, in *LBH*, 2:566; Hawkins to Henry Dearborn, [January ? 1802], in *LBH*, 2:434; Toulmin to Claiborne, July 23, 1813, Harry Toulmin Papers, ADAH; Hawkins to Eustis, July 21, 1810, in *LBH*, 2:565–66; Driesbach to Draper, July 1, 1874, Georgia, Alabama, and South Carolina Papers, DM.

20. Harriet Turner Corbin, "A History and Genealogy of Chief William McIntosh, Jr. and his Known Descendants," 23–24 (undated typescript, Mississippi Department of Archives and History, Jackson, Mississippi).

21. John Fleming to David Green, January 23, 1836, Papers of the American Board of Commissioners for Foreign Missions, Missions on the American Continents, 1811–1919, Library of Congress.

22. William Capers to William McKendree, August 27, 1822, William McKendree Papers, Special Collections and Archives, Robert W. Woodruff Library, Emory University; *Annual Reports of the Commissioner of Indian Affairs, 1824–31* (New York: AMS Press, 1976), 26, 33; Roland Hinds, "Early Creek Missions," *Chronicles of Oklahoma* 17 (March 1939): 48–61.

23. Thomas Henderson, "Indian Education," *American Baptist Magazine* 7 (February 1827): 49; Joe R. Goss, ed., *The Choctaw Academy: Official Correspondence, 1825–1841* (Conway AR: Oldbuck Press, 1992).

24. "Extracts from Rev. Mr. Compere's Journal, sent to the Corresponding Secretary," November 5, 1826, *Baptist Missionary Magazine* 7 (May 1827): 145.

25. Joseph G. Smoot, "An Account of Alabama Indian Missions and Presbyterian Churches in 1828 from the Travel Diary of William S. Potts," *Alabama Review* 18 (April 1965): 139.

26. *Niles Weekly Register*, August 3, 1822; Capers to Calhoun, May 17, 1824, LR, CA, OIA, M234, 219:37; Crowell to Calhoun, March 18, 1824, LR, CA, OIA, M234, 219:55–76; A. Hamill to Capers, March 25, 1823, LR, CA, OIA, M234, 219:204. As a result there were few Creek mechanics. Crowell to McKenney, February 4, 1820, LR, CA, OIA, M234, 222:303–5.

27. Henry Woodward to Earl of Shaftesbury, December 31, 1774, in *Collections of the South Carolina Historical Society* (Charleston: South Carolina Historical Society, 1897), 5:446–60; Francis Baily, *Journal of a Tour in Unsettled Parts of North America in 1796 & 1797* (London: Baily Brothers, 1856), 206, 368, 370–72; Bernhard, *Travels through North America*, 2:13–30; Milfort, *Memoirs*, 29; Joseph Morgan Wilcox to his father, January 1, 1814, *Narrative of the Life and Death of Lieut. Joseph Morgan*

Wilcox, Who was Massacred by the Creek Indians, On the Alabama River, (Miss. Ter.) On the 15th of January, 1814 (Marietta GA: R. Prentise, 1816), 6; Pope, *Tour Through the Southern and Western Territories*, 46–51.

28. Louis François Benjamin Dumont de Montigny, *Mémories historiques sur la Louisiane* (Paris: Chez Cl. J. B. Bauche, 1753), 248.

29. James M. Crawford, *The Mobilian Trade Language* (Knoxville: University of Tennessee Press, 1978); Emanuel J. Dreschel, "Mobilian Jargon in Southeastern Indian Anthropology," in Bonney and Paredes, *Anthropologists and Indians in the New South*, 175–78. Pamela J. Innes argues that the use of English and Muskogee in modern Creek society "signifies an ability to work within the Anglo-American community, which is necessary if one wishes to address many of the concerns of the traditional community." See Innes, "Demonstrating That One Can Work within Two Communities: Codeswitching in Muskogee (Creek) Political Discourse," *Florida Anthropologist* 50 (December 1997): 203.

30. SN, ADAH, 54–55; John H. Moore, "Mvskoke Personal Names," *Names* 43 (September 1995): 187–212; Woodward to Pickett, June 21, 1858, in Woodward, *Reminiscences*, 59.

31. Treaty with the Creeks at the Indians Springs, February 8, 1825, ASPIA, 2:564; Creeks to John Crowell, January 25, 1825, 2:579; Creek talk, January 25, 1825, 2:579–80; Georgia Commissioners to Governor Troup, July 16, 1825, 2:820–23; Statement of Josiah Gray, an Indian half-breed, July 3, 1825, 2:837; Interview with Loney Hardridge, January 1, 1937, IPHC, 38:5163.

32. T. Frederick Davis, "Milly Francis and Duncan McKrimmon: An Authentic Florida Pocahontas," FHQ 21 (January 1943): 256; Grant Foreman, ed., *A Traveler in Indian Territory: The Journal of Ethan Allen Hitchcock, Late Major-General in the United States Army* (Cedar Rapids IA: Torch Press, 1930), 102, 105; Pickett, *History of Alabama*, 2:128. Others went by Barbary among the Creeks and Barbara in colonial society. Wright, *Creeks and Seminoles*, 81.

33. Woodward to Hooper, June 13, 1858, in Woodward, *Reminiscences*, 48.

34. Phonetic barriers continue to shape cross-cultural barriers. See Richard Doss and Allan M. Gross, "The Effects of Black English and Code-Switching on Intraracial Perceptions," *Journal of Black Psychology* 20 (August 1994): 282–93.

35. Woodward to Hooper, November 3, 1858, in Woodward, *Reminiscences*, 109–13; O'Neill to Miró, December 22, 1788, AGI 38, PKY.

36. February 21, 1797, in LBH, 1:49; Interview with Thomas Barnett, June 24, 1937, IPHC, 5:6479; Benjamin Hawkins to Thomas Pinckney, September 5, 1814, in LBH, 2:695–701; John Peacock, "The Politics of Portraiture," in *Culture and Politics in Early Stuart England*, ed. Kevin Sharpe and Peter Lake (Stanford: Stanford University Press, 1993), 99–128; Kupperman, *Indians and English*, 42–43.

37. James C. Bonner, "Journal of a Mission to Georgia in 1827," GHQ 44 (March, 1960): 81.

38. This interpretation draws on Nathaniel Scheidley, "Unruly Men: Indians,

Settlers and the Ethos of Frontier Patriarchy in the Upper Tennessee Watershed, 1763–1815" (PhD diss., Princeton University, 1999).

39. Swanton, *Indians of the Southeastern United States*, 718–29, esp. 724; Swanton, *Early History of the Creek Indians*, 373–74; Swan, "Position and State of Manners," 270; SN, 40–41, 131–33; Christopher B. Rodning, "Mortuary Ritual and Gender Ideology in Protohistoric Southwestern North Carolina," in *Archaeological Studies of Gender in the Southeastern United States*, ed. Jane M. Eastman and Christopher B. Rodning (Gainesville: University Press of Florida, 2001), 77–100.

40. George Galphin's will, April 6, 1776, in CIL, 8. See Saunt, *New Order of Things*, 168–71.

41. Other fathers transferred their property before they died. For example, see Matthews to Barnard, August 17, 1787, in Hays, "Force Transcripts."

42. Extract of a letter from Panton to Leslie, August 28, 1793, EFP, bnd. 116L9, reel 44, PKY.

43. Hawkins to Eustis, August 27, 1809, in LBH, 2:556. See also Panton to Carondelet, February 20, 1793, in Caughey, *McGillivray of the Creeks*, 354; O'Neill to Baron de Carondelet, February 17, 1793, PC, leg. 39, 1424, reel 162, PKY.

44. Laws of the Creek Nation, June 12, 1818, Mitchell Papers.

45. November 29, 1796, in LBH, 1:5; Emma Lila Fundaburk, ed., *Southeastern Indians: Life Portraits; A Catalogue of Pictures, 1564–1860* (1958; reprint, Metuchen NJ: Scarecrow Reprint, 1969), prints 140–56. John R. Swanton, "Notes on the Mental Assimilation of Races," *Journal of the Washington Academy of Sciences* 16 (1926), 495–502.

46. Jane Hill to McKenney, May 29, 1828, LR, CA, OIA, M234, 221:821–25.

47. Bernhard, *Travels through North America*, 2:27.

48. Thomas Hart Benton, *Thirty Years View; or, A History of the Working of the American Government for Thirty Years, From 1820 to 1850*, 2 vols. (New York: D. Appleton, 1854), 1:163.

49. Testimony of John M. Bach, June 30, 1825, in ASPIA, 2:837.

50. "Von Reck's Journal," in Hvidt, *Von Reck's Voyage*, 45.

51. Stuart, *Three Years in North America*, 2:161.

52. Abigail Adams to Mary Cranch, August 8, 1790, in Stewart Mitchell, ed., *New Letters of Abigail Adams, 1788–1801* (Boston: Houghton Mifflin, 1947), 57. See Timothy J. Shannon, "Dressing for Success on the Mohawk Frontier: Hendrick, William Johnson, and the Indian Fashion," WMQ 53 (January 1996): 13–42.

53. Zéspedes to Gálvez, August 16, 1784, in LC, PKY; emphasis added.

54. James Schouler, *History of the United States, Under the Constitution*, 7 vols. (New York: Dodd, Mead, 1880), 1:171–72.

55. James Mooney, "Myths of the Cherokee," *James Mooney's History, Myths, and Sacred Formulas of the Cherokees* (Asheville: Bright Mountain Books, 1992), 210.

56. Stuart, *Three Years in North America*, 2:134.

57. Seagrove to the Secretary of War [Henry Knox], November 30, 1793, in ASPIA, 1:472.

58. December 1, 1796, in LBH, 1:6; Hawkins to Elizabeth House Trist, March 4, 1797, 1:87.

59. Deposition Jonathan Fitzpatrick, October 8, 1791, in Louise Frederick Hays, "Indian Letters, 1782–1839," 17 (typescript, GDAH); February 28, 1772, in "Journal of David Taitt's Travels," 512.

60. May 27, 1798, in LBH, 1:186.

61. Efau Haujo, May 28, 1798, in LBH, 1:187; Hawkins to James McHenry, June 22, 1798, in LBH, 1:209–10.

62. Hawkins to George Wells Foster, June 22, 1798, in LBH, 2:210. See also Pickett, *History of Alabama*, 2:256.

63. Hawkins to Mitchell, November 21, 1813, in LBH, 2:663; Hawkins to John Armstrong, November 21, 1813, in LBH, 2:665; Hawkins to Crawford, in LBH, 2:768–69; Big Warrior and Little Prince to Hawkins, September 24, 1813, in CIL, 820–21; Extract of a communication from the chiefs at Coweta to Hawkins, September 16, 1813, in ASPIA, 1:853.

64. December 18, 1796, in LBH, 1:21–22.

65. Hawkins to Armstrong, September 21, 1813, in LBH, 2:655; Henry S. Hallbert and Timothy Horton Ball, *The Creek War of 1813 and 1814* (Chicago: Donohue & Henneberry, 1895), 164–66.

5. IN TWO WORLDS

1. *Niles Weekly Register*, August 16, 1817.

2. Several scholars have alluded to the prevalence of children of intermarriages who served as interpreters and go-betweens. See William C. Sturtevant, "Commentary," in *Eighteenth-Century Florida and Its Borderlands*, ed. Samuel Proctor (Gainesville: University Press of Florida, 1975), 44; Braund, *Deerskins and Duffels*, 41; David H. Corkran, *The Creek Frontier, 1540–1783* (Norman: University of Oklahoma Press, 1967), 124–25; 219, 226–27.

3. For recent treatments of Coosaponakeesa, see Fisher, "Mary Musgrove"; Gillespie, "Sexual Politics of Race and Gender," 187–201; Green, "Mary Musgrove," 29–47.

4. "Oglethorpe's Treaty with the Lower Creek Indians," GHQ 4 (March 1920): 3–16; A Young Gentleman, "A New Voyage to Georgia," in *Collections of Georgia Historical Society* (Savannah: Savannah Morning News Print, 1904), 2:52.

5. Gillespie, "Sexual Politics of Race and Gender," 196.

6. Christie to Oglethorpe, December 14, 1734, in Lane, *General Oglethorpe's Georgia*, 1:68. See also John Musgrove to Oglethorpe, January 24, 1735, in Lane, *General Oglethorpe's Georgia*, 1:115; Quincy to Gordon, March 3, 1735, in Lane, *General Oglethorpe's Georgia*, 1:129–30; Causton to Oglethorpe, March 24, 1735, in Lane, *General Oglethorpe's Georgia*, 1:140; Causton to the Board of Trustees, January 16,

1735, in CRG, 30:172–76; Pat Tailfer, *A True and Historical Narrative of the Colony of Georgia*, ed. Clarence L. Ver Steeg (Athens: University of Georgia Press, 1960), 57.

7. Coulter, *Journal of William Stephens*, 123 n.

8. September 10, 1752, in "A Journal of a Mission to the Lower Creeks at Coweta Town, by Thomas Bosomworth, 1752," ed. Louise Frederick Hays (typescript, GDAH), 4.

9. July 21, 1744, July 22, 1744, and August 20, 1744, in Coulter, *Journal of William Stephens*, 127–28, 136.

10. Statement of the officers of Oglethorpe's regiment and the principal inhabitants of Frederica about the character and importance of Mary Musgrove, December 17, 1744, in CRG, 27:17.

11. John Pitts Corry, "Some New Lights on the Bosomworth Claims," GHQ 25 (September 1941): 195–224; Fisher, "Mary Musgrove," 226.

12. Harman Verelst to Stephens, July 25, 1746, in CRG, 31:44; Proposal of Thomas Bosomworth, to Lieutenant Governor Henry Ellis, October 31, 1757, PRO CO, 5/646; Benjamin Martyn to Stephens, November 1, 1745, in CRG, 31:29; Martyn to Richard Nevil Aldwortth, January 10, 1750, in CRG, 31:182.

13. Braund, *Deerskins and Duffels*, 78–79; Wright, *Creeks and Seminoles*, 146.

14. Seagrove to Irwin, April 18, 1796, in CIL, 477. See also White Lieutenant to Seagrove, June 23, 1793, in ASPIA, 1:401.

15. Statement of Creek Chiefs, May 14, 1825, LR, OIA, M234, 219:1099–1100. See Forrester to Stuart, September 18, 1768, PRO CO 5/70; Stuart to Earl of Hillsborough, April 27, 1771, 5/72; Mico Lucko to Stuart, April 19, 1772, 5/73; Stuart to Gage, November 1, 1766, Gage Papers, American Series.

16. Treaty signed by Tustunnuggee Thlucco, Speaker of the Nation, Upper Creeks and a number of other Chiefs, August 9, 1814, in ASPIA, 1:837–38.

17. Hawkins to Cornells, March 8, 1798, in LBH, 1:180; Tustunnuggee Hopuie and Little Prince to John Floyd, January 5, 1814, Floyd-McAdoo Family Papers, Library of Congress.

18. Hawkins to Armstrong, April 26, 1813, in ASPIA, 1:841.

19. Floyd to Pinckney, January 27, 1814, in *Raleigh Register*, February 11, 1814.

20. Lord Loudoun, Queries to the Governors, [April] 1756, Lord Loudoun Papers, HL; "At a Meeting of the Honorable the Members of His Majesty's Council, at Pensacola," November 22, 1766, in *The Minutes, Journal and Acts of the General Assembly of British West Florida*, ed. Robert R. Rea and Milo B. Howard Jr. (University: University of Alabama Press, 1979), 16; Zéspedes to Juan Ignacio de Urriza, September 16, 1784, in LC, PKY; Navarro to Galvez, April 15, 1786, in LC, PKY; Galvez to Intendent of Louisiana, March 18, 1782, Ayer Collection, Newberry Library; McKenney to Brearley, May 23, 1825, LS, OIA, M21, 3:84–85.

21. McKenney to Barbour, November 12, 1825, LS, OIA, M21, 2:228–31. See Abstract of a Letter from George Munro Traders in the Creek Nation, May 31, 1769, PRO CO 5/70.

22. Stuart to Hillsborough, September 15, 1768, PRO CO 5/69. Stuart repeatedly relied on bilingual traders to obtain intimate information about the inner workings of Creek villages. These spies often provided compromising information. See Stuart to Gage, June 2, 1763, Gage Papers, American Series.

23. Betton to McKenney, November 4, 1827, LR, OIA, M234, 221:96–101.

24. Warren Jourdan and W. Williamson to Gaines, July 1, 1825, LR, OIA, M234, 219:456; Creek Talk, March 15, 1817, WD, LR, M271, 2:61–64.

25. Seagrove to Henry Knox, May 24, 1792, in *ASPIA*, 1:296. See Taitt to Stuart, July, 7, 1776, in Davies, *Documents of the American Revolution*, 12:160; "Journal of an Expedition against the Rebels on the Frontiers of East Florida," July 11, 1778, PRO CO, 5/80; *Georgia Gazette*, February 2, 1774; Barnard to Seagrove, May 10, 1792, in *ASPIA*, 1:297; Seagrove to Fine Bones, Chief of Broken Arrow, November 20, 1793, in *ASPIA*, 1:376; Barnard to Matthews, June 8, 1787, Barnard to [?], August 1, 1787, Barnard to [?], July 2, 1790, Telemon Cuyler Collection, UGA; Hawkins to William Faulkener, November 25, 1797, in *LBH*, 1:161.

26. Hawkins to Lewis, February 16, 1814, Pickett Manuscripts, ADAH; Andrew Ellicott, *The Journal of Andrew Ellicott: Late Commissioner on Behalf of the United States . . . for Determining the Boundary Between the United States and the Possessions of His Catholic Majesty* (1803; reprint, Chicago: Quadrangle Books, 1962), 213; Hawkins to Armstrong, March 1, 1813, in *ASPIA*, 1:838.

27. Efau Haujo to Hawkins, June 29, 1802, in *ASPIA*, 1:681; A Talk from the head men of the buzzard roust and Cussetas to the Governor of Georgia, May 1, 1787, in CIL, 155.

28. February 21, 1797, in *LBH*, 1:49; Interview with Thomas Barnett, June 24, 1937, IPHC, 5:6479; Hawkins to Pinckney, September 5, 1814, in *LBH*, 2:695–701.

29. Efau Haujo to Hawkins, June 29, 1802, in *ASPIA*, 1:681.

30. Mitchell to Gaines, February 23, 1818, David B, Mitchell Papers, Newberry Library. See James C. Bonner, "Tustunugee Hutkee and Creek Factionalism on the Georgia-Alabama Frontier," *Alabama Review* 10 (April 1957): 124.

31. January 26, 1797, in *LBH*, 1:39. See Hawkins to Hopkins, March 17, 1799, in *LBH*, 1:242–43; Hawkins to Dearborn, January 23, 1807, in *LBH*, 2:511–12; Hawkins to Crawford, January 19, 1816, in *LBH*, 2:768–69; Hawkins to Pinckney, September 5, 1814, in *LBH*, 2:695–701; Hawkins to Jackson, August 6, 1814, in *LBH*, 2:690–91; November 24, 1796, to January 10, 1797, in *LBH*, 1:1–36.

32. Roderick McIntosh to Stuart, February, 2, 1768, Gage Papers, American Series.

33. Stuart, *Three Years in North America*, 2:135.

34. December 14, 1796, in *LBH*, 1:18; December 11, 1796, in *LBH*, 1:15.

35. Alexander Miln to Governor William Henry Lyttleton, February 24, 1760, in McDowell, *Documents Relating to Indian Affairs*, 2:498. Officials also used the term "gentlemen" to indicate the acceptable status of informants. See Col. Gage to Taylor, December 29, 1767, Gage Papers, American Series.

36. Paternal identities did not soothe all fears. See Gaines to Brown, January 31, 1829, in ASPMA, 4:130; Loomis, *Scenes in the Indian Country*, 199–200.

37. Milledge to Mitchell, April 25, 1804, GLB, GDAH.

38. Hawkins to Ellicott, April 5, 1799, in LBH, 1:243.

39. Hawkins to Hopkins, April 5, 1799, in LBH, 1:242.

40. Cornell to Seagrove, January 6, 1793, in ASPIA, 1:375.

41. Seagrove to Cornell, February 20, 1793, in ASPIA, 1:375.

42. Cowkeeper, for example, repeatedly relied on English traders to pass information on to British officials. See Major Francis Ogilvie to Gage, July 20, 1764, in Gage Papers, American Series.

43. Hawkins to Dearborn, April 20, 1805, in LBH, 1:492.

44. December 7, 1796, in LBH, 1:12.

45. Mauelshagen and Davis, *Partners in the Lord's Work*, 41–47, 71–74.

46. Hernando de Soto to the Justice and Board of Magistrates in Santiago de Cuba, July 9, 1539, in Bourne, *Narratives of Hernando de Soto*, 2:162.

47. Mauelshagen and Davis, *Partners in the Lord's Work*, 30, 47–48.

48. Jane Lyon (Compere) Pipkin, "E. L. Compere, Border Missionary," (typescript, Southern Baptist Historical Library and Archives, Nashville), 13.

49. William Sparks, *Memories of Fifty Years: Containing Brief Biographical Notices of Distinguished Americans, and Anecdotes of Remarkable Men* (Philadelphia: Claxton, Remsen & Haffelfinger, 1872), 478.

50. October 29, 1826, in "Extracts from Rev. Mr. Compere's Journal, sent to the Corresponding Secretary," *Baptist Missionary Magazine* 7 (May 1827): 145.

51. Compere to Pickett, April 6, 1848, Pickett Manuscripts, ADAH.

52. "Mission to the Creeks," *Baptist Missionary Magazine* 12 (June 1833): 183; January 21, 1827, "Extracts from Mr. Compere's Journal," *Baptist Missionary Magazine* 7 (June 1827): 181–83; October 28, 1826, "Extracts from Rev. Mr. Compere's Journal, sent to the Corresponding Secretary," *Baptist Missionary Magazine* 7 (May 1827): 144.

53. Compere to Corresponding Secretary, September 21, 1826, *Baptist Missionary Magazine* 7 (March 1827): 85–86. See also Smoot, "Account of Alabama Indian Missions," 142–43; January 21, 1827, "Extracts from Mr. Compere's Journal," *Baptist Missionary Magazine* 7 (June 1827): 181.

54. Compere to Corresponding Secretary, September 21, 1826, *Baptist Missionary Magazine* 7 (March 1827): 86.

55. February 18, 1827, "Extracts from Mr. Compere's Journal," *Baptist Missionary Magazine*, 7 (June 1827): 182. See Miscellaneous Writings, Henry Sale Halbert Papers, ADAH.

56. February 25, 1827, "Extracts from Mr. Compere's Journal," *Baptist Missionary Magazine* 7 (June 1827): 182–83; "Mission to the Creeks," *Baptist Missionary Magazine* 12 (June 1833): 183–84.

57. Simms, "Broken Arrow," 111; Benton, *Thirty Years View*, 163.

58. Hodgson to [?], April 3, 1820, in Hodgson, *Letters from North Ameri5ca*, 1:127; Testimony of James Moss, June 28, 1825, in U.S. Congress, *Report and Resolutions of the Legislature of Georgia with Accompanying Documents*, 19th Cong., 2nd sess., 1825, H. Doc. 59.

59. Board of Commissioners for Indian Affairs to Telfair, November 8, 1786, William Bacon Stevens Papers, GHS; McGillivray to Benjamin James, August 10, 1792, AGI, PKY, C:205; O'Neill to Ezpeleta, October 19, 1783, C:36; Milfort, *Memoirs*, 30–31, 61, 71.

60. William M. Willett, *A Narrative of The Military Actions of Colonel Marinus Willett, Taken Chiefly From His Own Manuscript* (New York: G. & C. & H. Carvill, 1831), 101, 103–5; Pope, *Tour Through the Southern and Western Territories*, 46–51; Margaret Hunter Hall, *The Aristocratic Journey: Being the Outspoken Letters of Mrs. Basil Hall Written during a Fourteen Months' Sojourn in America, 1827–1828*, ed. Una Pope-Hennessey (New York: Putnam, 1931), 240; James C. Bonner, "Journal of a Mission to Georgia in 1827," *GHQ* 44 (March 1960): 74–85; William B. Hesseltine and Larry Gara, "Across Georgia and into Alabama, 1817–1818," *GHQ* 37 (December 1953): 334; Bernhard, *Travels through North America*, 2:13–30; "Journal of David Taitt's Travels," 507; George Gilmer, *Sketches of Some of the First Settlers of Upper Georgia, of the Cherokees, and the Author* (Americus GA: Americus Book, 1926), 264–65.

61. Gregory A. Waselkov and Kathryn E. Holland Braund, eds., *William Bartram and the Southeastern Indians* (Lincoln: University of Nebraska Press, 1995), 42, 45–46, 49–51, 55–63, 65, 69, 71–74, 97–100, 122.

62. Dearborn to Hawkins, February 11, 1804, in Carter, *Territorial Papers of the United States*, 5:306–7.

63. Hodgson to [?], March 24, 1820 in Hodgson, *Letters from North America*, 2:118–19. See Lorenzo Dow, *History of Cosmopolite; or, the Writings of Rev. Lorenzo Dow: Containing His Experiences and Travels, in Europe and America, up to Near his Fiftieth Year* (Cincinnati: H. M. Rulison, 1856), 162–63, 222; Samuel Wilson Jr., ed., *Southern Travels: Journal of John H. B. Latrobe, 1834* (New Orleans: Historic New Orleans Collection, 1986), 97.

64. *Niles Weekly Register*, October 2, 1813.

65. Hodgson to [?], March 24, 1820, in Hodgson, *Letters from North America*, 2:123.

6. TUSTUNNUGGEE HUTKEE AND THE LIMITS OF DUAL IDENTITIES

1. Affidavit of Harris Allen and Francis Flournoy, May 16, 1825, in "The Murder of General William McIntosh, Treaties of Indian Springs 1821–1825, also Report of Joseph Vallance Bevan, Letters, Treaties, Executive Reports, and the Trial of John Crowell," ed. Louise Frederick Hays (typescript, GDAH). See also the *Missionary* (Mount Zion GA), May 9, 1825; *Missionary*, May 16, 1825; *Niles Weekly Register*, May 28, 1825; George M. Troup to Joseph Marshall, May 3, 1825, in *ASPIA*, 2:767–68.

2. Diary entry for May 15, 1825, in Charles Francis Adams, ed., *Memoirs of John*

Quincy Adams, Comprising Portions of His Diary from 1795 to 1848, 12 vols. (Philadelphia: J. B. Lippincott, 1874–77), 7:5.

3. *Niles Weekly Register*, May 28, 1825.

4. Treaty with the Creeks at the Indians Springs, February 28, 1825, in ASPIA, 2:563–64; McKenney to Adams, June 23, 1825, OIA, LS, M21, 2:59–61; Duncan Campbell to Calhoun, January 8, 1825, in ASPIA, 2:575–76; Troup to Senators and Representatives in Congress from Georgia, February 17, 1825, in ASPIA, 2:756; "At a general meeting of the Indians friendly to General McIntosh, and who feel themselves aggrieved of the injuries done by the Indians inimical to the late treaty held at the Indian Springs, the following address was unanimously agreed to, and for the same to be published in the Georgia Messenger and one of the Milledgeville papers," May 17, 1825, in ASPIA, 2:772–73; *Niles Weekly Register*, May 28, August 6, August 13, 1825; Samuel Hawkins to George M. Troup, April 12, 1825, in ASPIA, 2:766; George M. Troup, Report on the Commissioners, July, 26, 1825, GLB, GDAH; Governor's Message [George M. Troup], November 7, 1826, "Report and Resolutions of the Legislature of Georgia with Accompanying Documents," *House Documents* 59 (19–2); William Blount to Joseph M. White, December 10, 1827, OIA, LR, M234, 2:316–20.

5. This interpretation was repeated by several scholars. The flaws of this interpretation should be apparent. For example, see Woodward to Pickett, April 25, 1858, in Woodward, *Reminiscences*, 45.

6. Address to Creek Indians, May 17, 1825, in ASPIA, 2:772–73. A good description of reciprocity can be found in Martin, *Sacred Revolt*, 27–29.

7. Michael D. Green, *The Politics of Indian Removal: Creek Government and Society in Crisis* (Lincoln: University of Nebraska Press, 1982), 96.

8. The most explicit statement that the children of intermarriages were not true Indians comes from Jean and Joyotpaul Chaudhuri. They have recently asserted that McIntosh and other "mixed-bloods" often served in "double-agent roles between the Creeks and the English" and helped the Americans in their "divide-and-conquer" ambitions. See Chaudhuri and Chaudhuri, *Sacred Path*, 141, 143–48.

9. Griffith, *McIntosh and Weatherford*, 3–5, 11; Creek Chiefs to Mitchell, November 21, November 22, 1819, David Mitchell Papers. For a close reading and explanation of the rise of a Seminole leader, see Susan A. Miller, *Coacoochee's Bones: A Seminole Saga* (Lawrence: University Press of Kansas, 2003).

10. Not surprisingly McIntosh's maternal uncles were three of the greatest beneficiaries of his efforts and his most consistent supporters. See Abstract of Payments made by D. B. Mitchell, Indian agent, to a brigade of Creek warriors, commanded by General McIntosh, and called into the service of the United States in 1818, [?], in ASPMA, 2:109; Extract from the convention between the Creek and Cherokee nations of Indians, December 11, 1821, ASPIA, 2:741.

11. Henry DeLeon Southerland Jr. and Jerry Elijah Brown, *The Federal Road through Georgia, the Creek Nation, and Alabama, 1806–1836* (Tuscaloosa: University of Alabama Press, 1989), 126; Simms, "Broken Arrow," 113.

12. *Niles Weekly Register*, November 7, 1818.

13. Thomas L. McKenney and James Hall, *History of the Indian Tribes of North America with Biographical Sketches and Anecdotes of the Principal Chiefs* (Philadelphia: Frederick W. Greenough, 1838), 133.

14. Barbour to Chilly McIntosh, Inter lefty McIntosh, Bru. Doulazau and Jim Doulozou, May 17, 1825, OIA, M21, 2:14; Saunt, *New Order of Things*, 139–232.

15. Woodward, *Reminiscences*, 55. See also Southerland and Brown, *Federal Road through Georgia*, 124; John H. Goff, "The Path to Oakfuskee Upper Trading Route in Georgia to the Creek Indians," GHQ 39 (March 1955): 24; Antonio Waring to James C. Bonner, February 3, 1818, Antonio J. Waring Jr. Papers, GHS; Mitchell to Calhoun, February 3, 1818, in Carter, *Territorial Papers of the United States*, 18:244; *Niles Weekly Register*, May 21, 1825, June 26, 1824, December 7, 1816, August 31, 1816.

16. Mauelshagen and Davis, *Partners in the Lord's Work*, 73–74.

17. Baily, *Journal of a Tour*, 371.

18. Adam Hodgson to [?], April 3, 1820, in Hodgson, *Letters from North America*, 2:127–29. See Benjamin W. Griffith, *McIntosh and Weatherford: Creek Indian Leaders* (Tuscaloosa: University of Alabama Press, 1988), 230.

19. Thomas Flournoy to Mitchell, September 18, 1820, Andrew Pickens Papers, HL. See McKenney to Barbour, January 5, 1826, OIA, M21, 2:345–49, esp. 346.

20. McKenney and Hall, *History of the Indian Tribes*, 19.

21. William Gilmore Simms to the City Gazette, March 31, 1831, in Simms, *The Letters of William Gilmore Simms*, ed. Mary C. Simms Oliphant, Alfred Taylor Odell, and T. C. Duncan Eaves, 6 vols. (Columbia: University of South Carolina Press, 1952–82), 27.

22. Stuart, *Three Years in North America*, 2:134.

23. Cummins, *Summary Geography of Alabama*, 23–24.

24. Griffith, *McIntosh and Weatherford*, 87; James C. Bonner, "William McIntosh," in *Georgians in Profile: Historical Essays in Honor of Ellis Merton Coulter*, ed. Horace Montgomery (Athens: University of Georgia Press, 1958), 114–43.

25. Troup to the President, May 3, 1825, GLB, GDAH.

26. Absalom H. Chappell, *Miscellanies of Georgia: Historical, Biographical, Descriptive, &c.* 3 parts (Columbus GA: Gilbert Printing, 1928), 3:24; Warrick Lane Jones, "A Lettered Portrait of William McIntosh: Leader of the Creek Nation," *Chronicles of Oklahoma* 74 (Spring 1996): 77; Green, *Politics of Indian Removal*, 63–66.

27. Lawson, *New Voyage to Carolina*, 46, 190; Martin, *Sacred Revolt*, 77.

28. Alexander Ware to George M. Troup, May 19, 1825, in Hays, "Murder of General William McIntosh."

29. Address to the King of England from the Indians, August 15, 1818, in ASPFA, 4:552–53; Creeks to John Crowell, January 25, 1825, in ASPIA, 2:579; Troup to Honorable Senators and Representatives in Congress from Georgia, February 17, 1825, GLB, GDAH.

30. Creek Talk, January 25, 1825, in *ASPIA*, 2:579.

31. Jackson to Pinckney, March 28, 1814, in *Niles Weekly Register*, April 23, 1814.

32. McIntosh to Georgia Legislature, April 12, 1825, in *ASPIA*, 2:757.

33. Jackson to Crawford, June 10, 1816, in *ASPIA*, 2:110–11.

34. *Niles Weekly Register*, July 27, August 31, 1816. See also Robert Butler to Daniel Parker, May 3, 1818, in *ASPIA*, 1:704; Hawkins to Mitchell, August 12, 1813, PLP, reel 19; *Niles Weekly Register*, June 13, 1818; E. Merton Coulter, "The Chehaw Affair," GHQ 49 (December 1965): 369–95.

35. Hawkins to Dearborn, July 23, 1807, in *LBH*, 2:522; Hallbert and Ball, *Creek War of 1813 and 1814*, 92–93. For a detailed discussion of the sustained opposition to McIntosh, see Green, *Politics of Indian Removal*, 69–97.

36. Treaty of Fort Jackson, in Kappler, *Indian Treaties*, 2:109.

37. Hawkins to Dearborn, November 24, 1805, in *LBH*, 2:500–501; Hawkins to Dearborn, February 24, 1807, in *LBH*, 2:513–14.

38. Hawkins to Tustunnuggee Thlucco, Alexander Cornells, and McIntosh, April 24, 1813, in *LBH*, 2:636; Hawkins to Pinckney, September 5, 1814, in *LBH*, 2:695; *Niles Weekly Register*, May 20, 1815.

39. U.S. Congress, *Report of the Select Committee of the House of Representatives*, report no. 98, 19th Congress, 2nd sess., March 3, 1827, 416.

40. Creek Agency Records, Accounts 1817–18, Mitchell Papers.

41. Jackson to Mitchell, July 8, 1818, PLP, PKY, Reel 21.

42. Treaty with the Creeks, in Kappler, *Indian Treaties*, 1:155–56.

43. *ASPMA*, 2:109, 119; Troops Raised Without the Consent of Congress, February 28, 1820, in *ASPIA*, 2:92–132; Abstract of Payments made by D. B. Mitchell, Indian agent, to a brigade of Creek warriors, commanded by General McIntosh, and called into the service of the United States in 1818, in *ASPIA*, 2:109; Payroll of the general, field, and staff officers of General William McIntosh's brigade of Creek Warriors, lately in the service of the United States, January 14, 1820, in *ASPIA*, 2:109; Mitchell to McIntosh, October 27, 1819, in Meriwether, *Papers of John C. Calhoun*, 4:387–88.

44. Kappler, *Indian Treaties*, 2:215.

45. Samuel Hawkins to Troup, April 12, 1825, in *ASPIA*, 2:766.

46. John Crowell to Calhoun, August 21, 1823, Waring Papers.

47. Troup to McIntosh, March 29, April 4, 1825, GLB, GDAH; "Extract from the convention between the Creek and Cherokee nations of Indians, held December 11, 1821, on the subject of their boundary," in *ASPIA*, 2:741; *Niles Weekly Register*, December 7, 1816.

48. Hodgson, *Letters from North America*, 129.

49. Interview between the Secretary & the McIntosh Party, December 10, 1825, OIA, LS, M21, 2:288–92.

50. Thomas Crowell to Barbour, February 13, 1825, in Hays, "Murder of General William McIntosh," GDAH.

51. Little Prince and others [a declaration], August 24, 1826, Creek Indian Manuscripts, UGA.

52. O'Donnell, "Alexander McGillivray: Training for Leadership," 172–86; Green, "Alexander McGillivray," 41–63; Albert James Pickett, "McGillivray and the Creeks," *Alabama Historical Quarterly* 1 (Summer 1930): 126–48; Caughey, *McGillivray of the Creeks*, 3–57.

53. Elisha P. Douglass, "The Adventurer Bowles," WMQ 6 (January 1949): 3–23; Lyle N. McAlister, "The Marine Forces of William Augustus Bowles and His State of Muscogee," FHQ 32 (July 1953): 3–27; Lyle N. McAlister, "William Augustus Bowles and the State of Muskogee," FHQ 40 (April 1962): 317–28; Wright, *William Augustus Bowles*.

7. THE INSISTENCE OF RACE

1. Abstract of a letter from David Taitt, September 21, 1772, PRO CO, 5/74.

2. Affidavit of James Maxwell, June 12, 1751, in McDowell, *Documents Relating to Indian Affairs*, 2:70. See also Capt. Jenkins to Gage, May 16, 1767, Gage Papers, American Series; "Journal of David Taitt's Travels." 504–5, 512, 514, 568; Affidavit of James Maxwell, June 12, 1751, in McDowell, *Documents Relating to Indian Affairs*, 2:70; Abstract of a letter from David Taitt, September 21, 1772, PRO CO, 5/74. The term was more frequently used to describe African women. For a more detailed treatment of the use of the term *wenches* to describe female Native Americans and African Americans, see Kathleen M. Brown, *Good Wives, Nasty Wenches & Anxious Patriarchs: Gender, Race, and Power in Colonial Virginia* (Chapel Hill: University of North Carolina Press, 1996).

3. Luis de Unzaga to O'Neill, January 22, 1783, AGI, PC, Leg 1336, PKY.

4. Henry Ellis to the Board of Trade, September 5, 1760, in CGR, 28, part 1:286–87. See also Adair, *Adair's History of the American Indians*, 278–79; *South Carolina Gazette*, June 14, 1760.

5. Tonyn to Taitt, [?] 1776, Davies, *Documents of the American Revolution*, 12:108–9.

6. Lewis Cass, [circa 1815], Regulation of Indian Affairs, Ayer Collection, Newberry Library.

7. Samuel Moniac, Deposition 1813, Halbert Papers.

8. *Niles Weekly Register*, July 8, 1819.

9. Gilbert Russell to Secretary of State James Monroe, July 9, 1815, in Carter, *Territorial Papers of the United States*, 6:540. See Treaty of Fort Jackson, 1814, in Kappler, *Indian Treaties*, 107–10.

10. April 9, 1816, *Annals of the Congress of the United States*, 14th Cong., 1st sess. (Washington DC: Gales and Seaton, 1854), 1806–7.

11. Petition to Congress by Citizens on Mobile and Tombigbee Rivers, January 17, 1817, in Carter, *Territorial Papers of the United States*, 6:752.

12. *Journal of the House of Representatives of the United States, at the second session of the Fourteenth Congress . . . Washington City*, (Washington: William A.

Davis, 1816 [1817]), 216; see also *Annals of the Congress of the United States*, 14th Cong., 1st sess. (Washington DC: Gales and Seaton, 1854), 342, 353, 362, 1357, 1366, 1380; *Annals of the Congress of the United States*, 14th Cong., 2nd sess. (Washington DC: Gales and Seaton, 1854), 202, 203, 215, 406, 769, 1053, 1058, 1065; Richard S. Lackey, ed., *Frontier Claims in the Lower South* (New Orleans: Polyanthos, 1977), 26–29, quote on 29; see also various other claims, esp. 49, 51–52, 62.

13. Address to King from Creeks, August 15, 1818, in ASPFR, 5:552–53.

14. Hawkins to Crawford, January 19, 1816, WD, LR, M271, 1:1100–1107.

15. Dearborn to Hawkins, January 24, 1803, WD, LS, M15, A:306–8.

16. White Lieutenant to Seagrove, June 23, 1793, ASPIA, 1:401. See [?] to Galphin, October 16, 1772, Habersham Papers, GHS.

17. Crowell to Calhoun, April 6, 1824, OIA, CA, LR, M234, 219:78–79.

18. Crowell to Calhoun, November 23, 1824, OIA, CA, LR, M234, 219:123–26.

19. Crowell to Calhoun, November 23, 1824, OIA, CA, LR, M234, 219:123–26.

20. Cuyler to Crowell, July 14, 1825, Waring Papers; Thomas McKenney to Crowell, December 10, 1824, OIA, LS, M21, 1:261.

21. David H. White, "The Indian Policy of Juan Vicente Folch, Governor of Spanish Mobile, 1787–1792," *Alabama Review* 28 (October 1975): 260–75.

22. McGillivray to Juan Vicente Folch, May 14, 1789, in Caughey, *McGillivray of the Creeks*, 231–32; Folch to McGillivray, June 14, 1789, in Caughey, *McGillivray of the Creeks*, 237–38.

23. Michael D. Green explains that the acquittal likely resulted from "the influence and popularity of the two star witnesses, David B. Mitchell and William McIntosh." Green, *Politics of Indian Removal*, 62.

24. Law of McIntosh in 1818, June 12, 1818, Mitchell Papers.

25. Thus when "the Jackson administration made total Indian removal a national policy," historian Edward Countryman writes, "they accepted that Indians could remain as individuals on white terms." Countryman and other scholars, however, presume that this was an unexplored option; it was optimistic rhetoric rather than reality. Edward Countryman, "Indians, the Colonial Order, and the Social Significance of the American Revolution," WMQ 53 (April 1995): 357.

26. Jackson to the Creek Indians, March 23, 1829, OIA, LS, M21, 5:373–75. See also John Eaton to the Creek Indians west of the Mississippi, August 3, 1829, OIA, LS, M21, 6:61–64.

27. J. Terhune to Wilson Lumpkin, October 23, 1833, in Hays, "Indian Letters," 247. For examples of scholars who have expressed doubt as to the ability of reality to match the rhetoric of assimilation, see Wright, *Creeks and Seminoles*, 231; Mary Elizabeth Young, *Redskins, Ruffleshirts, and Rednecks: Indian Allotments in Alabama and Mississippi, 1830–1860* (Norman: University of Oklahoma Press, 1961), 38–39, 73–74.

28. McKenney to Barbour, November 29, 1827, OIA, LS, M21 4:153–57.

29. Driesbach to Draper, July 1, 1874, Georgia, Alabama, and South Carolina

Papers, DM; J. F. H. Claiborne, *Life and Times of Gen. Sam Dale, the Mississippi Partisan* (New York: Harper and Brothers, 1860), 128–29; J. Anthony Paredes, "Federal Recognition of the Poarch Creek," in *Indians of the Southeastern United States in the Late 20th Century*, ed. J. Anthony Paredes (Tuscaloosa: University of Alabama Press, 1992), 120–21.

30. J. M. Wilcox to his father, January 1, 1814, in *Narrative of the Life and Death of Lieut. Joseph Morgan Wilcox, Who was Massacred by the Creek Indians, On the Alabama River, (Miss. Ter.) On the 15th of January, 1814* (Marietta GA: R. Prentise, 1816), 6.

31. Hawkins to Mitchell, August 17, 1813, in *LBH*, 2:655–56; Jackson to David Holmes, April 18, 1814, in Bassett, *Correspondence of Andrew Jackson*, 1:504–5; *Niles Weekly Register*, May 21, 1814; Braund, "Creek Indians, Blacks and Slavery," 636.

32. Daniel Beasley to Ferdinand L. Claiborne, August 14, 1813, in "Letters Relating to the Tragedy of Fort Mims: August–September, 1813," ed. James F. Doster, *Alabama Review* 14 (October 1959): 275.

33. Marquis James, *Andrew Jackson: The Border Captain* (Indianapolis IN: Bobbs-Merrill, 1933), 183.

34. Woodward to Pickett, April 25, 1858, in Woodward, *Reminiscences*, 43.

35. Anne Royall to Matt [?], December 15, 1815, in Anne Royall, *Letters from Alabama, 1817–1822* (University: University of Alabama Press, 1930), 91–92. See Jackson to Willie Blount Bassett, April 18, 1814, in Bassett, *Correspondence of Andrew Jackson*, 1:503; Jackson to Holmes, April 18, 1814, in Bassett, *Correspondence of Andrew Jackson*, 1:504.

36. *Niles Weekly Register*, May 21, 1814.

37. Claiborne, *Life and Times of Gen. Sam Dale*, 129; see Woodward to Hooper, October 20, 1858, in Woodward, *Reminiscences*, 83.

38. Woodward to Hooper, October 31, 1858, in Woodward, *Reminiscences*, 96. Also see Pickett, *History of Alabama*, 267–68; Driesbach to Lyman Draper, July [?], 1874, Georgia, Alabama, and South Carolina Papers, DM.

39. March 16, 1824, *Mobile Commercial Register*.

40. Gillespie, "Sexual Politics of Race and Gender," 187–201; Winthrop Jordan, *White over Black: American Attitudes toward the Negro: 1550–1812* (New York: W. W. Norton, 1969), 90–91, 162.

41. Wright, *Creeks and Seminoles*, 75, 121, 170, 187, 274, 287; Martin, *Sacred Revolt*, 118, Woodward, *Reminiscences*; Littlefield, *Africans and Creeks*, 94.

42. Woodward to Hooper, December 20, 1858, in Woodward, *Reminiscences*, 153–62, esp. 160.

43. Wright, *Creeks and Seminoles*, 61, 75.

44. SN, ADAH, 1, 6, 35; emphasis added.

45. SN, ADAH, 42, 75.

46. Pickett, *History of Alabama*, 87; Peter A. Brannon, "Tukacahchi Sons-In-Law:

White Men Noted in Early Record Who Had Indian Wives," *Arrow Points* 3 (May 1929): 43.

47. Smoot, "Account of Alabama Indian Missions," 140. See also Littlefield, *Africans and Creeks*, 85–86; Jane E. Hill to McKenney, May 29, 1828, OIA, LR, M234, 221:84; Andrew Hamill to Peter B. Porter, September 12, 1828, 221:815; Brearley to Porter, June 27, 1828, 236:25.

48. Marion Elias Lazenby, *History of Methodism in Alabama and West Florida: Bring an Account of the Amazing March of Methodism through Alabama and West Florida* ([Nashville?], 1960), 171–72; Anson West, *A History of Methodism in Alabama* (Spartanburg SC: Reprint Company, 1983) 376.

49. Driesbach to Draper, July [?], 1874, DM. See also Daniel F. Littlefield Jr., *Seminole Burning: A Story of Racial Violence* (Jackson: University Press of Mississippi, 1996), 20–32; Angie Debo, *The Road to Disappearance: A History of the Creek Indians* (Norman: University of Oklahoma Press, 1941), 265–66, 369–73; William W. Quinn Jr., "The Southeast Syndrome: Notes on Indian Descendant Recruitment Organizations and Their Perceptions of Native American Culture," *American Indian Quarterly* 14 (Spring 1990): 147–54.

50. James B. Sellers, *The First Methodist Church of Tuscaloosa, Alabama* (Tuscaloosa: Weatherford Printing, 1968), 73.

51. Interview with Thomas Barnnett, June 24, 1937, IPHC, 5:6479; Interview with Jasper Bell, August 3, 1937, IPHC 7:7077; Interview with Alec. Berryhill, May 12, 1937, IPHC 7:5876; Interview with Timmie Fife, February 28, 1938, IPHC 30:13104; Interview with Lee Hawkins, August 4, 1937, IPHC 40:7427; Interview with Sam J. Haynes, February 18, 1939, IPHC 40:12992.

52. Charles M. Hudson, *Southeastern Indians* (Knoxville: University of Tennessee Press, 1976), 460–61; Wright, *Creeks and Seminoles*, 221–43, 284–88; Eakins, "Some Information Respecting the Creeks," 1:265–83.

53. *Niles Weekly Register*, May 21, 1825; Chilly McIntosh, Intullasky McIntosh, Ben Daulawza and Jim Daulawza to James Barbour, May 17, 1825, in *Niles Weekly Register*, July 16, 1825; *Niles Weekly Register*, September 20, 1828; December 9, 1825, in Adams, *Memoirs of John Quincy Adams*, 7:76; Chilly McIntosh and Others [A declaration], August 28, 1826, Creek Indian Manuscripts; Debo, *Road to Disappearance*, 90; Grant Foreman, *Indian Removal: The Emigration of the Five Civilized Tribes* (Norman: University of Oklahoma Press, 1952), 90; Green, *Politics of Indian Removal*, 98–101, 104–8; Wright, *Creeks and Seminoles*, 242–53.

54. Riaford to Pickett, February 8, 1850, Pickett Manuscripts, ADAH. See also Thomas Ellis to Pickett, August 26, 1847, Pickett Manuscripts, ADAH; Bernhard, *Travels through North America*, 2:30; Testimony of James Moss, June 28, 1825, in U.S. Congress, *Report and Resolutions of the Legislature of Georgia with Accompanying Documents*, 19th Cong., 2nd sess., 1825, H. Doc. 59.

55. Riaford to Pickett, February 8, 1850, Pickett Manuscripts, ADAH (emphasis added). Elsewhere, Riaford saw no contradiction when he claimed that Lewis "was

the only *white man* with the Indian Regiment at the blowing up of the negro fort in 1816. While living with Col. Hawkins [years earlier] he took an Indian wife and from that day has been *identified with the Creek Indians,* he is a national chief of great influence, a good liver, and a most hospitable man."

56. Margaret Hunter Hall, *Aristocratic Journey,* 240–41. Mauelshagen and Davis, *Partners in the Lord's Work,* 43; on March 24, 1828, Smoot, "Account of Alabama Indian Missions," 140–41.

57. Anne Kendrick Walker, *Russell County in Retrospect: An Epic of the Far Southeast* (Richmond VA: Dietz Press, 1950), 72.

EPILOGUE

1. Swanton, *Myths and Tales of the Southeastern Indians,* 74.

2. Toulmin to Holmes, August 27, 1813, J. F. H Claiborne Collection in Mississippi State Department of Archives and History, Jackson. See also Holmes to Armstrong, July 27, 1813, in Carter, *Territorial Papers of the United States,* 6:389.

3. Hawkins, September 17, 1813, in LBH, 2:665. See also Martin, *Sacred Revolt,* 156; Saunt, *New Order of Things,* 263–64.

4. Toulmin to Claiborne, July 23, 1813, Toulmin Papers.

5. Hawkins to Armstrong, June 28, 1813, in LBH, 2:643. For a similar claim, see Frank L. Owsley Jr., "Prophet of War: Josiah Francis and the Creek War," *American Indian Quarterly* 9 (Summer 1985): 273–74.

6. McIntosh and others to Mitchell, June 12, 1818, Mitchell Papers; Crowell to Barbour, September 10, 1827, OIA, CA, LR, M234, 221:248–49.

7. McKenney and Hall, *History of the Indian Tribes,* 1:82–83.

Selected Bibliography

MANUSCRIPT COLLECTIONS

Alabama Department of Archives and History, Montgomery

Alabama Governor Reward Files, 1822–24
Albert James Pickett Manuscripts
George Stiggins Papers
Harry Toulmin Papers
Henry Sale Halbert Collection

Florida State University Library, Tallahassee

Indian Pioneer History Collection, originals in Grant Foreman Collection, Oklahoma Historical Society, Oklahoma City, Oklahoma (microfilm)

Georgia Department of Archives and History, Atlanta

Governors Letter Books
Louise Frederick Hays, ed., "Creek Indian Letters, Talks and Treaties, 1705–1839"
Louise Frederick Hays, ed., "Indian Depredations, 1787–1825"
Louise Frederick Hays, "Indian Letters, 1782–1839"
Louise Frederick Hays, ed., "The Murder of General William McIntosh, Treaties of Indian Springs, 1821–25, also Report of Joseph Vallance Bevan, Letters Treaties, Executive Reports, and the Trial of John Crowell" (typescript)
Louise Frederick Hays, ed., "Unpublished Letters of Timothy Barnard, 1784–1820" (typescript)
Louise Frederick Hays, ed., "Unpublished Letters of Benjamin Hawkins" (typescript)
Louise Frederick Hays, ed., "Force Transcripts, Georgia Records Council Correspondence, 1782–1789" (typescript)

Georgia Historical Society, Savannah

Joseph Vallence Bevan Papers
Henry Ellis Papers
James Habersham Papers
William Bacon Stevens Papers
Antonio J. Waring Jr. Papers

Henry E. Huntington Library, San Marino, California

Eaton Papers

Letter Book of James Glen
Huntington Manuscripts
Lord Loudoun Papers
Andrew Pickens Papers
Rhees Collection

Library of Congress, Washington DC

Floyd-McAdoo Family Papers

National Archives and Records Services

East Florida Papers
Records of the Bureau of Indian Affairs, Correspondence of the Office of Indian Affairs (Central Office) and Related Records, Letters Received, 1824–81, Microcopy 234
Records of the Bureau of Indian Affairs, Letter Book, Creek Trading House, 1795–1816, Microcopy 4
Records of the Bureau of Indian Affairs, Letters Received by the Office of the Secretary of War Relating to Indian Affairs, 1800–23, Microcopy 271
Records of the Bureau of Indian Affairs, Letters Sent by the Office of Indian Affairs, 1824–81, Microcopy 21
Records of the Bureau of Indian Affairs, Letters Sent by the Secretary of War Relating to Indian Affairs, 1800–24, Microcopy 15
Records of the Bureau of Indian Affairs, Letters Sent by the Superintendent of Indian Trade, 1807–23, Microcopy 16

Newberry Library, Chicago, Illinois

Ayer Collection
Mitchell Papers

Southern Baptist Historical Library and Archives, Nashville

Ebenezer Lee Compere Collection

University of Florida, P. K. Yonge Library of Florida History, Gainesville

Archivo General de Indias, Seville, Spain (microfilm)
Archivo General de la Nación, Mexico City, Mexico (microfilm)
Lyman Draper Manuscripts, State Historical Society of Wisconsin, Madison (microfilm)
Gage Papers, American Series, William Clements Library, University of Michigan, Ann Arbor (microfilm)
Gage Papers, English Series, William Clements Library, University of Michigan, Ann Arbor (microfilm)
Joseph B. Lockey Collection

Public Record Office, Colonial Office series 5 and 323
Santo Domingo Papers, Archivo de Indias, Seville, Spain

University of Georgia Library, Hargrett Rare Book and Manuscript Library, Athens
Telemon Cuyler Collection
Benjamin Hawkins Papers

University of West Florida Library, Pensacola
Panton, Leslie and Company Papers, Microfilm

NEWSPAPERS

Baptist Missionary Magazine (Boston)
Georgia Gazette (Savannah)
The Missionary (Mount Zion GA)
Niles Weekly Register (Baltimore)
South Carolina Gazette (Charleston)

PUBLISHED SOURCES

Adair, James. *Adair's History of the American Indians.* Ed. Samuel Cole Williams. 1775. Reprint, New York: Promontory Press, 1930.

Alcoff, Linda. "Mestizo Identity." In *American Mixed Race: The Culture of Microdiversity,* ed. Naomi Zack, 257–78. Lanham MD: Rowman & Littlefield, 1995.

Alden, John Richard. *John Stuart and the Southern Colonial Frontier: A Study of Indian Relations, War, Trade, and Land Problems in the Southern Wilderness, 1754–1775.* New York: Gordion Press, 1966.

American State Papers, Class 1: Foreign Relations. 6 vols. Washington DC: Gales & Seaton, 1833–59. (ASPFR)

American State Papers, Class 2: Indian Affairs. 2 vols. Washington DC: Gales & Seaton, 1832–34). (ASPIA)

American State Papers, Class 5: Military Affairs. 7 vols. Washington DC: Gales & Seaton, 1832–61. (ASPMA)

Archdale, John. *A New Description of That Fertile and Pleasant Province of Carolina: With a Brief Account of its Discovery, Settling, and the Government Thereof to this Time. With Several Remarkable Passages of Divine Providence during my Time.* London: John Wyat, 1707.

Aron, Stephen. "Pigs and Hunters: 'Rights in the Woods' on the Trans-Appalachian Frontier." In *Contact Points: American Frontiers from the Mohawk Valley to the Mississippi, 1750–1830,* ed. Andrew R. L. Cayton and Fredrika J. Teute, 175–204. Chapel Hill: University of North Carolina Press, 1998.

Axtell, James. *The European and the Indian: Essays in the Ethnohistory of Colonial North America.* New York: Oxford University Press, 1981.

———. *The Invasion Within: The Contest of Cultures in Colonial North America.* New York: Oxford University Press, 1985.

————. "The White Indians of Colonial America." *WMQ* 32 (January 1975): 55–88.

Baily, Francis. *Journal of a Tour in Unsettled Parts of North America in 1796 & 1797*. London: Baily Brothers, 1856.

Baird, W. David. "Are There 'Real' Indians in Oklahoma? Historical Perceptions of the Five Civilized Tribes." *Chronicles of Oklahoma* 68 (Spring 1990): 4–23.

Bassett, John Spencer, ed. *Correspondence of Andrew Jackson* 7 vols. Washington DC: Carnegie Institute, 1926–27.

Benton, Thomas Hart. *Thirty Years View; or, A History of the Working of the American Government for Thirty Years, From 1820 to 1850*. 2 vols. New York: D. Appleton, 1854.

Berkhofer, Robert F., Jr. *Salvation and the Savage: An Analysis of Protestant Missions and American Indian Response, 1787–1862*. Lexington: University of Kentucky Press, 1965.

————. *The White Man's Indian: Images of the American Indian from Columbus to the Present*. New York: Vintage Press, 1978.

Bernhard, Karl. *Travels through North America, During the years 1825 and 1826*. 2 vols. Philadelphia: Carey, Lea & Carey, 1828.

Blu, Karen. *The Lumbee Problem: The Making of an Indian People*. New York: Cambridge University Press, 1980.

————. "Region and Recognition: Southern Indians, Anthropologists, and Presumed Biology." In *Anthropologists and Indians in the New South*, ed. Rachel A. Bonney and J. Anthony Paredes, 71–85. Tuscaloosa: University of Alabama Press, 2001.

Bolton, Herbert Eugene. *The Spanish Borderlands: A Chronicle of Old Florida and the Southwest*. New Haven CT: Yale University Press, 1921.

Bonner, James C. "Journal of a Mission to Georgia in 1827." *GHQ* 44 (March 1960): 74–85.

Bossu, Jean-Bernard. *Travels in the Interior of North America, 1751–1762*. Trans. and ed. Seymour Feiler. Norman: University of Oklahoma Press, 1962.

Boyd, Julian P., ed. *The Papers of Thomas Jefferson*. 21 vols. Princeton NJ: Princeton University Press, 1952.

Braund, Kathryn E. Holland. "The Creek Indians, Blacks and Slavery." *Journal of Southern History* 57 (November 1991): 601–36.

————. *Deerskins and Duffels: Creek Indian Trade with Anglo-America, 1685–1815*. Lincoln: University of Nebraska Press, 1993.

————. "Guardians of Tradition and Handmaidens to Change: Women's Roles in Creek Economic and Social Life during the Eighteenth Century." *American Indian Quarterly* 14 (Summer 1990): 239–58.

Calloway, Colin G. "Neither White nor Red: White Renegades on the American Indian Frontier." *Western History Quarterly* 17 (January 1986): 43–66.

Calmes, Alan Royse. "Indian Cultural Traditions and European Conquest of the Georgia–South Carolina Coastal plain, 3000 BC–1733 AD: A Combined Archaeological and Historical Investigation." PhD diss., University of South Carolina, 1968.

Candler, Allen D., Kenneth Coleman, and Milton Ready, eds. *The Colonial Records of the State of Georgia.* 32 vols. Atlanta: Franklin Printing and Publishing, 1904–16. (CRG)

Carroll, B. R. ed., *Historical Collections of South Carolina.* 2 vols. New York: Harper and Brothers, 1836).

Carson, James Taylor. *Searching for the Bright Path: The Mississippi Choctaws from Prehistory to Removal.* Lincoln: University of Nebraska Press, 1999.

Carter, Clarence Edwin, ed. *The Correspondence of General Thomas Gage with the Secretaries of State, 1763–1775.* 2 vols. New Haven: Yale University Press, 1931.

————, ed. *The Territorial Papers of the United States.* 28 vols. Washington DC: United States Printing Office, 1934–49.

Cashin, Edward J., Jr. *Lachlan McGillivray, Indian Trader: The Shaping of the Southern Colonial Frontier.* Athens: University of Georgia Press, 1992.

Catesby, Mark. *The Natural History of Carolina, Florida, and the Bahama Islands: Containing the Figures of Birds, Beasts, Fishes, Serpents, Insects, and Plants.* 2 vols. London: Benjamin White, 1771.

Caughey, John Walton. *McGillivray of the Creeks.* Norman: University of Oklahoma, 1938.

Champagne, Duane. *Social Order and Political Change: Constitutional Governments among the Cherokee, the Choctaw, the Chickasaw, and the Creek.* Stanford CA: Stanford University Press, 1992.

Chaplin, Joyce E. "Natural Philosophy and an Early Racial Idiom in North America: Comparing English and Indian Bodies." WMQ 54 (January 1997): 229–52. Chaudhuri, Jean, and Joyotpaul Chaudhuri. *A Sacred Path: The Way of the Muscogee Creeks.* Los Angeles: UCLA American Indian Studies Center, 2001.

Clayton, Lawrence E., Vernon James Knight Jr., and Edward C. Moore, eds. *The de Soto Chronicles: The Expedition of Hernando de Soto to North America in 1539–1543.* 2 vols. Tuscaloosa: University of Alabama Press, 1992.

Coker, William S., and Thomas D. Watson. *Indian Traders of the Southeastern Spanish Borderlands: Panton, Leslie & Company and John Forbes & Company, 1783–1847.* Pensacola: University of West Florida, 1986.

Corkran, David H. *The Creek Frontier, 1540–1783.* Norman: University of Oklahoma Press, 1967.

Coulter, E. Merton, ed. *Journal of William Stephens, 1671–1753.* 2 vols. Athens: University of Georgia Press, 1958–59.

Crawford, James M. *The Mobilian Trade Language.* Knoxville: University of Tennessee Press, 1978.

Crosby, Alfred W., Jr. *Ecological Imperialism and the Biological Expansion of Europe.* New York: Cambridge University Press, 1986.

————. "Virgin Soil Epidemics as a Factor in the Aboriginal Depopulation in America," *WMQ* 33 (April 1976): 289–99.

Cummins, Ebenezer H. *Summary Geography of Alabama, One of the United States.* Philadelphia: William Brown, 1819.

Davies, Kenneth G., ed. *Documents of the American Revolution, 1770–1783.* 21 vols. Dublin: Irish University Press, 1972–79.

Deagan, Kathleen A. "Sex, Status and Role in the Mestizaje of Spanish Colonial Florida." PhD diss., University of Florida, 1974.

Debo, Angie. *The Road to Disappearance: A History of the Creek Indians.* Norman: University of Oklahoma Press, 1941.

De Vorsey, Louis, Jr., ed. *DeBrahm's Report of the General Survey in the Southern District of North America.* Columbia: University of South Carolina Press, 1971.

————. *The Indian Boundary in the Southern Colonies, 1763–1775.* Chapel Hill: University of North Carolina Press, 1961.

Dobyns, Henry F. *Their Number Become Thinned: Native American Population Dynamics in Eastern North America.* Knoxville: University of Tennessee Press, 1983.

Doster, James F. *The Creek Indians and Their Florida Lands, 1740–1823.* 2 vols. New York: Garland, 1974.

Dow, Lorenzo. *History of Cosmopolite; or the Writings of rev. Lorenzo Dow: Containing His Experiences and Travels, in Europe and America, up to Near his Fiftieth Year.* Cincinnati OH: H. M. Rulison, 1856.

Dowd, Gregory Evans. *A Spirited Resistance: The North American Indian Struggle for Unity, 1745–1815.* Baltimore MD: Johns Hopkins University Press, 1992.

Downs, Dorothy. "British Influences on Creek and Seminole Men's Clothing, 1733–1858." *Florida Anthropologist* 33 (June 1980): 46–65.

Drayton, John. *A View of South-Carolina, As Respects Her Natural and Civil Concerns.* Charleston SC: W. P. Young, 1802.

Dysart, Jane E. "Another Road to Disappearance: Assimilation of Creek Indians in Pensacola, Florida, during the Nineteenth Century." *FHQ* 61 (July 1982): 37–48.

Ethridge, Robbie. *Creek Country: The Creek Indians and Their World.* Chapel Hill: University of North Carolina Press, 2003.

Felldin, Jeanne Robey, and Charlotte Magee Tucker. *1832 Census of Creek Indians Taken by Parsons and Abbot.* Tomball TX: Genealogical Publications, 1978.

Fisher, Doris Debrman. "Mary Musgrove: Creek Englishwoman." PhD diss., Emory University, 1990.

Forbes, Jack D. *Africans and Native Americans: The Language of Race and the Evolution of Red-Black Peoples.* Urbana: University of Illinois Press, 1993.

Ford, Paul Leicester, ed. *The Works of Thomas Jefferson.* 12 vols. New York: G. P. Putnam's Sons, 1892–99.

Foreman, Grant. *Indian Removal: The Emigration of the Five Civilized Tribes.* Norman: University of Oklahoma Press, 1952.

Fundaburk, Emma Lila, ed. *Southeastern Indians: Life Portraits; A Catalogue of Pictures, 1564–1860*. Metuchen NJ: Scarecrow Reprint, 1969.

Galloway, Patricia Kay. *Choctaw Genesis, 1500–1700*. Lincoln: University of Nebraska Press, 1995.

Gatschet, Albert S. *A Migration Legend of the Creek Indians, with a Linguistic, Historic and Ethnographic Introduction*. 1884. Reprint, New York: AMS Press, 1969.

Gillespie, Michele. "The Sexual Politics of Race and Gender: Mary Musgrove and the Georgia Trustees." In *The Devil's Lane: Sex and Race in the Early South*, ed. Catherine Clinton and Michele Gillespie, 187–201. New York: Oxford University Press, 1997.

Ginsberg, Elaine K., ed. *Passing and the Fictions of Identity in Early America*. Durham NC: Duke University Press, 1996.

Grant, C. L., ed. *Letters, Journals and Writings of Benjamin Hawkins*. 2 vols. Savannah: Beehive Press, 1980. (*LBH*)

Green, Michael D. "Mary Musgrove: Creating a New World." In *Sifters: Native American Women's Lives*, ed. Theda Perdue, 29–47. New York: Oxford University Press, 2001.

————. *The Politics of Indian Removal: Creek Government and Society in Crisis*. Lincoln: University of Nebraska Press, 1982.

Griffith, Benjamin W. *McIntosh and Weatherford: Creek Indian Leaders*. Tuscaloosa: University of Alabama Press, 1988.

Hagan, William T. "Full Blood, Mixed Blood, Generic, and Ersatz: The Problem of Indian Identity." *Arizona and the West* 27 (Winter 1985): 309–26.

Hagedorn, Nancy L. "'A Friend to Go between Them': The Interpreter as Cultural Broker during Anglo-Iroquois Councils, 1740–70." *Ethnohistory* 35 (Winter 1988): 60–80.

Hall, Leslie. *Land and Allegiance in Revolutionary Georgia*. Athens: University of Georgia Press, 2002.

Hall, Margaret Hunter. *The Aristocratic Journey: Being the Outspoken Letters of Mrs. Basil Hall Written during a Fourteen Months' Sojourn in America, 1827–1828*. Ed. Una Pope-Hennessey. New York: Putnam, 1931.

Hallbert, Henry S., and Timothy Horton Ball. *The Creek War of 1813 and 1814*. Chicago: Donohue & Henneberry, 1895.

Harrison, Faye V. "The Persistent Power of 'Race' in the Cultural and Political Economy of Racism." *Annual Review of Anthropology* 24 (1995): 47–74.

Hatley, M. Thomas. *The Dividing Path: Cherokees and South Carolinians through the Revolutionary Era*. New York: Oxford University Press, 1995.

Henri, Florette. *The Southern Indians and Benjamin Hawkins, 1796–1816*. Norman: University of Oklahoma Press, 1986.

Hewitt, J. N. B. "Notes on the Creek Indians." In Smithsonian Institution, *Bureau of American Ethnology Bulletin*, no. 123, ed. J. R. Swanton. Washington DC: Government Printing Office, 1939.

Hodgson, Adam. *Letters from North America, Written During a Tour in the United States and Canada.* London: Hurst, Robinson, 1824.

Hodgson, William Brown. *Creek Indian History as Comprised in Creek Confederacy.* Americus GA: Americus Book, 1938.

Hoffman, Ronald, Mechal Sobel, and Fredrika J. Teute, eds. *Through a Glass Darkly: Reflections on Personal Identity in Early America.* Chapel Hill: University of North Carolina Press, 1997.

Hudson, Charles M. "The Hernando de Soto Expedition, 1539–1543." In *The Forgotten Centuries: Indians and Europeans in the American South, 1521–1704,* ed. Charles M. Hudson and Charmen Chaves Tesser, 74–103. Athens: University of Georgia Press, 1994.

————. *Southeastern Indians.* Knoxville: University of Tennessee Press, 1976.

Hudson, Charles M., and Charmen Chaves Tesser, eds. *The Forgotten Centuries: Indians and Europeans in the American South, 1521–1704.* Athens: University of Georgia Press, 1994.

Hvidt, Kristian, ed. *Von Reck's Voyage: Drawings and Journal of Philip Georg Friedrich von Reck.* Savannah: Beehive Press, 1980.

Jacobs, Wilbur R., ed. *Indians on the Southern Colonial Frontier: The Edmond Atkin Report and Plan of 1755.* Columbia: University of South Carolina Press, 1954.

Jaimes, M. Annette. "Some Kind of Indian: On Race, Eugenics, and Mixed Bloods." In *American Mixed Race: The Culture of Microdiversity,* ed. Naomi Zack, 133–53. Lanham MD: Rowman & Littlefield, 1995.

Jennings, Francis. *The Invasion of America: Indians, Colonialism, and the Cant of Conquest.* New York: W. W. Norton, 1975.

Johnston, J. H. "Documentary Evidence of the Relations of Negroes and Indians." *Journal of Negro History* 14 (January 1929): 21–43.

Kappler, Charles J., ed. *Indian Treaties, 1778–1883.* Washington DC: Government Printing Office, 1904.

Karttunen, Frances E. *Between Worlds: Interpreters, Guides, and Survivors.* New Brunswick NJ: Rutgers University Press, 1994.

Kawashima, Yasuhide. "Forest Diplomats: The Role of Interpreters in Indian-White Relations on the Early American Frontier." *American Indian Quarterly* 13 (Winter 1989): 1–14.

Kidwell, Clara Sue. "Indian Women as Cultural Mediators." *Ethnohistory* 39 (Spring 1992): 97–107.

Klein, Rachel N. *Unification of a Slave State: The Rise of the Planter Class in the South Carolina Backcountry, 1760–1808.* Chapel Hill: University of North Carolina Press, 1990.

Klingberd, Frank J., ed. *The Carolina Chronicle of Dr. Francis Le Jau, 1706–1717.* Berkeley: University of California Press, 1956.

Knight, Vernon James. "The Formation of the Creeks." In *The Forgotten Centuries:*

Indians and Europeans in the American South 1521–1704. ed. Charles M. Hudson and Carmen Chaves Tesser, 373–92. Athens: University of Georgia Press, 1994.

Kupperman, Karen Ordahl. *Indians and English: Facing Off in Early America.* Ithaca NY: Cornell University Press, 2000.

———. *Settling with the Indians: The Meeting of English and Indian Cultures in America, 1580–1640.* Totowa NJ: Rowman & Littlefield, 1980.

Lackey, Richard S., ed. *Frontier Claims in the Lower South.* New Orleans: Polyanthos, 1977.

Landers, Jane. *Black Society in Spanish Florida.* Urbana: University of Illinois Press, 1999.

Lane, Mills, ed. *General Oglethorpe's Georgia: Colonial Letters, 1733–1743.* 2 vols. Savannah: Beehive Press, 1975.

Lawson, John. *A New Voyage to Carolina.* Ed. Hugh Talmage Lefler. Chapel Hill: University of North Carolina Press, 1967.

Le Moyne, Lacque. *Narrative of Le Moyne, An Artist who Accompanied the French Expedition to Florida Under Laudonniére, 1564.* Boston: James R. Osgood, 1875.

Liancourt, Duke de la Rochefoucault. *Travels through the United States of North America, the Country of the Iroquois, and Upper Canada, in the Years 1795, 1796, and 1797.* London: R. Phillips, 1799.

Littlefield, Daniel F., Jr. *Africans and Creeks: From the Colonial Period to the Civil War.* Westport CT: Greenwood Press, 1979.

Loomis, Augustus. *Scenes in the Indian Country.* Philadelphia: Presbyterian Board of Publication, 1818.

Martin, Joel W. *Sacred Revolt: The Muskogee's Struggle for a New World.* Boston: Beacon Press, 1991.

May, Katja. *African Americans and Native Americans in the Creek and Cherokee Nations, 1830s to 1920s.* New York: Garland, 1996.

Mauelshagen, Carl, and Gerald H. Davis, eds. and trans. *Partners in the Lord's Work: The Diary of Two Moravian Missionaries in the Creek Indian Country, 1807–1813.* Atlanta: Georgia State College, 1969.

McCoy, Isaac. *History of Baptist Indian Missions: Embracing Remarks on the Former and Present Condition of the Aboriginal Tribes; Their Settlements within the Indian Territory, and their Future Prospects.* New York: H. and S. Raynor, 1840.

McDowell, William L., Jr., ed. *Documents Relating to Indian Affairs.* Vol. 1: *May 21, 1750–August 7, 1754.* Columbia: South Carolina Archives Department, 1958. Vol. 2: *1754–1765.* Columbia: University of South Carolina Press, 1970.

———, ed., *Journals of the Commissioners of the Indian Trade, September 20, 1710– April 12, 1715.* Columbia: South Carolina Archives Department, 1926.

McEwen, Bonnie G., ed. *Indians of the Greater Southeast: Historical Archaeology and Ethnohistory.* Gainesville: University Press of Florida, 2000.

McKenney, Thomas L., and James Hall. *History of the Indian Tribes of North Amer-*

ica with Biographical Sketches and Anecdotes of the Principal Chiefs. Philadelphia: Frederick W. Greenough, 1838.

McLoughlin, William G. *Cherokees and Missionaries, 1789–1839.* Norman: University of Oklahoma Press, 1984.

————. "Red Indians, Black Slavery and White Racism: America's Slaveholding Indians." *American Quarterly* 26 (October 1974): 367–85.

Meek, Alexander Beufort. *Romantic Passages of Southwest History; Including Orations, Sketches, and Essays.* New York: S. H. Goetzel, 1857.

Mereness, Newton D., ed. *Travels in the American Colonies.* New York: Macmillan, 1916.

Meriwether, Robert Lee. *The Expansion of South Carolina, 1729–1765.* Kingsport TN: Southern, 1940.

Merrell, James H. "'The Cast of His Countenance': Reading Andrew Montour." In *Through a Glass Darkly: Reflections on Personal Identity in Early America,* ed. Ronald Hoffman, Mechal Sobel, and Fredrika J. Teute, eds., 13–39. Chapel Hill: University of North Carolina Press, 1997.

————. *The Indians' New World: Catawbas and Their Neighbors from European Contact through the Era of Removal.* New York: W. W. Norton, 1989.

————. *Into the American Woods: Negotiators on the Pennsylvania Frontier.* New York: W. W. Norton, 1999.

————. "The Racial Education of the Catawba Indians." *Journal of Southern History* 50 (August 1984): 363–84.

Milanich, Jerald T. *Florida Indians and the Invasion from Europe.* Gainesville: University Press of Florida, 1995.

Milanich, Jerald T., and Samuel Proctor, eds. *Tacachale: Essays on the Indians of Florida and Southeastern Georgia in the Historic Period.* Gainesville: University Press of Florida, 1978, 1994.

Milfort, Louis. *Memoirs; or, A Quick Glance at My Various Travels and My Sojourn in the Creek Nation.* Ed. and trans. Ben C. McCary. 1802. Reprint, Kennesaw GA: Continental Book, 1959.

Moore, Alexander, ed. *Nairne's Muskhogean Journals: The 1708 Expedition to the Mississippi River.* Jackson: University Press of Mississippi, 1988.

Moore, John H. "Mvskoke Personal Names." *Names* 43 (September 1995): 187–212.

Nunez, Theron A., Jr. "Creek Nativism and the Creek War of 1813–1814." *Ethnohistory* 5 (Winter 1958): 1–47; 5 (Spring 1858): 131–75; 5 (Summer 1958): 292–301.

O'Brien, Greg. *Choctaws in a Revolutionary Age, 1750–1830.* Lincoln: University of Nebraska Press, 2002.

O'Donnell, James H. *Southern Indians in the American Revolution.* Knoxville: University of Tennessee Press, 1973.

Okamura, J. Y. "Situational Ethnicity." *Ethnic and Racial Studies* 4 (October 1981): 452–65.

Owsley, Frank L., Jr. "Prophet of War: Josiah Francis and the Creek War," *American Indian Quarterly* 9 (Summer 1985): 273–93.

Paredes, J. Anthony, and Kenneth J. Plante. "A Reexamination of Creek Indian Population Trends: 1738–1832." *American Indian Culture and Research Journal* 6, no. 4 (1982): 3–28.

Perdue, Theda. *Cherokee Women: Gender and Culture Change, 1700–1835.* Lincoln: University of Nebraska Press, 1998.

———. *"Mixed Blood" Indians: Racial Construction in the Early South.* Athens: University of Georgia Press, 2003.

———. *Slavery and the Evolution of Cherokee Society.* Knoxville: University of Tennessee Press, 1979.

Peterson, Jacqueline, and Jennifer S. H. Brown, eds. *The New Peoples: Being and Becoming Métis in North America.* Lincoln: University of Nebraska Press, 1985.

Pickett, Albert James. *History of Alabama and Incidentally of Georgia and Mississippi, from the Earliest Period.* 2 vols. Charleston SC: Walker & James, 1851.

Piker, Joshua Aaron. "'Peculiarly Connected': The Creek Town of Oakfuskee and the Study of Colonial American Communities, 1708–1785." PhD diss., Cornell University, 1998.

Pope, John. *A Tour Through the Southern and Western Territories of the United States of North-America; the Spanish Dominions on the River Mississippi, and the Floridas; the Countries of the Creek Nations; and Many Uninhabited Parts.* Richmond VA: John Dixon, 1792.

Richter, Daniel K. "Cultural Brokers and Intercultural Politics: New York–Iroquois Relations, 1664–1701." *Journal of American History* 75 (June 1988): 40–67.

———. *Facing East from Indian Country: A Native History of Early America.* Cambridge: Harvard University Press, 2001.

———. *The Ordeal of the Longhouse: The Peoples of the Iroquois Lead in the Era of European Civilization.* Chapel Hill: University of North Carolina Press, 1992.

Riordan, Patrick. "Finding Freedom in Florida: Native Peoples, African Americans, and Colonists, 1670–1816." *FHQ* 75 (Summer 1996): 24–43.

Rodning, Christopher B. "Mortuary Ritual and Gender Ideology in Protohistoric Southwestern North Carolina." In *Archaeological Studies of Gender in the Southeastern United States,* ed. Jane M. Eastman and Christopher Rodning. Gainesville: University Press of Florida, 2001.

Rogin, Michael Paul. *Fathers and Children: Andrew Jackson and the Subjugation of the American Indian.* New York: Vintage Books, 1975.

Romans, Bernard. *A Concise Natural History of East and West Florida.* Ed. Rembert W. Patrick. 1775. Reprint, Gainesville: University of Florida Press, 1962.

Root, Maria P., ed. *Racially Mixed People in America.* Newberry Park CA: Sage, 1992.

Rowland, Dunbar, ed. *Mississippi Provincial Archives, 1763–1766, English Dominion.* Nashville: Press of Brandon Printing, 1911.

Rowland, Dunbar, and Albert Godfrey Sanders, eds. *Mississippi Provincial Archives,*

French Dominion. 5 vols. Jackson: Press of the Mississippi Department of Archives and History, 1927–84.

Royall, Anne. *Letters from Alabama, 1817–1822.* University: University of Alabama Press, 1975.

Saunt, Claudio. *A New Order of Things: Property, Power, and the Transformation of the Creek Indians, 1733–1816.* Cambridge: Cambridge University Press, 1999.

Scheidley, Nathaniel. "Unruly Men: Indians, Settlers and the Ethos of Frontier Patriarchy in the Upper Tennessee Watershed, 1763–1815." PhD diss., Princeton University, 1999.

Schoolcraft, Henry R., ed. *Information Respecting the History, Condition and Prospects of the Indian Tribes of the United States: Collected and Prepared Under the Direction of the Bureau of Indian Affairs, Per Act of Congress of March 3d, 1847.* 5 vols. Philadelphia: Lippincott, Grambo, 1853.

Shannon, Timothy J. "Dressing for Success on the Mohawk Frontier: Hendrick, William Johnson, and the Indian Fashion." *WMQ*, 53 (January 1996): 13–42.

Sheehan, Bernard W. *The Seeds of Extinction: Jeffersonian Philanthropy and the American Indian.* New York: W. W. Norton, 1973.

Shoemaker, Nancy. "How Indians Got to Be Red." *American Historical Review* 102 (June 1997): 625–44.

———, ed. *Negotiators of Change: Historical Perspectives on Native American Women.* New York: Routledge, 1995.

Sider, Gerald M. *Lubee Indian Histories: Race, Ethnicity, and Indian Identity in the Southern United States.* New York: Cambridge University Press, 1993.

Smedley, Audrey. *Race in North America: Origin and Evolution of a Worldview.* Boulder CO: Westview Press, 1993.

Smith, Marvin T. "Aboriginal Depopulation in the Postcontact Southeast." In *The Forgotten Centuries: Indians and Europeans in the American South, 1521–1704*, ed. Charles M. Hudson and Charmen Chaves Tesser, 257–76. Athens: University of Georgia Press, 1994.

———. *Archaeology of Aboriginal Culture Change in the Interior Southeast.* Gainesville: University Presses of Florida, 1987.

———. "Depopulation and Culture Change in the Early Historic Period Interior Southeast." PhD diss., University of Florida, 1984.

Smoot, Joseph G. "An Account of Alabama Indian Missions and Presbyterian Churches in 1828 from the Travel Diary of William S. Potts." *Alabama Review* 18 (April 1965): 134–52.

Smythe, John F. D. *Tour in the United States of America.* 2 vols. 1784. Reprint, New York: New York Times and Arno Press, 1968.

Sollars, Werner. *Beyond Ethnicity: Consent and Descent in American Cultures.* New York: Oxford University Press, 1986.

Southerland, Henry DeLeon, Jr., and Jerry Elijah Brown. *The Federal Road through*

Georgia, the Creek Nation, and Alabama, 1806–1836. Tuscaloosa: University of Alabama Press, 1989.

Spoehr, Alexander. *Changing Kinship Systems: A Study in the Acculturation of the Creek, Cherokee, and Choctaw.* Chicago: Field Museum of Natural History, 1947.

Strictures Addressed to James Madison on the Celebrated Report of William H. Crawford Recommending the Intermarriage of Americans with Indian Tribes. Philadelphia: Jesper Harding, 1824.

Strum, Circe, *Blood Politics: Race, Culture, and Identity in the Cherokee Nation of Oklahoma.* Berkeley: University of California Press, 2002.

Stuart, James. *Three Years in North America.* 2 vols. Edinburgh: Robert Cadell, 1833.

Sturtevant, William C. "Commentary." In *Eighteenth-Century Florida and Its Borderlands,* ed. Samuel Proctor, 40–47. Gainesville: University of Presses of Florida, 1975.

Swan, Caleb. "Position and State of Manners and Arts in the Creek, or Muscogee Nation in 1791." In *Information Respecting the History, Condition and Prospects of the Indian Tribes of the United States: Collected and Prepared Under the Direction of the Bureau of Indian Affairs, Department of the Interior Per Act of Congress of March 3d, 1847,* ed. Henry R. Schoolcraft, 5:251–83. Philadelphia: J. B. Lippincott.

Swanton, John R. *Early History of the Creek Indians and Their Neighbors.* Washington DC: Government Printing Office, 1922.

———. *The Indians of the Southeastern United States.* Washington DC: United States Government Printing Office, 1946.

———. *Indian Tribes of the Lower Mississippi Valley and Adjacent Coast of the Gulf of Mexico.* Washington DC: Government Printing Office, 1911.

———. *Myths and Tales of the Southeastern Indians.* 1929. Reprint, Norman: University of Oklahoma Press, 1995.

———. "Notes on the Mental Assimilation of Races." *Journal of the Washington Academy of Sciences* 16 (1926): 495–502.

———. "Religious Beliefs and Medical Practices of the Creek Indians." In *Forty Second Annual Report of the Bureau of American Ethnology to the Secretary of the Smithsonian Institution,* 473–672. Washington DC: United States Government Printing Office, 1928.

———. "Social Organization and Social Usages of the Indians of the Creek Confederacy." In *Forty Second Annual Report of the Bureau of American Ethnology to the Secretary of the Smithsonian Institution.* Washington DC: United States Government Printing Office, 1928.

Szasz, Ferenc Morton. *Scots in the North American West, 1790–1917.* Norman: University of Oklahoma Press, 2000.

Szasz, Margaret Connell, ed. *Between Indian and White Worlds: The Cultural Broker.* Norman: University of Oklahoma Press, 1994.

———. *Indian Education in the American Colonies, 1607–1783.* Albuquerque: University of New Mexico Press, 1985.

Tailfer, Pat. *A True and Historical Narrative of the Colony of Georgia.* Ed. Clarence L. Ver Steeg. Athens: University of Georgia Press, 1960.

Thicknesse, Philip. *Memoirs and Anecdotes of Philip Thicknesse, Late Lieutenant Governor of Land Guard Fort, and Unfortunately Father to George Touchet, Baron Audley.* (London?): author, 1788.

Usner, Daniel H., Jr. "American Indians on the Cotton Frontier: Changing Economic Relations with Citizens and Slaves in the Mississippi Territory." *Journal of American History* 72 (September 1985): 297–317.

———. "The Frontier Exchange Economy of the Lower Mississippi Valley in the Eighteenth Century." *WMQ* 44 (April 1987): 165–92.

———. *Indians, Settlers, and Slaves in a Frontier Exchange Economy: The Lower Mississippi Valley before 1783.* Chapel Hill: University of North Carolina Press, 1992.

Vaughan, Alden T. "From White Man to Redskin: Changing Anglo-American Perceptions of the American Indian." In *Roots of American Racism: Essays on the Colonial Experience,* ed. Alden T. Vaughan, 3–33. New York: Oxford University Press, 1995.

Vaughan, Alden T., and Daniel D. Richter. "Crossing the Cultural Divide: Indians and New Englanders, 1605–1763." In *Roots of American Racism: Essays on the Colonial Experience,* ed. Alden T. Vaughan, 213–52. New York: Oxford University Press, 1995.

Waselkov, Gregory A., and Kathryn E. Holland Braund, eds. *William Bartram and the Southeastern Indians.* Lincoln: University of Nebraska Press, 1995.

Waselkov, Gregory A., and Brian M. Wood. "The Creek War of 1813–1814: Effects on Creek Society and Settlement Pattern." *Journal of Alabama Archaeology* 32 (June 1986): 1–24.

Washburn, Wilcomb E., ed. *The Garland Library of Narratives of North American Indian Captivities.* New York: Garland, 1977.

Waters, Mary C. *Ethnic Options: Choosing Identities in America.* Berkeley: University of California Press, 1990.

White, George. *Historical Collections of Georgia Containing the Most Interesting Facts, Traditions, Biographical Sketches, Anecdotes, Etc., Relating To Its History and Antiquities From Its First Settlement to the Present Time; Compiled From Original Records and Official Documents.* New York: Pudney & Russell, 1855.

White, Richard. *The Middle Ground: Indians, Empires, and Republics in the Great Lakes Region, 1650–1815.* New York: Cambridge University Press, 1991.

———. *The Roots of Dependency: Subsistence, Environment, and Social Changes among the Choctaws, Pawnees, and Navajos.* Lincoln: University of Nebraska Press, 1983.

Wilhelm, Paul. *Travels in North America, 1822–1824.* Trans. W. Robert Nitske. Ed. Savoie Lottinville. Norman: University of Oklahoma Press, 1973.

Williams, Samuel Cole, ed. *Early Travels in the Tennessee Country*. Johnson City TN: Watuga Press, 1938.

Willis, William S. "Divide and Rule: Red, White, and Black in the Southeast." *Journal of Negro History* 48 (July 1963): 157–76.

Wilson, Samuel, Jr., ed. *Southern Travels: Journal of John H. B. Latrobe, 1834*. New Orleans: Historic New Orleans Collection, 1986.

Wilson, Terry P. "Blood Quantum: Native American Mixed Bloods." In *Racially Mixed People in America*, ed. Maria P. P. Root, 108–25. Newbury Park CA: Sage, 1992.

Wood, Peter H. *Black Majority: Negroes in Colonial South Carolina from 1670 through the Stono Rebellion*. New York: W. W. Norton, 1974.

Wood, Peter H., Gregory A. Waselkov, and M. Thomas Hatley, eds. *Powhatan's Mantle: Indians in the Colonial Southeast*. Lincoln: University of Nebraska Press, 1989.

Woods, Michael Leonard. *Personal Reminiscences of Colonel Albert James Pickett*. Montgomery: Alabama Historical Society, 1904.

Woodward, Thomas Simpson. *Woodward's Reminiscences of the Creek, or Muscogee Indians, Contained in Letters to Friends in Georgia and Alabama*. Montgomery AL: Barrett & Wimbish, 1859.

Wright, J. Leitch, Jr. *Creeks and Seminoles: The Destruction and Regeneration of the Muscogulge People*. Lincoln: University of Nebraska Press, 1986.

———. *William Augustus Bowles: Director General of the Creek Nation*. Athens: University of Georgia Press, 1967.

Wyatt-Brown, Bertram. *Southern Honor: Ethics and Violence in the Old South*. New York: Oxford University Press, 1982.

Young, Mary Elizabeth. *Redskins, Ruffleshirts, and Rednecks: Indian Allotments in Alabama and Mississippi, 1830–1860*. Norman: University of Oklahoma Press, 1961.

Zack, Naomi, ed. *American Mixed Race: The Culture of Microdiversity*. Lanham MD: Rowman & Littlefield, 1995.

Index

Abihka Indians, 14, 20
Acorn Town (Lockchau Talofau), 102
Adair, James, 18
Adams, Abigail, 73
adoption, 5, 9, 11, 14–18, 24–25, 29, 30, 35, 46–47, 54–55, 59, 85, 90, 114, 116, 118–19, 129
adultery, 37, 54, 75, 89
African American–Creek intermixture, 6–7, 11, 21, 38, 43, 48, 55, 72, 78, 91–92, 124, 127, 129
African Americans, 31, 48, 52–53, 55, 63, 78, 90, 92, 129, 131. See also slavery
agriculture, 11, 48, 50, 67, 86, 108
Alabama, 2, 11, 42–43, 65, 91, 106, 116, 120, 122–25
Alabama Indians, 8, 12, 19–20, 25, 70
Altamaha, 12
American Revolution, 17–18, 24, 32–33, 39–40, 44, 49, 64, 74, 85, 93, 115
annuities, 105–6, 108–10, 117
Apalachee, 12
Archdale, John, 51
Asbury mission, 66, 124, 125
Ashe, Thomas, 53
Augusta GA, 54, 101, 103
authority, 23, 96–114, 126

Bach, John, 72
Bailey, Daniel, 76
Bailey, Dixon, 75
Bailey, James, 76
Bailey, Polly Sizemore Fisher, 76, 85
Bailey, Richard, Jr., 75, 120
Bailey, Richard, Sr., 34, 74–75, 120
Baily, Francis, 102
baptism, 52, 64, 124–25
Barber, Eunice, 15–17, 55–56

Barbour, James, 101
Barnard, Billy, 85
Barnard, Homanhidge, 69, 85
Barnard, Timothy, 40, 69, 85–86
Barnard, Timpochee (Timothy Jr.), 69, 85–86
Barnard, Tuccohoppe, 69, 85
Barnett, Slafecha, 77–78
Bartram, William, 34–35, 49, 93
Battis, Mary Ann, 72, 124
Battle of Horseshoe Bend, 121
Benton, Thomas Hart, 72, 92
Betton, Solomon, 84
Big Springs, 42
Big Warrior. See Tustunnuggee Thlucco
bilingualism and multilingualism, 2–3, 12, 18–19, 31, 43, 62–63, 67, 76–77, 80, 82, 85–86, 90, 95, 100
black drink, 2, 13, 22–23
blacksmiths, 16, 43, 127
blood quantum, 5, 129, 131
Bosomworth, Mary Musgrove Matthews. See Coosaponakeesa
Bosomworth, Thomas, 80–81
Bossu, Jean-Bernard, 55–56
Bowles, William Augustus, 40, 44, 113
Brims, 78
Brissert, Ambrose, 1–3, 5–6, 114
Broken Arrow, 42, 98, 111
Brown, George, 17
Brown, Jane, 17
Brown, Jesse, 125
Buffon, George Louis Leclerc, 53
Bullock, James, 32
burial norms, 13, 52, 70–71
Burkard, Johann Christian, 23, 42, 89–90, 127
Byrd, William, 56

captives of war, 14–18, 30–31, 55–56, 90

Carr, Paddy, 84

Carr, Thomas, 125

Carson, James Taylor, 4

cases of mistaken identity, 1–3, 97–100, 114–19

Cass, Lewis, 115–16

Catawba, 15

Catesby, Mark, 51

cattle, 2, 6, 30, 39, 44, 62, 70–71, 97, 100–102, 108–9, 121–22

Charleston SC, 64

Cherokee Indians, 15, 18, 33–34, 44, 48–49, 57, 104–5

Chickasaw, 15, 18–19

Chigellie, 37–38

children of European American–Creek inter-marriages, 2–10; and confusion of identity, 114–19; as cultural brokers 77–95; ethnic options of 120–27; as members of Creek society, 36, 39, 45, 47; as political leaders, 96–113; and potential for "civilization," 57–58; problem of definition of, 27, 29; socialization of, 62–76

Chisholm, John, 40

Choctaw Academy, 66

Choctaw Indians, 15, 18, 20, 48, 54

Christianity, 27, 42, 47, 51, 65, 67, 90–91, 124–25

"civilization plan," 24, 66, 76, 86, 108

clan, 1–2, 4–6, 8–11, 14–16, 20–22, 30–36, 45, 55, 61–64, 66, 70–72, 80–81, 85, 98–100, 126, 129–31. *See also specific clans*

clothing, 1, 5, 21, 27, 32, 49–50, 52, 59, 62, 73–74, 76, 103, 108, 115

Coe, Susannah, 104–5

Colvert, George, 69

Compere, Lee, 14, 52, 67, 90–92

Coosa, 12–14, 19, 20, 24

Coosaponakeesa (Mary Musgrove Matthews Bosomworth), 64, 78–81, 96, 112–13

Cornell, Abraham, 88–89

Cornell, David (Davy), 68, 88

Cornell, Joseph, 88

Cornells, Alexander, 82–83, 89–90

Cornells, George, 69

cotton growing, 32, 48, 62, 67, 93, 101–2

cotton spinning, 76, 86

Coweta, 14, 19–20, 24, 111

Cowkeeper, 160n42

Creek Agency, 89, 93

Creek Confederacy, formation of, 11–20

Creek demographics, 12–13, 18, 26–30

Creek National Council, 98–99, 130

Creek political advisers, 9, 43, 77, 85, 92, 95

Creek political structure, 11, 19–20, 23–24, 40, 105–6, 110–11

Creek religious leaders, 16, 23–24, 123

Crevecoeur, J. Hector St. John, 58

Crowell, John, 104, 110–11, 118

Crowell, Thomas, 110

cultural brokers, 3–4, 7, 77–95, 99, 114

Cummins, Ebenezer H., 103–4

Cusseta Indians, 86

Cuyler, Jeremiah, 118

Dale, Sam, 122

Davis, John, 91

Dearborn, Henry, 93–94, 117

Deer clan, 55

deerskin trade and traders, 1–2, 5–6, 9, 18, 26, 28–30, 32–42, 44–45, 48–49, 57–59, 62–64, 67–69, 74–76, 78–85, 87, 93, 106, 109, 110, 116, 118

desertion, soldiers, 40–41, 44

disease, 12–14

Dubois, Barrent, 124

Durant, Laughlin, 69

Durant, Sophia, 71, 76, 117

Durouzeaux, James, 35, 90

education, European American, 46, 61, 62–67, 69–70, 74–76, 78, 102, 124. *See also* schools

Efau Haujo, 75, 85–86

Ellis, Henry, 115

ethnic diversity, within Creek society, 5, 11, 14–15, 18–20, 24

Etome Tustunnuggee, 97

Everard, Richard, 37–38

eviction, 11, 26, 33–34, 75, 78, 120

Federal Road, 70, 93–94, 106, 108

fences, 2, 62, 67, 102

ferries, 32, 69–70, 85, 94–95, 102, 106, 126

First Seminole War, 96, 101–2, 109, 116–17

Fisher, Josiah, 76

Fisher, Peggy, 76

Fitzwalter, Joseph, 38

Fletcher, Elizabeth, 76

Florida, 2, 11, 40–41, 44, 64–65, 69, 115, 119

Folch, Vicente, 119

Fontaine, Jacques, 51

Forrester, Stephen, 82

Fort Mims, 76, 121–22, 125, 130

Fort Mitchell, 110

Francis, Josiah, 68, 116

fugitives from justice, 30–31, 42–44, 59, 75, 80, 87, 119, 126

Fus-hatchee, 24, 114

Galphin, George, 18, 24, 32, 70–71, 115

Galphin, John, 84

Garzón, Juan, 84

gender norms, 11, 48, 52, 53, 57, 61, 63, 67, 69, 79, 101, 120

Georgia, 2, 11, 14, 19, 31–32, 39, 41–44, 48, 51, 53–54, 65, 74–76, 79–81, 85, 91, 98–99, 104, 107, 115, 119–21

Glen, James, 15, 61–62

Green Corn Ceremony, 2, 13–14, 22, 89

Green, Michael D., 99

Grierson, Eliza, 104

Grierson, Robert, 87

Griffin, Edward, 64, 78

gunsmiths, 16

Hague, John, 30

hair, 3, 6, 47, 53, 54–55, 69, 72

Hale, Hannah, 30

Hall, Margaret Hunter, 127

Hambly, William, 83

Handsome Fellow, 115

Hawkins, Benjamin, 21, 28, 30, 43–44, 57–58, 61–62, 71, 74–76, 83, 85–90, 93, 108, 117

Hawkins, Eliza, 72, 105

Hawkins, Samuel, 104–5, 110

Hay, David, 28

Haynes, Sam J., 15

Henry, Jim, 41

herding, 2, 6, 39, 48, 62, 67, 86, 100–102

Hewitt, J. N. B., 63

Hickory Ground, 39

High Headed Jim, 54

Hilibi, 87, 111

Hitchiti Indians, 8, 19–20, 25

Hodgson, Adam, 94, 102, 111

hogs, 30, 97, 101–2

Hollinger, Adam, 70

Hopie of Thlothlagalga, 75

horses, 30, 44, 64, 70–71, 75, 97, 102

hospitality, 37, 80, 93–94

Howard Heniha, 100

Hunter, Thomas, 42–43

hunting, 10–11, 21, 26–27, 37, 50, 63, 67, 79, 100, 132

Hutton, James, 82

Indian countrymen, 2–3, 5–7, 9, 22; and ability to appear Creek, 47–49, 54–56, 59; and confusion of identity, 1, 114–19; as cultural brokers, 80–82, 85, 89–90; during Indian removal, 120–21, 123–27; and entrance into Creek villages, 11, 26–36, 38–45; as fathers of Creek children, 62–72, 74–76

Indian removal, 4, 28, 42, 44, 46–47, 49, 85, 109, 114, 119–27

Indian Springs, 102–3, 109

inheritance, 66, 70–72, 117

inns, 69–70, 93–95, 102–3, 106

intermarriage: French policy regarding, 57–58; proposals to promote, among Creeks, 56–59

interpreters, 2, 9, 16, 18, 21, 35, 43, 65, 67–70, 74, 77–93, 95, 112, 114

Jackson, Andrew, 46, 50, 106–7, 109, 120–22

Jackson, Rachel, 46

Jefferson, Thomas, 40, 51, 53, 57, 61

Jemison, Robert, Jr., 125

Johnson, Samuel, 65

Kasihta, 14, 24

Killgore, Robert, 34

law, within Creek society, 71, 86, 97–99, 111–
   12, 117, 131
Law Menders, 97–98, 100, 110
Lawson, John, 34, 39, 54
legal trials, 65–66, 79, 118–19
Le Jau, Francis, 17
Lessly, Francis, 34
Lewis, Kendall, 38, 43–44, 89, 92–93, 126–27
liquor, 1, 75, 118
literacy, 52, 62–63, 67, 73, 75–76, 90, 102, 132
Little Prince, 107, 111
Little Tallassee, 71
Logan, John, 43
Lovett, George, 84
Loyalists, 39–41, 44, 59, 69, 113
Luna, Tristán de, 13
Lyncoya, 46
Lyons, Samuel, 34
Lyons, William, 34
Lyttleton, William Henry, 87

Mackay, Robert, 41
Macnac, Samuel, 130
Mankiller, 36
marriage and cohabitation, 6, 14–15, 18, 21–
   22, 25–30, 32–39, 42, 52, 56–59, 61–62, 69,
   79–80, 85–87, 103–5, 115, 122, 124, 130–31
Marshall, Joseph, 85, 125
Marshall, Thomas, 28
Martin, Joel, 23
maternal uncles, 10, 61, 63, 66, 69, 100
matrilineal distribution of property, 66, 70–
   72, 117, 131
Matthews, Jacob, 80
Mayfield, Alexander, 84
Mayfield, George, 82
McCoy, Isaac, 50–51
McDonald, Daniel, 68
McDonald, David, 87
McGee, Len, 88
McGillivray, Alexander, 1, 17, 22, 27, 30–31, 34,
   39, 40, 53, 64–66, 68, 71, 73–74, 92–93, 96,
   113, 119
McGillivray, Lachlan, 18, 32, 39–40, 64, 71
McGirth, Billy, 69
McIntosh, Barbara, 104

McIntosh, Chilly, 111, 126
McIntosh, John, 104
McIntosh, Peggy, 104–5
McIntosh, Roderick, 87
McIntosh, William, Jr. *See* Tustunnuggee
   Hutkee
McIntosh, William, Sr., 66, 104
McIntosh, William R., 104
McKenney, Thomas L., 43, 101, 103
McLatchy, Charles, 22
McQueen, James, 41, 96
Meigs, Return, 57
Merrell, James, 3
messengers, 69, 77, 84–85, 87–88, 92, 95
Métis, 8
Milfort, Louis, 27–28
Milledge, John, 88
Milledgeville GA, 124
Miln, Alexander, 87
Mims, Samuel, 32, 40, 125
missionaries, Christian, 23, 28, 30, 37, 42–43,
   47, 50–52, 58, 59, 66, 67, 80, 83, 86, 89–93.
   See also Asbury mission
Mississippian chiefdoms, 12–13, 19
Mitchell, David B., 65, 103–4, 107–10
Mobilian language, 68
Moniac, David, 65, 70
Moniac, Sam, 70, 84
Montiano, Manuel de, 16
Montour, Andrew, 3
Moore, Frank, 39
Mordecai, Abraham (Abram), 38, 40–41
Morrison, Ambrose, 42
Musgrove, Johnny, 79
Muskogee Indians, 8, 11, 14–15, 18
Muskogee language, 8, 10–11, 15, 18–19, 33, 63,
   68, 77, 80, 84, 89, 91

names, as indicators of identity, 23, 54–55,
   68–69, 121, 125
Narváez, Pánfilo de, 90
Natchez Indians, 19–20
New York, 65, 73, 75, 102

O'Neill, Arturo, 2, 6, 58
O'Riley, John, 30

Oakfusgee, 115
Oglethorpe, John, 38, 42, 64, 79, 80, 112
oral traditions, regarding race, 77–78, 129, 131–32
orchards, 70, 75
Ortiz, Juan, 56, 90

packhorsemen, 26, 32, 34
paint, face and body, 1–2, 5, 47, 52–56, 59, 115
Panton, Leslie, and Forbes Company, 5
Panton, William, 71
Pardo, Juan, 13
parenting, 52, 61–76
Parson, Enoch, 28–29
Parton, James, 46
paternalism, 46, 50, 107, 122
paternity, 2, 4, 7–10, 20, 27–28, 57, 61–62, 69, 83, 87–88, 98–101, 104, 112–13, 130–31
Pensacola FL, 1, 44, 54, 103, 114
Perdue, Theda, 4
Perryman, Betsy, 43
Petersen, Karsten, 23, 42, 89–90, 127
Pettit, Rachel, 72
Philadelphia, 65, 75–76
physical appearance, 1–3, 5–6, 14, 21, 27, 45–48, 51–56, 59, 69, 72–74, 76, 78, 101, 103, 105, 124, 131. *See also* clothing; piercing, body; race; skin color; tattoos
Pickens, Israel, 43
Pickett, Albert James, 22, 44, 56, 124
Pierce, John, 65
piercing, body, 2–3, 52, 74
plantations, 40, 64–65, 67, 75, 93, 97, 102–3, 109, 121
polygamy, 28–29, 104–5
Potts, William, 127
pre-Columbian chiefdoms. *See* Mississippian chiefdoms
prenuptial agreements, 131
Priber, Christopher Gotlieb, 31
punishments, 22, 26, 33, 36, 54, 63, 75, 78–89, 97, 110, 117–18

race, 1–11, 27, 29, 46–53, 55, 58, 73, 90–91, 114–17, 127–32. *See also* skin color
ransoms and bounties, 13, 15, 17, 30–31, 43

reciprocity, 11–12, 96–98, 100, 105–11
Red Stick War, 32, 36, 46, 65, 83, 85–86, 96, 98, 106–8, 116, 121–22, 125, 130 *See also* War of 1812
Red String Affair, 41
redistribution, 96, 100, 106, 108–10
Romans, Bernard, 20
Russell, Gilbert, 116
Russell, James, 40

Sandoval, Juan Antonio, 84
Savannah GA, 38, 64, 66, 74, 103–4, 119
scalping, 54, 88, 115
schools, 46, 63–67, 101–2. *See also* education
Scotland, 65–66
Seagrove, James, 74, 82, 85, 88–89, 117
Seminole Indians, 18, 44, 48, 73, 117
servitude, indentured, 30–31, 41–42, 80
sex, 27, 29, 31, 34–38, 41
Shawnee Indians, 15, 17, 19, 21
Sheehan, Bernard, 47
Shirley, John, 34
Simms, William Gilmore, 50, 92, 101, 103
Simory, William, 41
skin color, 1, 5, 47, 51–52, 72–73, 103, 117, 124, 129–31. *See also* race
slave raids, 13–14, 44, 75
slave trade, internal, 1–2, 5, 17
slavery, 1–2, 6–7, 17, 22, 30–32, 39, 43, 44, 46, 48, 62, 64, 67, 70–71, 78, 90, 93, 97, 100–102, 121, 131–32. *See also* African Americans
Smith, Isaac, 91
Smythe, John, 35–36
sobriety, 50, 88
Soto, Hernando de, 12–13, 53, 56, 90
South Carolina, 14, 31–32, 39, 40, 54, 57, 64, 78
sovereignty, 116, 118–19, 131
Spain, Drury, 94
Spalding, Thomas, 104
Sparks, William, 90
St. Andrews Society of the State of New York, 65
St. Augustine FL, 16, 41
Steiner, Abraham, 37
Stephens, William, 41, 54
Stiggins, George, 19–21, 28, 123–24

Stiggins, Mary, 122
Stinson, George, 110, 118–19
Stuart, James, 72–73
Stuart, John, 32, 39, 84, 87
Sullivan, Peggy, 85
Swan, Caleb, 26–29, 40

Taitt, David, 115
Talisi, 12–13
Talladego, 111
Tammany Society of the Columbian Order, 73–74
Tate, David, 65–66
tattoos, 5, 23, 47, 52, 55–56, 59, 63, 74, 115
taverns, 70, 93–95, 102, 106, 126
Tecumseh, 21, 108, 130
Tensaw District, 64–65
terminology, 4, 7–9, 87, 129, 135n4
Thicknesse, Philip, 52
Tiger, Turner, 19
toll roads, 69, 93, 95, 102
Tomochichi, 14
Tomoc Mico, 100
Tonyn, Patrick, 39, 115
torture, 16–17
trade goods, 1, 30, 32, 35–36, 39, 48–49, 62, 67, 70–71, 96–97, 99–101, 105–10, 117–18, 130–31
trade regulations, 32–33, 117–18
travel guides, 9, 77, 84, 86, 89–91, 93, 95, 127
travel, within Creek country, 64, 69, 83–84, 86, 89–95, 102–3
treaties, 9, 31, 82, 86, 92, 94, 105–6, 109, 112. *See also specific treaties*
Treaty of Indian Springs (1821), 109
Treaty of Indian Springs (1825), 86, 97–99, 109–11
Treaty of New York (1790), 65, 73, 75
Treaty of Washington (1805), 106
Troup, George M., 104
Tuckabahchee, 24
Tuscaloosa AL, 125
Tuskegee Indians, 30
Tuskenahah, 100
Tustunnuggee Hutkee (William McIntosh Jr.), 66, 72, 93–94, 96–12, 114, 117, 126
Tustunnuggee Thlucco (Big Warrior), 14, 43, 62, 82–83, 85, 92, 110, 124, 126, 149n23

Tybee Island, 115

Uchee Indians, 14, 19–20, 30
Unzaga, Luis de, 2, 115

village loyalty, 11, 15, 23, 40, 130–31
Von Reck, Frederick, 17, 53, 72

Wall, Jesse, 70, 93
Walsh, James, 40
War of 1812, 46, 101–2, 106, 116–17, 121. *See also* Red Stick War
Ware, Alexander, 105
Washington, George, 78
Waters, Sarah, 74
Watson, Joseph, 79–80
Weatherford, Charles, 34, 119, 121
Weatherford, William, 68, 96, 121–23
weaving, 67, 86, 108
Wellbank, George, 40
wench, use of term to describe Native women, 36, 105, 115
Wesley, John, 64
West Point, U.S. Military Academy, 46, 65
White, Nicholas, 29
White Lieutenant, 74, 117
Wind clan, 1, 11, 34, 35, 60, 79, 100, 144n32
Winelett, John, 125
Withington Station, 52, 66, 92
Wolf King, 80
women, Creek, 1–2, 4–5, 8–9, 21, 26–30, 33–44, 53, 56–58, 61–64, 66–67, 69–72, 74–76, 78–82, 85–87, 96, 100, 104–5, 112, 115, 117–18, 124, 126–27
women, European American, 27, 33–34
Woodward, Thomas Simpson, 28, 41, 102, 123
Wright, J. Leitch, Jr., 19
Wright, James, 42
Wright, Thomas, 42
Wright, William, 88

Yamacraw Indians, 14–15, 52
Yamasee Indians, 14–15
Yamasee War, 14, 33
Yazoo Indians, 67
Yellow Hair, 54

Zéspedes, Manuel de, 73 ,

The Payne-Butrick Papers, Volumes 1, 2, 3
The Payne-Butrick Papers, Volumes 4, 5, 6
Edited and annotated by
William L. Anderson, Jane L. Brown,
and Anne F. Rogers

Deerskins and Duffels: The Creek Indian
Trade with Anglo-America, 1685–1815
By Kathryn E. Holland Braund

Searching for the Bright Path: The Mississippi
Choctaws from Prehistory to Removal
By James Taylor Carson

Demanding the Cherokee Nation: Indian
Autonomy and American Culture, 1830–1900
By Andrew Denson

The Second Creek War: Interethnic Conflict
and Collusion on a Collapsing Frontier
By John T. Ellisor

Cherokee Americans: The Eastern Band
of Cherokees in the Twentieth Century
By John R. Finger

Creeks and Southerners:
Biculturalism on the Early American Frontier
By Andrew K. Frank

Choctaw Genesis, 1500–1700
By Patricia Galloway

The Southeastern Ceremonial Complex:
Artifacts and Analysis
The Cottonlandia Conference
Edited by Patricia Galloway
Exhibition Catalog by David H. Dye
and Camille Wharey

The Invention of the Creek Nation, 1670–1763
By Steven C. Hahn

Bad Fruits of the Civilized Tree: Alcohol and
the Sovereignty of the Cherokee Nation
By Izumi Ishii

Epidemics and Enslavement:
Biological Catastrophe in the
Native Southeast, 1492–1715
By Paul Kelton

An Assumption of Sovereignty:
Social and Political Transformation among
the Florida Seminoles, 1953–1979
By Harry A. Kersey Jr.

Up from These Hills:
Memories of a Cherokee Boyhood
By Leonard Carson Lambert Jr.
As told to Michael Lambert

The Caddo Chiefdoms:
Caddo Economics and Politics, 700–1835
By David La Vere

The Moravian Springplace Mission
to the Cherokees, Volume 1: 1805–1813
The Moravian Springplace Mission
to the Cherokees, Volume 2: 1814–1821
Edited and introduced
by Rowena McClinton

The Moravian Springplace Mission
to the Cherokees, Abridged Edition
Edited and with an introduction
by Rowena McClinton

Keeping the Circle: American Indian Identity
in Eastern North Carolina, 1885–2004
By Christopher Arris Oakley

Choctaws in a Revolutionary Age, 1750–1830
By Greg O'Brien

CPSIA information can be obtained
at www.ICGtesting.com
Printed in the USA
LVOW11s1559021216
515417LV00033B/180/P